The Law
(In Plain English)®
for
Small
Business

Second Edition

Leonard D. DuBoff
Attorney at Law

SPHINX® PUBLISHING
AN IMPRINT OF SOURCEBOOKS, INC.®
NAPERVILLE, ILLINOIS
www.SphinxLegal.com

Second Edition, 2007

Published by: **Sphinx® Publishing, An Imprint of Sourcebooks, Inc.®**

Naperville Office
P.O. Box 4410
Naperville, Illinois 60567-4410
630-961-3900
Fax: 630-961-2168
www.sourcebooks.com
www.SphinxLegal.com

This publication is designed to provide accurate and authoritative information in regard to the subject matter covered. It is sold with the understanding that the publisher is not engaged in rendering legal, accounting, or other professional service. If legal advice or other expert assistance is required, the services of a competent professional person should be sought.

From a Declaration of Principles Jointly Adopted by a Committee of the American Bar Association and a Committee of Publishers and Associations

This product is not a substitute for legal advice.

Disclaimer required by Texas statutes.

Library of Congress Cataloging-in-Publication Data
DuBoff, Leonard D.
  Law (in plain English) for small business / by Leonard D. DuBoff. -- 2nd
ed.
      p. cm.
  Includes index.
  ISBN-13: 978-1-57248-599-0 (pbk. : alk. paper)
  ISBN-10: 1-57248-599-X (pbk. : alk. paper)
  1. Business law--United States. 2. Small business--United States. I.
Title.
KF390.B84D828 2006
346.73'0652--dc22
                                                                    2006035227

Printed and bound in the United States of America.
SB — 10 9 8 7 6 5 4 3 2 1

Dedication

To my wife, Mary Ann Crawford DuBoff,
for all you have done and for all we have together,
and to my mother, Millicent DuBoff,
for giving me the tools necessary to create this work
and the drive to actually do it.
Finally, to my grandson, Brian,
with hopes that he will carry on the tradition.

Acknowledgments

There is a host of individuals who have aided me in preparing this edition of *The Law (in Plain English)® for Small Business* for publication. It is impossible to identify all of them within these pages, but some deserve special recognition. I would like to thank the following friends, colleagues, former students, and associates for their valuable assistance.

In particular, I would like to thank Christy O. King, principal in the law firm The DuBoff Law Group, LLC, for her aid in spearheading much of the revision work that contributed to this book. Without her attention to detail, this revision would not have been possible.

Jed Macy of The Macy Company was extraordinarily helpful in providing up-to-date and accurate information about pensions and profit-sharing plans.

I am also indebted to John Stevko, CPA, speaker and former CEO of the tax and accounting education company Gear Up, Inc., for his aid with the numerous changes in tax law. I would also like to thank Laurie Miller, CPA, and William Paxton, CPA, of the accounting firm of Paxton & Miller, LLC, for their help in revising the tax chapter of this book. John, Bill, and Laurie are exceptionally knowledgeable with respect to small business tax issues.

My colleague and former student, Emil Berg, was extremely helpful in providing recommendations with respect to the material contained in the chapter on insurance law. I would also like to thank Bert Krages, Esq., for his help in reviewing the section on hazardous substances in the employment chapter.

I also appreciate the assistance of Steve Silver, Senior Vice President and Financial Advisor at Morgan Stanley, for his help in obtaining information with respect to securities and the securities market.

I would also like to express my sincere appreciation to Gene W. Arant, Esq., a registered patent attorney and an author himself, for his help in reviewing the patent chapter. Gene's knowledge of patent law is extraordinary, and his help in understanding some of the newer, more complex developments has been important to the quality of that chapter. Dennis McLaughlin, Esq., of Dennis McLaughlin & Associates, a franchise law expert, was extremely helpful in updating the chapter on franchising.

A special thanks to my brother, Michael H. DuBoff, of the law firm of Snow Becker Krauss, P.C., for his astute comments and recommendations.

I would also like to thank everyone, and I mean everyone, at Sphinx Publishing for their cheerful service with this book. In particular, I would like to recognize the special help of my editor, Michael Bowen.

I am also indebted to Lynn Della for the countless days she spent assisting me in reworking the earlier version and compiling the myriad of changes that have occurred in the law. Lynn's knowledge of law and business and their real-world applications have proved to be a valuable resource. I could not have revised this book without her help. My secretary, Peggy Reckow, deserves special recognition for her extra effort in converting my numerous interlinings and cryptic notes into a readable volume. Her special talent in working with the foibles of the computer system and transmitting the manuscript to the editors has been extremely beneficial.

Finally, I would like to recognize the aid of my partner in law and in life, Mary Ann Crawford DuBoff, for all of her work on this text. Words are inadequate to express the appreciation I feel for all she has contributed to this and all of my projects.

Contents

Preface

When I first began writing *The Law (In Plain English)*® series more than a quarter century ago, my goal was to educate nonlawyers on the business aspects of their businesses and professions. At the time, I was a full-time law professor, and as an educator, I felt that one of my missions was to provide educational tools. Later, as a full-time lawyer, I realized the importance of this series in educating my clients so that they could more effectively communicate with me. It became clear that the more knowledgeable my clients were about the myriad of legal issues they faced in their businesses and professions, the more effectively they could aid me in helping them. It is for this reason that I continue this series. Today, there are *In Plain English*® books for writers, high-tech entrepreneurs, health care professionals, craftspeople, gallery operators, photographers, restauranteurs, and this volume for those who are involved with every aspect of small businesses.

The word *small*, as used in the title, is not intended to limit this text to operators of ma-and-pa operations. Rather, it is intended to encompass all businesses that are not publicly traded and listed on national securities exchanges. It is likely that companies of that size would have in-house counsel trained in the various subjects discussed in this volume. However, even the principals of such companies might gain a clearer understanding of the legal issues with which they deal with by reading an In Plain English® book.

This book is not intended to be a substitute for the advice of a professional. Instead, it is designed to sensitize you to the issues that may require the aid of a skilled attorney or other expert. It is my sincere hope that this book will, like its predecessors in the series, be practical, useful, and readable. One of my goals in preparing this book is to enable the reader to identify problem areas and seek the aid of a skilled professional when necessary—or preferably before it becomes necessary. It is quite common for the owners of small businesses to become embroiled in legal problems before they are able to appreciate the problem.

The law is quite complex and rapidly evolving. Since the first incarnation of this text was published in 1987, many changes have occurred. New business forms, such as limited liability companies and limited liability partnerships, have emerged. The World Wide Web has become a vehicle for communication and commerce, and the law has been scrambling to keep pace. In writing this edition, it was my intention to chronicle the changes and convert them into a clear and understandable text that will aid the reader in understanding the current state of business law. It is hoped that by my doing so, business readers will be able to more effectively communicate with their business associates and legal advisors when inevitable legal issues arise.

Leonard D. DuBoff
Portland, Oregon, 2006

NOTE: For an online newsletter that covers many of the issues discussed in this book and updates that information on a regular basis, go to **www.dubofflaw.com/ci.**

CHAPTER 1

Finding a Lawyer and an Accountant

Most businesspeople expect to seek the advice of a lawyer only occasionally, for counseling on important matters such as the decision to incorporate or the purchase of a building. If this is your concept of the attorney's role in your business, you need to reevaluate it. Most small businesses would operate more efficiently and more profitably in the long run if they had a relationship with a business attorney more like that between a family doctor and patient. An ongoing relationship that allows the attorney to get to know the business well enough to engage in preventive legal counseling and to assist in planning makes it possible to solve many problems before they occur.

If your business is small or undercapitalized, you are doubtless anxious to keep operating costs down. You probably do not relish the idea of paying an attorney to get to know your business if you are not involved in an immediate crisis. However, it is a good bet that a visit with a competent business lawyer right now will result in the raising of issues vital to the future of your business. There is good reason why larger, successful businesses employ one or more attorneys full time as in-house counsel. Ready access to legal advice is something you should not deny your business at any time, for any reason.

An attorney experienced in business law can give you important information regarding the risks unique to your business. Furthermore, a lawyer can advise you regarding your rights and obligations in your relationship with present and future employees, the rules that apply in your state regarding the hiring and firing of employees, permissible collection practices, and so forth. Ignorance of these issues and violation of the rules can result in financially devastating lawsuits and even criminal penalties. Since each state has its own laws covering certain business practices, state laws must be consulted on many areas covered in this book. A competent local business attorney is, therefore, your best source of information on many issues that will arise in the running of your business. Many law firms have attorneys who are licensed in several jurisdictions, and others have relationships with attorneys in other locales.

IN PLAIN ENGLISH

Most legal problems cost more to solve or defend after they arise than it would have cost to prevent their occurrence in the first place. Litigation is notoriously inefficient and expensive. You do not want to sue or to be sued, if you can help it.

FINDING A LAWYER

If you do not know any attorneys, ask other businesspeople if they know any good ones. You want either a lawyer who specializes in business or a general practitioner who has many satisfied business clients. Finding the lawyer who is right for you may require that you shop around a bit. Most local and state bar associations have referral services. A good tip is to find out who is in the business law section of the state or local bar association or who has served on special bar committees dealing with law reform. It may also be useful to find out if any articles covering the area of law with which you are concerned have been published in either scholarly journals or continuing legal education publications, and if the author is available to assist you.

It is a good idea to hire a specialist or law firm with a number of specialists rather than a general practitioner. While it is true that you may pay more per hour for the expert, you will not have to pay for the attorney's learning time. Experience is valuable. In this regard, you may wish to keep in mind that it is uncommon for a lawyer to specialize in business practice and also handle criminal matters. Thus, if you are faced with a criminal prosecution for the death of an employee, then you should be searching for an experienced criminal defense lawyer.

Evaluating a Lawyer

One method by which you can attempt to evaluate an attorney in regard to representing business clients is by consulting the Martindale-Hubbell Law Directory in your local county law library or online at **www.martindale.com**. While this may be useful, the mere fact that an attorney's name does not appear in the book should not be given too much weight, since there is a significant charge for being included and some lawyers may have chosen not to pay for the listing. You may also wish to search the World Wide Web. Many law firms have established websites. The larger firms usually include extensive information about the firm, its practice areas, and its attorneys.

After you have obtained several recommendations for attorneys, it is appropriate for you to talk with them for a short period of time to determine whether you would be comfortable working with them. Do not be afraid to ask about their background, experience, and whether they feel they can help you.

Using a Lawyer

Once you have completed the interview process, select the person who appears to best satisfy your needs. One of the first items you should discuss with your lawyer is the fee structure. You are entitled to an estimate. However, unless you enter into an agreement to the contrary with the attorney, the estimate is just that. Business lawyers generally charge by the hour, though you may be quoted a flat rate for a specific service, such as incorporation or a simple will.

Contact your lawyer whenever you believe a legal question has arisen. Your attorney should aid you in identifying which questions require legal action or advice and which require business decisions. Generally, lawyers will deal only with legal issues, though they may help you to evaluate business problems.

Some attorneys encourage clients to feel comfortable calling at the office during the day or at home in the evening. Other lawyers, however, may resent having their personal time invaded. Some, in fact, do not list their home telephone numbers. You should learn your attorney's preference early on.

The attorney-client relationship is such that you should feel comfortable when confiding in your attorney. This person will not disclose your confidential communications; in fact, a violation of this rule, depending on the circumstances, can be considered an ethical breach that could subject the attorney to professional sanctions. If you take the time to develop a good working relationship with your attorney, it may well prove to be one of your more valuable business assets.

FINDING AN ACCOUNTANT

In addition to an attorney, most small businesses will need the services of a competent accountant to aid with tax planning, the filing of periodic reports, and annual tax returns. Finding an accountant with whom your business is compatible is similar to finding an attorney. You should ask around and learn which accountants are servicing businesses similar to yours. State professional accounting associations may also provide a referral service or point you to a directory of accountants in your area. You should interview prospective accountants to determine whether you feel you can work with them and whether you feel their skills will be compatible with your business needs.

Like your attorney, your accountant can provide valuable assistance in planning for the future of your business. It is important to work with professionals you trust and with whom you are able to relate on a professional level.

CHAPTER 2

Organizing Your Business

Everyone in business knows that survival requires careful financial planning, yet few fully realize the importance of selecting the best legal form for the business. Small businesses have little need for the sophisticated organizational structures utilized in large, publicly traded corporations, but since all entrepreneurs must pay taxes, obtain loans, and expose themselves to potential liability with every sale they make, it only makes sense to structure one's business so as to address these issues.

Every business has an organizational form best suited to it. When I counsel people on organizing their businesses, I usually adopt a two-step approach. First, we discuss various aspects of taxes and liability in order to decide which of the basic legal structures is best. There are only a handful of basic forms—the sole proprietorship, the partnership, the corporation, the limited liability company, the limited liability partnership, and a few hybrids. Once we have decided which of these is most appropriate, we go into the organizational documents, such as partnership agreements, corporate bylaws, or operating agreements. These documents define the day-to-day operations of a business and must be tailored to individual situations.

What I offer here is an explanation of the features of each of these kinds of organizations, including their advantages and disadvantages. This should give you an idea of which form might be best for your business. I discuss potential problems, but since I cannot go into a full discussion of the more intricate details cannot be had here, you should consult an experienced business attorney before deciding to adopt any particular structure. My purpose is to facilitate your communication with your lawyer and to enable you to better understand the choices available.

SOLE PROPRIETORSHIPS

The technical name *sole proprietorship* may be unfamiliar to you, but chances are you are operating under this form now. The sole proprietorship is an unincorporated business owned by one person. As a form of business, it is elegant in its simplicity. All it requires is a little money and work. Legal requirements are few and simple. A business license and registering the name of the business, if you operate it under a name other than your own, are generally all you need.

Disadvantages

There are many financial risks involved in operating your business as a sole proprietor. If you recognize any of these dangers as a real threat, you probably should consider an alternative form of organization.

If you are the sole proprietor of a business venture, the property you personally own is at risk. In other words, if for any reason you owe more than the dollar value of your business, your creditors can force a sale of most of your personally owned property to satisfy the debt.

For many risks, insurance is available that shifts the loss from you to an insurance company, but there are some risks for which insurance simply is not available. For instance, insurance is generally not available to protect against a large rise in the cost or sudden unavailability of supplies, inventory, or raw materials. In addition, the cost of product liability insurance has become so high that, as a practical matter, it is unavailable to most small businesses. Even when pro-cured, every insurance policy has a limited, strictly defined scope of coverage. These liability risks, as well as many other uncertain economic factors, can drive a small business and its sole proprietor into bankruptcy.

Taxes

The sole proprietor is personally taxed on all profits of the business and may deduct losses. Of course, the rate of taxation will change with increases in income. Fortunately, there are ways to ease this tax burden.

IN PLAIN ENGLISH

Maximize your tax savings by establishing an approved IRA or contributing to a pen-sion fund. By deducting a specified amount of your net income for placement into an interest-bearing account, approved government securities, mutual funds, or company pension plan, you can withdraw the funds at a later date—when you are in a lower tax bracket. There may, however, be severe restrictions if you withdraw the money prior to retirement age. (See Chapter 24, "Pension Plans," for a more complete dis-cussion of this subject.)

For further information on tax planning devices, contact your local Internal Revenue Service (IRS) office and ask for free pamphlets, or use the services of an accountant experienced in dealing with business tax planning.

PARTNERSHIPS AND JOINT VENTURES

A partnership is defined by most state laws as an association of two or more per-sons to conduct, as co-owners, a business for profit. No formalities are required. In fact, in some cases, people have been held to be partners even though they never had any intention of forming a partnership. For example, if you lend a friend some money to start a business and the friend agrees to pay you a certain percentage of whatever profit is made, you may be your friend's partner in the eyes of the law, even though you take no part in running the business. This is important, because each partner is subject to unlimited personal liability for the debts of the partnership. Each partner is also liable for the negligence of another partner and of the partnership's employees when a negligent act occurs in the usual course of business.

A joint venture is a partnership for a limited or specific purpose, rather than one that continues for an indefinite or specified time. For example, an arrangement whereby two or more persons or businesses agree to build a single house and sell it for profit is a joint venture. An agreement to develop numerous properties over a period of time is a partnership.

Advantages and Disadvantages

The economic advantages of doing business in a partnership form are:
- the pooling of capital;
- the collaboration of skills;
- easier access to credit enhanced by the collective credit rating; and,
- a potentially more efficient allocation of labor and resources.

A major disadvantage is that, as noted above, each partner is fully and personally liable for all the debts of the partnership, even if not personally involved in incurring those debts.

This means that if you are getting involved in a partnership, you should be especially cautious in two areas. First, since the involvement of a partner increases your potential liability, you should choose a responsible partner. Second, the partnership should be adequately insured to protect both the assets of the partnership and the personal assets of each partner.

Formalities

No formalities are required to create a partnership. If the partners do not have a formal agreement defining the terms of the partnership, such as control of the partnership or the distribution of profits, state law dictates the terms. State laws are based on the fundamental characteristics of the typical partnership and attempt to correspond to the reasonable expectations of the partners. The most important of these legally presumed characteristics are:

- no one can become an actual member of a partnership without the unanimous consent of all partners;
- every member has an equal vote in the management of the partnership regardless of the partner's percentage interest in it;
- all partners share equally in the profits and losses of the partnership, no matter how much capital each has contributed;
- a simple majority vote is required for decisions in the ordinary course of business and a unanimous vote is required to change the fundamental character of the business; and,
- a partnership is terminable at will by any partner. A partner can withdraw from the partnership at any time, and this withdrawal will cause a dissolution of the partnership.

Most state laws contain a provision that allows the partners to make their own agreements regarding the management structure and division of profits that best suits the needs of the individual partners.

Partnership Agreements

A comprehensive partnership agreement is no simple matter. Some major considerations in preparing a partnership agreement include the name of the partnership, a description of the business, contributions of capital by the partners, duration of the partnership, distribution of profits, management responsibilities, duties of partners, prohibited acts, and provisions for the dissolution of the partnership. (These items are detailed in Chapter 3.) It is essential for potential partners to devote time and considerable care to the preparation of an agreement.

IN PLAIN ENGLISH

Enlist the services of a competent business lawyer. The expense of a lawyer to help you put together an agreement suited to the needs of your partnership is usually well justified by the economic savings recouped in the smooth organization, operation, and, when necessary, the final dissolution of the partnership.

Taxes

A partnership does not possess any special tax advantages over a sole proprietorship. Each partner pays tax on his or her share of the profits, whether distributed or retained, and each is entitled to the same proportion of the partnership deductions and credits. The partnership must prepare an annual information return for the IRS known as Schedule K-1, Form 1065. It details each partner's share of income, credits, and deductions that the IRS uses to check against the individual returns filed by the partners.

LIMITED PARTNERSHIPS

The limited partnership is a hybrid containing elements of both partnerships and corporations. A limited partnership may be formed by parties who wish to invest in a business and share in its profits, but seek to limit their risk to the amount of their investment. The law provides such limited risk for the limited partner, but only so long as the limited partner plays no active role in the day-to-day management and operation of the business. In effect, the limited partner is very much like an investor who buys a few shares of stock in a corporation, but has no significant role in running the business.

Formation

In order to establish a limited partnership, it is necessary to have one or more general partners who run the business (and have full personal liability) and one or more limited partners who play a passive role. Forming a limited partnership requires documentation to be filed with the proper state agency. If not filed or improperly filed, a limited partner could be treated as a general partner and lose the benefit of limited liability. In addition, the limited partner must refrain from becoming involved in the day-to-day operation of the partnership. Otherwise, the limited partner might be found to be actively participating in the business and thereby held to be a general partner with unlimited personal liability.

Uses

Limited partnership is a convenient form for securing needed financial backers who wish to share in the profits of an enterprise without undue exposure to personal liability when forming a corporation or limited liability company (LLC) may not be appropriate, i.e., when one does not meet all the requirements for an S corporation or when one does not desire ownership in an LLC.

IN PLAIN ENGLISH

A limited partnership can be used to attract investors when credit is hard to get or is too expensive. In return for investing, the limited partner may receive a designated share of the profits. From the entrepreneur's point of view, this may be an attractive way to fund a business, since the limited partner receives nothing if there are no profits. Had the entrepreneur borrowed money from a creditor, he or she would be at risk to repay the loan regardless of the success or failure of the business.

Another use of the limited partnership is to facilitate reorganization of a general partnership after the death or retirement of a general partner. Remember, a partnership can be terminated upon the request of any partner. Although the original partnership is technically dissolved when one partner retires, it is not uncommon for the remaining partners to agree to buy out the retiring partner's share—that is, to return that person's capital contribution and keep the business going. Some state laws establish this as the rule unless the parties agree otherwise.

Raising enough cash to buy out the retiring partner, however, could jeopardize the business by forcing the remaining partners to liquidate certain partnership assets. A convenient way to avoid such a detrimental liquidation is for the retiree to step into a limited partner status. Thus, he or she can continue to share in the profits (which to some extent flow from that partner's past labor), while removing personal assets from the risk of partnership liabilities. In the meantime, the remaining partners are afforded the opportunity to restructure the partnership funding under more favorable terms.

Unintended Partners

Whether yours is a straightforward general partnership or a limited partnership, one arrangement you want to avoid is the unintended partnership. This can occur when you work together with another person and your relationship is not described formally. For example, if you and another person decide to import, market, and sell small electronic appliances from Asia, it is essential for you to spell out in detail the arrangements between the two of you. If you do not, you could find that the other person is your partner and entitled to half the income you receive, even though his or her contribution was minimal. You can avoid this by simply hiring the other person as an employee or independent contractor. Whichever arrangement you choose, be sure to have a detailed written agreement.

CORPORATIONS

The word *corporation* may call to mind a vision of a large company with hundreds or thousands of employees. In fact, the vast majority of corporations in the United States are small or moderate-sized companies. There are, of course, advantages and disadvantages to incorporating. If it appears advantageous to incorporate, you will find it can be done with surprising ease and little expense. You should, however, use the services of a knowledgeable business lawyer to ensure compliance with state formalities, completion of corporate mechanics, and to obtain advice on corporate taxation.

Compared to Partnerships

In describing the corporate form, it is useful to compare it to a partnership.

Liability

The owners of the corporation are not, as a rule, personally liable for the corporation's debts. They stand to lose only their investment. Unlike a limited partner, a shareholder is allowed full participation in the control of the corporation through the shareholder's voting privileges—the higher the percentage of outstanding shares owned, the more significant the control.

For the small corporation, however, limited liability may be something of an illusion. Very often creditors will require that the owners personally cosign for any credit extended, including credit cards. In addition, individuals remain responsible for their own wrongful acts. A shareholder who negligently causes an injury while engaged in corporate business has not only subjected the corporation to liability, but also remains personally liable. If the other party to a contract with the corporation has agreed to look only to the corporation for responsibility, the corporate liability shield does protect a shareholder from liability for breach of contract.

The corporate shield also offers protection in situations where an agent hired by the corporation has committed a wrongful act while working for the corporation. For example, if a management consultant negligently injures a pedestrian while driving somewhere on corporate business, the consultant will be liable for the wrongful act and the corporation may be liable; however, the shareholder who owns stock in the corporation will probably not be held personally liable.

Continuity of Existence

Another difference between a corporation and a partnership relates to continuity of existence. Many of the events that can cause the dissolution of a partnership do not have the same effect on a corporation. In fact, it is common for a corporation to have perpetual existence. Shareholders, unlike partners, cannot decide to withdraw and demand a return of capital from the corporation—all they can do is sell their stock. A corporation may, therefore, have both legal and economic continuity.

IN PLAIN ENGLISH

This can be a tremendous disadvantage to shareholders (or their heirs) if they want to sell stock when there are no buyers for it. *Buy-sell agreements* can, however, be made that guarantee return of capital to the estate of a shareholder who dies or to a shareholder who decides to withdraw.

Transferability of Ownership

The third difference relates to transferability of ownership. No one can become a partner without unanimous consent of the other partners, unless otherwise agreed. In a corporation, shareholders can generally sell all or any number of their shares to whomever and whenever they wish. If the owners of a small corporation do not want it to be open to outside ownership, however, transferability may be restricted by agreement of the shareholders.

Management and Control

The fourth difference is in the structure of management and control. Common shareholders are given a vote in proportion to their ownership in the corporation. Other kinds of stock can be created, with or without voting rights. A voting shareholder uses his or her vote to elect a board of directors and to create rules under which the board will operate.

The basic rules of the corporation are stated in its *articles of incorporation*, which are filed with the state. These serve as the constitution for the corporation and can be amended by shareholder vote. More detailed operational rules— *bylaws*—should also be prepared. Both shareholders and directors may have the power to create or amend bylaws. This varies from state to state and may be determined by the shareholders themselves. The board of directors then makes operational decisions for the corporation, typically delegating day-to-day control to a president or chief executive officer.

A shareholder, even one who owns all the stock, may not preempt a decision of the board of directors. If the board has exceeded the powers granted it by the articles or bylaws, any shareholder may sue for a court order remedying the situation. If the board is within its powers, the shareholders then have no recourse except to remove the board or any board member. In a few more progressive states, a small corporation may entirely forgo having a board of directors. In these cases, the corporation is authorized to allow the shareholders to vote directly on business decisions, just as in a partnership.

Raising Additional Capital
The fifth distinction between partnerships and corporations is the greater variety of means available to the corporation for raising additional capital. Partnerships are quite restricted in this regard. They can borrow money or, if all the partners agree, they can take on additional partners. A corporation, on the other hand, may issue more stock. This stock can be of many different varieties: recallable at a set price, for example, or convertible into another kind of stock.

A process frequently used to attract a new investor is the issuance of preferred stock. The corporation agrees to pay the preferred shareholder some predetermined amount, known as a *dividend preference*, before it pays any dividends to other shareholders. It also means, if the corporation should go bankrupt, the preferred shareholder will generally be paid out of the proceeds of liquidation before the common shareholders, although after the corporation's creditors are paid.

In most cases, the issuance of new stock merely requires approval by a majority of the existing shareholders. In addition, corporations can borrow money on a short-term basis by issuing notes or for a longer period by issuing debentures or bonds.

IN PLAIN ENGLISH

Actually, a corporation's ability to raise additional capital is limited only by its lawyer's creativity and the economics of the marketplace.

Taxes

Under both state and federal laws, the profits of the corporation are taxed to the corporation before they are paid out as dividends. Then, because the dividends constitute income to the shareholders, they are taxed again as the shareholder's personal income. This double taxation constitutes the major disadvantage of conducting business in the corporate form.

Avoiding Double Taxation

There are several methods of avoiding double taxation. First, a corporation can plan its business so as not to have much profit. This can be done by drawing off what would be profit in payments to shareholders for a variety of services. For example, a shareholder can be paid a salary, rent for property leased to the corporation, or interest on a loan made to the corporation. All of these are legal deductions from the corporate income.

Deducting Benefits

A corporation can also deduct the cost of various benefits provided for its employees. For example, a corporation can deduct all its payments made for certain qualified employee life insurance plans, while the employees pay no personal income tax on this benefit. Sole proprietors or partnerships, on the other hand, may not be entitled to deduct these expenses.

Retained Earnings

A corporation can also reinvest its profits for reasonable business expansion. This undistributed money is not taxed as income to the shareholders, though the corporation must pay corporate tax on it. By contrast, the retained earnings of a partnership are taxed to the individual partners even though the money is not distributed.

Corporate reinvestment has two advantages. First, the business can be built up with money that has been taxed only at the corporate level and on which no individual shareholder needs to pay any tax. Second, within reasonable limits, the corporation can delay the distribution of corporate earnings until, for example, a time of lower personal income of the shareholder and, therefore, lower personal tax rates.

If, however, the amount withheld for expansion is deemed by the IRS to be unreasonably high, then the corporation may be exposed to a penalty. It is, therefore, wise to work with an experienced tax planner on a regular basis.

S CORPORATIONS

Congress created a hybrid organizational form that allows the owners of a small corporation to take advantage of many of the corporate features described above, but that is taxed in a manner similar to a sole proprietorship or partnership (and avoid most of the double-taxation problems). In this form of organization, called an S corporation, income and losses flow directly to shareholders and the corporation pays no income tax. This form can be particularly advantageous in the early years of a corporation, because the owners can deduct almost all the corporate losses from their personal incomes. They cannot do so in a standard, or C corporation. They can have this favorable tax situation while simultaneously enjoying the limited liability of the corporate form.

IN PLAIN ENGLISH

If the corporation is likely to sustain major losses and shareholders have other sources of income against which they wish to write off those losses, the S corporation is likely to be a desirable form for the business.

Small corporation, as defined by the tax law, does not refer to the amount of business generated; rather, it refers to the number of owners. In order to qualify for S status, the corporation may not have more than one hundred owners, each of whom must be a human being or a certain kind of trust or nonprofit corporation. Additionally, there cannot be more than one class of voting stock. An S corporation can own stock in another S corporation.

Taxes

S corporations are generally taxed in the same way as partnerships or sole proprietorships. Unfortunately, the tax rules for S corporations are not as simple as those for partnerships or individuals. Generally speaking, the owner of an S corporation can be taxed on his or her pro rata share of the distributable profits and may deduct his or her share of distributable losses.

LIMITED LIABILITY COMPANIES AND LIMITED LIABILITY PARTNERSHIPS

The *limited liability company* (LLC) combines the limited liability features of a corporation with all the tax advantages available to the sole proprietor or partnership. The law in most states permits those conducting business as an LLC to create the most flexible and user-friendly organizational structure. They can elect to have the LLC's business conducted by a *manager* or by the *members* (owners) themselves. They may, but are not required to, have periodic meetings, and in fact, the owners can, through the operating agreement (equivalent to a corporation's bylaws), create whatever organizational structure they consider appropriate.

An entrepreneur conducting business through an LLC can shield his or her personal assets from the risk of the business for all situations except the individual's own wrongful acts. This liability shield is identical to the one offered by the corporate form. The owners of an LLC can also enjoy all the tax features accorded to sole proprietors or partners in a partnership.

Limited liability companies do not have the same restrictions imposed on S corporations regarding the number of owners and the type of owners (i.e., human beings or specified business forms). In fact, business corporations, partnerships, and other business entities can own interests in LLCs. Limited liability companies may also have more than one class of voting ownership.

Keep in mind that the LLC form is relatively new, so there is not yet any significant body of case law interpreting the meaning of the new statutes that created it. It is, however, extremely flexible and, in 1997, the Internal Revenue Code was amended to permit LLCs to be taxed like C corporations if they so choose, or like sole proprietorships and partnerships.

When LLCs were first created, most professional associations declared them analogous to business corporations and prohibited their use by professionals. The one profession that did permit the use of LLCs was accounting. The LLP was created as a permitted business form for all professionals.

Limited Liability Partnerships

For businesses that have been conducted in the partnership form and desire a liability shield, the *limited liability partnership* (LLP) is available. This business form parallels the LLC in most respects. It is created by converting a partnership into an LLP, and it is available for professionals who, in many states, may not conduct business through LLCs.

> **NOTE:** Licensed professionals who desire some form of liability shield may also create professional corporations.

Minority Owners

Dissolving a corporation is not only painful because of certain tax penalties, but it is almost always impossible without the consent of the majority of the owners. This may be true of LLCs and LLPs, as well. If you are involved in the formation of a business entity and will be a minority owner, you must realize that the majority owners will have ultimate and absolute control unless minority owners take certain precautions from the start. There are numerous horror stories relating to what some majority owners have done to minority owners. Avoiding these problems is no more difficult than drafting an appropriate agreement among the owners. Both LLCs and LLPs have operating agreements that can be structured for minority protection. You should always retain your own attorney to represent you during the business entity's formation, rather than waiting until it is too late.

HYBRIDS

It is important to determine which business form will be most advantageous for your business. In addition to the business forms previously discussed, many states permit the creation of hybrid forms of business organization, such as limited liability limited partnerships (LLLPs) and business trusts. It is important for you to consult with an experienced business lawyer in order to determine which business forms are available in your state and which would best serve your business objectives.

CHAPTER 3

Business Organization Checklist

As discussed in the previous chapter, there is a host of business forms available for the entrepreneur. These forms range from the simplest—sole proprietorships—to more structured organizations, such as partnerships, corporations, limited liability companies, and limited liability partnerships. The structure of your business will depend upon a number of considerations. Creating any of these business forms is a rather simple process, but to do it right and enjoy all the advantages, it is highly recommended that you consult a competent business lawyer. Of course, a lawyer's time costs money, but you can save some money if you come properly prepared. The following are some of the points you should be prepared to discuss with your lawyer.

ACCOUNTANT

Other than yourself, the most important person with whom your attorney will work is your accountant. The accountant will provide valuable input on the business's financial structure, funding, capitalization, allocation of ownership, and other issues.

BUSINESS NAME

Regardless of its form, every business will have a name. Contact your attorney ahead of time with the proposed name of the business. A quick inquiry to the corporation commissioner or secretary of state will establish whether the proposed name is available. Many corporation division offices have online services that could enable you to begin the process yourself. You or your attorney can reserve your chosen business name until you are ready to use it. You will also have to consider whether the business will have a special mark or logo that needs trademark protection. (For a discussion of trademarks, see Chapter 12.)

BUSINESS STRUCTURE

It is also important to determine which business form your operation will adopt, since each available structure has benefits and drawbacks. The forms to consider and their pros and cons are discussed below and in Chapter 2.

Partnership

If it is determined that you will conduct your business in the partnership form, it is essential that you have a formal written agreement prepared by a skilled business attorney. The more time you and your prospective partners spend on being well prepared by discussing these details in advance of meeting with a lawyer, the less such a meeting is likely to cost you.

Following are the basic items of a partnership agreement that you should consider.

Name

As noted, every business will have a name. Most partnerships simply use the surnames of the principal partners. The choice in that case is nothing more than the order of the names—which depends on various factors from prestige to the way the names sound in a particular order. If the business name does not include the partners' full names, it will be necessary to file the proposed business name with the appropriate agency. Care should be taken to choose a name that is distinctive and not already in use. If the name is not distinctive, others can use it. If the name is already in use, you could be liable for trade name or trademark infringement.

Description of the Business

In describing the business, the partners should agree on the basic scope of the business—its requirements in regard to capital and labor, each party's individual contributions of capital and labor, and perhaps some plans regarding future growth.

Capital

After determining how much capital each partner will contribute, the partners must decide when it will be contributed, how to value the property contributed, and whether a partner can contribute or withdraw any property at a later date.

Duration

Sometimes partnerships are organized for a fixed amount of time or are automatically dissolved on certain conditions, such as the completion of a project.

Distribution of Profits

You can make whatever arrangement you want for distribution of profits. Although ordinarily a partner is not paid, it is possible to give an active partner a salary in addition to a share of the profits. Since the partnership's profits can be determined only at the close of a business year, distributions ordinarily are not made until that time. It is, however, possible to allow the partners a monthly draw of money against their share of the final profits. In some cases, it may also be necessary or desirable to allow limited expense accounts for some partners.

Not all the profits of the partnership need to be distributed at year's end. Some can be retained for expansion. This arrangement can be provided for in the partnership agreement. Whether or not the profits are distributed, all partners must pay tax on their shares of the profit. The tax code refers directly to the partnership agreement to determine what that share is. This further demonstrates the importance of a partnership agreement.

Management

The power in the partnership can be divided many ways. All partners can be given the same voice or some may be given more than others. A few partners might be allowed to manage the business entirely, with the remaining partners being given a vote only on specifically designated issues.

Besides voting, three other areas of management should be covered. First is the question of who can sign checks, place orders, or enter into contracts on behalf of the partnership. Under state partnership laws, any partner may do these things so long as they occur in the usual course of business. Since such a broad delegation of authority can lead to confusion, it might be best to delegate this authority more narrowly. Second, it is a good idea to determine a regular date for partnership meetings. Finally, some consideration should be given to the possibility of a disagreement arising among the partners that leads to a deadlock. One way to avoid this is to distribute the voting power so as to make a deadlock impossible. In a two-person partnership, however, this would mean that one partner would be in absolute control. That might be unacceptable to the other partner. If power is divided equally among an even number of partners, as is often the case, the agreement should stipulate a neutral party or arbitrator who could settle any dispute and thereby avoid a dissolution of the partnership.

Prohibited Acts

By law, each partner owes the partnership certain duties by virtue of being an agent of the partnership. First is the duty of diligence. This means the partner must exercise reasonable care in acting as a partner. Second is a duty of obedience. The partner must obey the rules of the partnership and, most importantly, must not exceed the authority that the partnership has entrusted in him or her. Finally, there is a duty of loyalty.

A partner may not, without approval of the other partners, compete with the partnership in another business. A partner also may not seize upon a business opportunity that would be of value to the partnership without first telling the partnership about it and allowing the partnership to pursue it, if the partnership so desires. A list of prohibited acts should be made a part of the partnership agreement, elaborating and expanding on these fundamental duties.

Dissolution and Liquidation

A partnership is automatically dissolved upon the death, withdrawal, or expulsion of a partner. Dissolution identifies the legal end of the partnership, but need not affect its economic life if the partnership agreement has provided for the continuation of the business after a dissolution. Nonetheless, a dissolution will affect the business, because the partner who withdraws or is expelled, or the estate of a deceased partner, will be entitled to a return of the proportionate share of capital that the departing partner contributed.

Details, such as how this capital will be returned, should be decided before dissolution. At the time of dissolution, it may be impossible to negotiate. One method of handling this is to provide for a return of the capital in cash over a period of time. Some provision should be made so that each of the remaining partners will know how much of a departing partner's interest they may purchase.

After a partner leaves, the partnership may need to be reorganized and recapitalized. Again, provisions for this should be worked out in advance if possible. Finally, since it is always possible that the partners will eventually want to liquidate the partnership, it should be decided in advance who will liquidate the assets, which assets will be distributed, and what property will be returned to its original contributor.

Corporations, LLCs, and LLPs

There are usually two reasons for creating a business form such as a corporation, LLC, or LLP—limiting personal liability and minimizing income tax liability. The second reason is generally applicable to a business that is earning a good deal of money.

IN PLAIN ENGLISH

Even if your business is not earning a great deal of money, you may nevertheless want to consider creating a business entity that limits your personal liability.

Corporations, LLCs, and LLPs are hypothetical, legal persons, and as such, are responsible for their own acts and contracts. Thus, if a consumer in a retail store slips on a banana peel, if a consultant's car negligently injures a pedestrian, or if the food your restaurant served causes food poisoning, the corporation, LLC, or LLP—and not its owners—will be liable (assuming the proper formalities have been adhered to).

NOTE: Any individual personally responsible for a wrongful act will also be liable.

Officers and Structure

State statutes generally require a corporation, LLC, or LLP to have some chief operating officer, such as a president or manager. In addition, state statutes may require other administrative officers, such as a secretary. The corporate bylaws or the LLC's or LLP's operating agreement should have a separate description for specialized officers. Note that most states permit LLCs to elect to be run by a single manager or by the members (owners).

Owners

Questions to ask yourself regarding owners include the following.
- How many shares of stock should your corporation be authorized to issue? (In the case of LLCs and LLPs, certificates of ownership, which resemble shares of stock in a corporation, are used and the same considerations for their issuance are present.)
- How many units should be issued when the business commences operations?

- How many units should be held in reserve for future issuance?
- Should there be separate classes of corporate shareholders and LLC or LLP members?

If the corporation or LLC is to be family-owned, ownership may be used to some extent as a means of estate planning or wealth-shifting. You might, therefore, also wish to ask your attorney about updating your will at the same time you incorporate or create an LLC. While LLPs may be used for this purpose, it is not as common.

Owner Agreements

Discuss with your lawyer the possibility of creating owner agreements that govern employment status of key individuals or commit owners to voting a certain way on specific issues. Ensure that a method has been established to prevent an owners' voting deadlock.

Buy-Sell Agreements

The first meeting with your lawyer is a good time to discuss buy-sell agreements. Buy-sell agreements resolve such matters as when one of the owners wishes to leave the business or under what circumstances an owner is able to sell to outsiders. In closely held corporations, the corporation or other shareholders are generally granted the first option to buy the stock. The same kind of procedure can be implemented for LLCs and LLPs.

Decide what circumstances should trigger the business's or other owners' right to buy the interest—death, disability, retirement, termination, and so forth. Also decide whether the buy-sell agreement should be tied to key-person insurance that would fund the purchase of ownership interest by the corporation, LLC, or LLP in the event of a key owner's death. Further, the buy-sell agreement can identify the mechanism for valuing the business—annual appraisal, book value, multiple earnings, arbitration, or some other method—when an owner departs.

Planning for Future Owners

If you anticipate bringing in some additional owners, you and your attorney should discuss the method by which this may be accomplished. There are legal restrictions that are imposed on the issuance and sale of additional shares of stock, as well as the sale and transfer of LLC or LLP interests. Planning for the future is best done at formation.

Capitalization

At this point, the attorney works closely with your accountant. Issues to resolve include the following.

- What will be the initial capitalization or funding of the corporation, LLC, or LLP?
- Will owners make loans to the business and contribute the rest in exchange for ownership interest?
- What is being contributed by owners in exchange for their interests—money, past services, equipment, assets of an ongoing business, licensing agreements, or other things?
- What value will be placed on assets that are contributed to the business?

Governing Board

An initial decision must be made as to who will be on the board of directors of a corporation or the governing board of an LLC or LLP and how many initial directors there will be. You must also decide whether owners will have the right to elect members of the board based on their percentages of ownership. If the LLC or LLP elects to be run by a manager, then a method for selecting that person should be specified.

IN PLAIN ENGLISH

It is a good idea for there to be an odd number of directors in order to avoid the potential for a voting deadlock.

Housekeeping

Your attorney will need to know several other details. For instance, the number of employees the business anticipates for the coming twelve-month period must be stated on the application for a federal taxpayer ID number. You must also decide whether the business tax year will end on December 31 or on another date.

> **NOTE:** S corporations and LLCs that are not taxable entities must adopt the calendar year.

Decisions on whether the business accounting method will be on a cash basis or accrual basis must be made. The amount of, if any, salaries for its officers or managers must be authorized. Set the date for the annual meeting. Selecting a registered agent (generally, your attorney will assume this role) and determining which bank your business will use are all preliminary decisions that must be made.

Employee Benefits

Be prepared to consider employee benefit plans, such as life and health insurance, profit-sharing, pension, or other retirement plans, and employee ownership programs, as well as other fringe benefits. Even if you do not plan to implement such programs when the corporation, LLC, or LLP is created, it is nonetheless a good idea to consider whether such programs may be instituted in the future.

Tax Treatment

Like corporations, LLCs and LLPs can elect to be taxed like corporations or choose to be mere conduits. This choice may be made when the entity is first created or when the first year's taxes are filed. Careful consideration must be given to the appropriate tax treatment, as you may not be able to change your decision later.

If the corporation is likely to sustain major losses and shareholders have other sources of income against which they wish to write off those losses, chances are the S election would be appropriate. For businesses that may not qualify for treatment as S corporations, the LLC may be the appropriate business form, and evaluation of whether the entity should elect to be taxed or choose to have profits and losses passed through to its owners should also be considered.

As you can see, there is much to discuss at the first meeting with your lawyer. A little time and thought prior to that meeting will prove to be a worthwhile investment.

CHAPTER **4**

Developing Your Business Plan

In order to establish a viable business, it is essential to plan. This means that the entrepreneurs must determine where they intend to have the business go; what it will sell; who it will compete against; and, how it will develop.

In addition, every business needs capital at one time or another. This funding might be sought as bank loans, other conventional forms of financing, or as venture capital. It might also be obtained through a public sale of securities (discussed in Chapter 6). No matter what the source of financing, an important first step is the preparation of a business plan. This can aid a banker, venture capitalist, or prospective owner in evaluating your company.

A business plan may be considered a road map to determine the course your business will travel from start-up to full operation. The structure and content of your business plan will vary depending upon such factors as the company's stage of development, the nature of the business, and the type of markets it will serve. There is a host of different formats that have been used for business plans. Although the order of presentation is by no means standard, each of the following topics should be addressed in structuring any business plan. In addition, there are numerous software packages available to assist you in creating your business plan.

EXECUTIVE SUMMARY

The executive summary provides the reader with a short overview of the key elements of the business plan. Sophisticated businesspeople are turned away by exaggeration. The summary must provide an accurate assessment of your business, while distinguishing your product or service and organization from others that are competing in the same market. The summary should also describe your management team, emphasizing experience and skills, but should not ignore management weaknesses and how you expect to overcome them. Another important part of the summary will be your key financial projections and funding requirements to meet those projections. Above all, the summary must be designed to catch the reader's attention. Unless the summary inspires one to read further, it has likely not served its purpose and the remainder of the plan may go unread.

HISTORY OF THE BUSINESS

Businesspeople want to know about the past performance of a business before they assess its potential. To this end, the business plan should provide a brief history of the business (including when it was founded), subsequent development and growth, how it has been organized (i.e., as a sole proprietorship, partnership, corporation, LLC, or LLP), and how well past performance can predict the future. If you have good reason to believe that the past performance is not indicative of the business's potential, be sure to state those reasons in this section.

PRODUCTS AND SERVICES

This section describes in detail the products or services of your business. Include a summary explaining any unique features, a statement about performance and present status, and any special services provided, such as newsletters or catalogs. Keep in mind, however, that investors may not have expertise with your business or even familiarity with your industry. This section should be written in language that is easily understood by businesspeople with nontechnical backgrounds.

THE MARKET

This section should contain a comprehensive description of the market your business intends to target. If the product or service you are selling is innovative, independent market research may need to be included to define both the initial and future markets. If the product or service you are involved with has been available for some time, the market has most likely already been defined. In that case, you may be able to rely on available data from similar businesses, industry professional associations, the Small Business Administration, chambers of commerce, or the like.

IN PLAIN ENGLISH

For purposes of obtaining investment capital, the market section may be the most important part of your business plan. To the banker, venture capitalist, or prospective owner, a business without a strong understanding of its targeted market is a bad risk, even if the service or product to be sold is first-rate.

The market description should be more detailed than the product or service description. This will indicate to potential investors that you understand the priority of market over product or service.

THE COMPETITION

Identify your competitors, discuss their relative strengths and weaknesses, and indicate the market share likely held by each. Include a forecast of the market share you expect to capture in the first three to five years and the sources from which you expect to draw customers. Be sure to spell out your rationale for each projection—more innovative products, creative promotion, marketing, favorable reviews, price, service, or other factors. As with all projections in the business plan, do not understate the strengths of your competition while overstating your own. Sophisticated businesspeople will not back a company that does not have a realistic view of its competition.

SOURCE OF WORK

Obtaining sought-after products or services at an economical price and having the ability to sell the work or provide the service expeditiously are key to making a profit. This section should discuss the trade shows that you attend, detail your suppliers, and identify those with whom you have exclusivity or other agreements. Additionally, you should explain the steps taken by you to expand your product or service line, as well as the markets for it, and whether you acquire products at wholesale or on consignment. In some businesses, such as those selling vehicles or equipment, it would be appropriate to discuss whether you handle resales, rebuilds, or only newly manufactured vehicles or equipment. You should also present information about the reputation of the product, including, for example, favorable reviews and relevant data from recognized publications.

MANAGEMENT

As a general rule, bankers, venture capitalists, and prospective owners would favor investing in a start-up business with first-rate management over an established business with mediocre management. This priority should be reflected in your business plan.

In this section, emphasize the experience of each key management executive. Include job descriptions and salaries and provide résumés detailing each executive's past business experience, education, publications, and any other information that will indicate to potential financiers that you have a qualified management team. If your current management team has weak spots, define them and explain how they will be overcome.

FINANCIAL DATA

Superior products or services and top-flight management count for nothing if your financial projections do not allow for a substantial return on investment. Consequently, this section is the bottom line of your business plan. Begin by summarizing previous financial performance. If your business is new, be sure that all financial projections are realistic and justifiable. Remember that most prospective investors and lenders are sophisticated and will check out other comparable businesses. If your projections deviate widely from the industry norm, you will lose credibility and jeopardize the financing you seek.

IN PLAIN ENGLISH

Do not inundate your potential investor with yards of computer-generated spreadsheets. Your financial data should be concise and easy to understand.

Finally, your financial section should discuss the financing itself. Indicate how much money the business needs, the form of financing sought, and how the money is to be used. Most important, discuss the projected return within the next five years of operation. As with all financial information, be realistic and support your projections with solid data and a sound rationale.

THE BUSINESS PLAN TEAM

The development of a well-written business plan is a considerable undertaking. It forces you to focus your ideas, ferret out weak spots in your organization, and turn abstract concepts into a concrete plan. Experienced professionals, such as lawyers, accountants, and other relevant professionals, can provide invaluable assistance in putting together a sound and attractive business plan. Your lawyer can help your business obtain the legal protection that it needs while steering you away from the legal pitfalls that face all new or expanding businesses. Your accountant can assist you with the myriad financial assessments you must make. Knowledgeable and respected professionals can lend credibility to your numbers and projections.

Beyond this, experienced lawyers and accountants have invaluable contacts within the venture capital and banking communities. They can tell you who has the capital, where it is being invested, and how you can best get a share. By enlisting the help of experienced professionals and following the suggestions presented here, you can develop a business plan that will help you attract the financing you need for your new or expanding business.

CHAPTER 5

Borrowing from Banks

Commercial loans can be a valuable source of needed capital for qualified business borrowers. Small businesses sometimes seek loans from institutional lenders, such as credit unions, insurance companies, and pension trusts. Unfortunately, institutional lenders other than banks will rarely deal with small businesses, particularly when the potential borrower does not have an extensive track record. It is for this reason the focus of this chapter is on bank lending. You should, however, consider these other sources of funds when seeking a loan. Most institutional lenders follow the same procedures as banks and demand the same type of information.

Lending policies vary dramatically from institution to institution. You should talk to several banks to determine which might be likely to lend to your business and which have the most favorable loan terms. While lenders, by nature, are conservative in their lending policies, you may discover some to be more flexible than others. To save time and increase the chances of loan approval, it makes sense to first approach those banks that are most likely to view your proposal favorably and whose lending criteria you feel you can meet.

You should not necessarily limit your search for a loan to your community. A statewide, regional, or even national search may be necessary before you find the right combination of willing lender and favorable terms. With the Internet, this is not as difficult as it once was.

IN PLAIN ENGLISH

Using your credit card as a source of financing is not a good idea, except in the most extreme cases. Interest rates are high and the terms are generally not good for business planning. You must also personally guarantee any business credit card.

After having shopped the marketplace and decided on a particular bank, you will be ready for the next step—preparing the loan proposal. The importance of being properly prepared before taking this critical step cannot be overemphasized. Loan officers are not likely to be impressed by a hastily prepared application containing vague, incomplete information and unsubstantiated claims. Many loan requests are doomed at this early stage because ill-prepared applicants failed to adequately present themselves and their businesses to the lender even though the proposed ventures are, in fact, sound.

LOAN PROPOSAL

Inexperience with the bank's lending procedures can result in an unexpected rejection. Knowing the bank's lending policy and following its procedure is, therefore, essential. At a minimum, a borrower should be prepared to satisfactorily address each of the following questions.

- Is your business creditworthy?
- For what purpose is the money needed?
- Do you need a short- or long-term loan?
- How much money do you really need?
- What kind of collateral do you and your business have to secure the loan?

The lender's decision to grant or refuse the loan request will be based on your answers to these questions.

Creditworthiness

The ability to obtain money when you need it may be as important to the operation of your business as having a good location and the right equipment. However, before an institution will agree to lend you money, the loan officer must be satisfied that you and your business constitute a good risk—that is, that you are creditworthy. This decision includes several considerations.

Good Character

The lender will want to know what sort of person you are and your reputation in the community. Your past credit history and the likelihood that you will repay the loan if your business falters or fails will be looked at and evaluated.

Despite its subjective nature, this character factor figures prominently in the lender's decision-making. It is not uncommon for a loan officer to deny a loan request, irrespective of the applicant's qualifications on paper, if the officer is not convinced of the borrower's good character. Even for signature loans—which require only the applicant's signature and are available only to businesses and entrepreneurs with the highest credit standing, business integrity, and management skills—the applicant's character will affect the institution's decision to make a loan.

Cushion

The lender will want to know if the borrower has included a suitable allowance for unexpected business developments in the loan request. That is, does the loan proposal realistically allow for the operation of a business and provide for alternative resources to meet the borrower's obligation if the business expectations are not met?

IN PLAIN ENGLISH

If the borrower is stretching the limit and leaving no margin for error so that repayment can be made only if the proposed venture is successful, the lender may consider the loan too risky.

Purpose

Once the bank has evaluated the creditworthiness of you and your business, you should be ready to explain the appropriateness of the kind of loan requested. It is important to be able to convince the lender that your proposed use of the borrowed money will generate the additional revenue needed to pay the loan during the agreed repayment period. The purpose of the loan will determine what type of loan—long- or short-term—the applicant should request.

Term of Loan

Loans needed to purchase inventory, especially where the applicant's business is highly seasonal, will generally be short-term loans requiring repayment within one year or less. This is because the bank will likely anticipate repayment from the sale of the assets financed by the loan.

Intermediate-term loans, which require payment in between one and five years, and long-term loans, which extend payments over ten or even fifteen years, are more appropriate for purchases of fixed assets. Repayment on the loans is expected to be made not from the sale of these assets, but from the earnings generated by the company's ongoing use of them. Those assets produce income at a much slower rate, hence the bank's willingness to allow repayment over a longer period. Bear in mind that commercial lenders are interested in offering funds to successful businesses in need of additional capital to expand and increase profitability. They are not particularly inclined to make loans to businesses that need the money to pay off existing debts.

Depending upon your credit reputation, short-term loans may be available with or without security. It is more likely that long-term loans will require adequate security (which may include securing the asset to be acquired) and necessitate a pledge of personal, as well as business, assets.

Loans that are characterized as lines of credit basically provide the business with the opportunity to borrow up to a specified amount at any given time. This can be used to facilitate purchases, help pay salaries when the business is experiencing cash flow problems, or the like. A line of credit is typically available on a long-term basis. Most lenders require the line to be paid off at least once a year, even though the money can be borrowed again immediately thereafter.

Repayment

When and how the loan will be repaid is closely associated with the questions of how much money is needed and for what purpose. The banker will use judgment and professional experience to assess your business ability and the likelihood of your future success. The banker will want to know whether or not the proposed use of the borrowed funds justifies the repayment schedule requested. As the borrower, you must be able to demonstrate that the cash flow anticipated from the proceeds of the loan will be adequate to meet the repayment terms if the loan is granted.

Amount Needed

The lender is also concerned about the amount of the loan being adequate, since an undercapitalized business is more likely to get into financial trouble. Similarly, a lender will be reluctant to approve a loan that is excessive, since the debt service may result in an unnecessarily high cash drain on the business. The loan should net the borrower the amount necessary to accomplish the desired goal with a slight cushion for error and no more.

Estimating the amounts needed to finance building construction, conversion, or expansion—long-term loans—is relatively easy, as is estimating the cost of fixed-asset acquisition. On the other hand, working-capital needs—short-term loans—

are more difficult to assess and depend upon the type and location of business. To plan your working capital requirements, it is important to know the cash flow of your business, present and anticipated. This involves a projection of all the elements of cash receipts and disbursements at the time they are likely to occur. These figures should be projected monthly to aid the bank in its evaluation.

Collateral

Sometimes loans will be made solely on the borrower's signature. More frequently, banks will require collateral to secure the loan. Acceptable collateral can take a variety of forms. The type and amount of collateral necessary in a given situation will depend on the particular bank's lending policies and the borrower's financial state. In general, banks will accept the following types of collateral as security for a business loan.

Sureties

You may have to get other people to sign a note in order to bolster your credit. These people—*sureties*—may cosign your note as endorsers, comakers, or guarantors. While the law makes some subtle distinctions as to when each of these sureties becomes liable for the borrower's debt, in essence, these parties will be expected to pay back the borrowed funds if the borrower fails to do so. The bank may or may not require sureties to pledge their own assets as security for their promise to pay upon the borrower's default. This will depend, to a great extent, on the surety's own creditworthiness.

Assignment of Leases

Assigning a lease as a form of security is particularly appropriate for franchise situations. If the bank lends a business franchise money for a building and takes back a mortgage, that mortgage may be secured by assigning to the lender the lease entered into between the franchisor and the franchisee that will occupy the building. If the franchisor fails to meet mortgage payments, the bank can directly receive the franchisee's lease payments in satisfaction of the franchisor's debt.

Warehouse Receipts

Banks will accept commodities as security by lending money on a warehouse receipt. Such a receipt is usually delivered directly to the bank and shows that the merchandise used as security either has been placed in a public warehouse, or has left the business's premises under the control of a bonded employee. Such loans are generally made only on standard, readily marketable goods.

Security Interests

Equipment loans may be secured by giving the bank a lien on the equipment you are buying. The amount loaned will likely be less than the purchase price. How much less will be determined by the present and future market value of the equipment and its rate of depreciation. You will be expected to adequately insure the equipment, to properly maintain it, and to protect it from damage.

Real Estate Holdings

You may be able to borrow against the equity in your personal real estate holdings, as well as those of the business. Again, you will likely be required to maintain the property in good condition and carry adequate insurance on the property for the benefit of the lender at least up to the amount of the loan.

Accounts Receivable

Many banks will lend money secured by your business accounts receivable. In effect, the bank is relying on your customers to pay off your obligation to the bank.

Savings Accounts and Life Insurance Policies

Sometimes you may get a loan by assigning your savings account to the lender. The lender will then flag the account, while notifying the savings account holder of the existence of the debt in order to ensure that the account will not be diminished during the term of the loan. In addition, the lender will likely limit or prohibit the use of debit cards and the like during the term of the loan. Loans can also be made up to the cash value of a life insurance policy but you must be prepared to assign the policy over to the lender.

Stocks and Bonds

Stocks and bonds may be accepted as collateral for a loan if they are readily marketable. However, banks will typically lend no more than 75% of the market value of a high-grade security. If the value of the securities drops below the lender's required margin, the borrower may be asked to provide additional security for the loan.

Inventory

As previously discussed, business inventory, either on hand or to be acquired, can be used as security for short-term loans. The lender will expect the loan to be repaid from the revenues generated by the sale of this inventory on a timely basis. Inventory may also be used as collateral for long-term loans when the lender establishes what is called a field warehousing arrangement. In this situation, the inventory is segregated and identified as collateral for a loan and an employee responsible to the lender is placed in charge of the field warehouse. This is quite common in the automotive sales industry.

Intellectual Property

Patents, copyrights, trademarks, and other forms of intellectual property may be used as collateral for a loan. There is an increasing body of case law surrounding the methods by which these assets may be secured. Unfortunately, many lenders are unfamiliar with methods of valuing the potential worth of intellectual properties, and thus, may not be willing to attribute a meaningful value to them. If you plan to pledge your intellectual property as security for a loan, it would be beneficial for you first to attempt to obtain an independent appraisal of it.

BUSINESS OUTLOOK

The lender will be evaluating the business outlook for your company in particular, and for your type of business in general, in light of contemporary economic realities. Part of the evaluation will be whether your proposed use of the loan can reasonably be expected to produce the anticipated increased revenues for your business. While your proposed plan may appear viable on paper, it may not be realistic given the state of the economy within which your company operates.

Financial Evidence

Remember that bankers prefer to make loans to solvent, profitable, growing enterprises. They seek assurance that the loan will contribute to that growth, since your repayment ability is directly related to your business success. As noted previously, bankers are not interested in lending money so that a business can pay off already existing loans.

To aid the bank in understanding the financial health of your business, you probably will be asked to provide specific financial data. Two basic financial documents are customarily submitted for this purpose—the business's balance sheet and its profit-and-loss statement. The balance sheet will aid the bank in evaluating your business viability, while the profit-and-loss statement summarizes the business's current performance. Unless yours is a new venture, you should be prepared to submit these financial reports for at least the past two or three years, since they are the principal means for measuring your company's stability and growth potential. Ideally, an independent accountant will have prepared these statements.

Analyzing Your Business Potential

In interviewing loan applicants and in studying the financial records of their businesses, the bank is especially interested in the following facts and figures.

General Information

The lender will be interested in the current condition of your business accounts payable and notes payable. If you are not presently able to meet existing debts, the lender will be hard-pressed to understand how you expect to be able to meet any additional obligations. Perhaps the requested funds will solve cash flow problems you now have and will also increase earnings so that you will be able to bring past-due accounts current while adequately handling the added debt. In this situation, you might overcome the lender's skepticism by presenting a well-thought-out, solid business plan that clearly demonstrates how the new loan will solve, rather than add to, the business's financial problems and will boost revenues.

Additionally, the lender will likely want to know the salaries of the owner or manager and other company officers to see if they are reasonable. Excessive salaries represent an unacceptable drain on company resources and profits that may adversely affect the company's ability to meet debt obligations.

The lender will also be interested in the size of your work force to determine whether it seems adequate to maximize the business potential or excessive compared to other similar businesses.

You should be prepared to discuss the adequacy of your company's insurance coverage, your present tax situation (whether all taxes are current), and if your business sells a product, the size, if any, of your order backlog. For services, the business's reputation will be particularly relevant. Existing business contracts will likely also be evaluated.

All these factors say something about the financial state of your business. Although the lender may inquire into other areas, the borrower who knows the type of general information of interest to a lender and can present it articulately greatly increases the chances of having the loan approved.

Fixed Assets

Since fixed assets can be used to secure the loan, the bank will likely be interested in the type, condition, age, and current market value of your company's equipment, machinery, etc. You should be prepared to explain how these assets have been depreciated, their useful life expectancy, and whether they have been previously mortgaged or pledged as collateral to another lender. In addition, be ready to discuss any need or plans to acquire fixed assets. This need could mean additional debt obligations in the near future or it could explain and justify your projected growth.

IN PLAIN ENGLISH

Banks are reluctant to loan money to companies with haphazardly kept records. Make sure yours are up-to-date, accurate, and in good condition.

Options for Owners of New Businesses

The preceding analysis applies primarily to loan requests made by established, proven businesses. New-business loan applicants will probably not be able to supply much of the information described earlier. While this will not necessarily preclude having a loan approved, it could make its approval more difficult. You should be aware that new-business loans constitute only approximately 5% of all business loans made.

This reluctance to finance unproven businesses, understandably frustrating to new-business owners, is consistent with the traditionally conservative nature of banks. In light of the extraordinarily high failure rate of new businesses, compounded by the fact that a new business generally cannot provide adequate financial data to evaluate its potential for success, the lender is hard-pressed to justify making high-risk loans. Even where the new-business borrower offers more than adequate collateral to secure the loan, the request may be denied.

Banks are comfortable lending money and earning profits from the interest charged on their loans. They are not comfortable in the role of an involuntary partner in the failing business of a delinquent debtor. Even though banks secure loans with a wide range of collateral, they understandably are not anxious to have to foreclose on that security. They are not in the business of selling business machinery or inventory, or of trying to collect a delinquent debtor's accounts receivable. Although banks try to protect themselves by lending only a fraction of the collateral's market value, they still may not obtain the full amount they are owed in a distress sale of that collateral, since this type of sale traditionally attracts bargain-hunters who will often buy only at prices well below true market value. With an understanding of these dynamics, a new-business loan applicant can better appreciate a bank's hesitation in approving a loan.

Nonetheless, banks do make some loans to new businesses. The entrepreneur will need to demonstrate a good reputation for paying debts and to offer evidence of business management skills. Perhaps you have firsthand knowledge and expertise in the type of business you propose to establish as a result of having previously been employed in the same or a closely related field. If so, emphasize that. In addition, provide a sound business plan to support your projections. You can further improve your chances of obtaining a loan if you have invested your own money in the business, thus indicating your confidence in its success. If possible, show that the business has a good debt-to-equity ratio and that it is not saddled with an inordinately high debt.

Even if your loan application is initially refused, it is important to establish a good working relationship with a bank. Any initial business success will impress upon the bank the soundness of your plan, thereby opening the door for future financing should the need arise.

APPLICATION

Having targeted the source for funds and having analyzed the business in terms you now know lenders look at, you are ready to develop the loan request. Though most lenders will require the application to include the same standard essential information, they often differ as to the prescribed format of the application. Some lenders may provide suggested formats, while others may require a specific format. The actual content, length, and formality will depend on the lender's familiarity with your business, the amount of money requested, and the proposed use of the borrowed funds. A simple application form and a conversation may be adequate for your local banker. The start-up business seeking substantial funds from lenders unfamiliar with it will be required to provide much more extensive documentation, including a detailed plan of the entire business.

The business loan applicant is typically asked to submit any or all of the following information.

- *Personal financial statements.* These indicate the applicant's personal net worth. This is helpful in evaluating creditworthiness and revealing potential sources of collateral, as well as estimating repayment capabilities.
- *Recent and current tax filings.* These should include filings of the individual and of the business, usually for the last three years, if available.
- *Business financial statements.* These ideally should extend back for at least two or three years and should have been prepared and authenticated by an independent accountant. The lender may also request cash flow statements and profit projections.
- *Business history.* This should include past profit or loss patterns, current debt-to-equity ratio, current and projected cash flow, and present and projected future earnings.
- *Business plan.* This should explain the proposed use of the requested funds and how the loan will benefit the business. The length and content of this plan will vary according to the financial health of the applicant's business and the amount and type of loan applied for.

Other documentation may also be requested. The individual lender will indicate what is needed in light of the given circumstances.

LENDER'S RULES AND LIMITATIONS

Once the loan has been approved in principle, it is likely that the bank will impose certain rules and constraints on you and your business. These serve to protect the lender against unnecessary risk and against the possibility of your engaging in poor management practices. You, your attorney, and your business advisor should evaluate all the terms and conditions of the loan in order to determine whether it is acceptable. If the bank's requirements are too onerous, it may be appropriate for you to decline the loan and seek alternative financing. Never agree to restrictions to which you cannot realistically adhere. On the other hand, if the terms and conditions of the loan are acceptable, even though they are demanding, it may be appropriate to take the loan. In fact, some borrowers view these limitations as an opportunity for improving their own management techniques and business profitability.

As a result of the bank's scrutiny of your company, the kinds of limitations imposed will depend, to a great extent, on the company itself. If the company is a good risk, only minimum limitations need be set. A poor risk, of course, should expect greater limitations to be placed on it. Three common types of limitations you are likely to encounter are repayment terms, use of pledged security, and periodic reporting.

Repayment Terms

The bank will want to set a loan-repayment schedule that accurately reflects your ability to earn revenues sufficient to meet the proposed obligation. Risky businesses can expect shorter terms, while proven enterprises may receive longer periods within which to repay the loan.

Use of Pledged Security

Once a lender agrees to accept collateral to secure a loan, it will understandably be keenly interested in assuring that, should the need arise, the collateral will still be available to satisfy the debt. To this end, the lender may take actual possession of the collateral if it is stocks, bonds, or other negotiable instruments. A bank is not likely to take physical possession of a business inventory or fixed assets and remove them to the bank's vault.

There are, however, other ways a bank can obtain possession of your fixed assets while allowing you to use them. For example, the lender could perfect—legally establish—a security interest in machinery and intellectual property, as well as equipment used in your plant or business. This is done by filing a financing statement in the appropriate state or county office. (A *security interest* is the legal term for a lender's rights in collateral.)

The bank may impose restrictions on the use of the collateral and require that it be properly maintained and adequately insured. The bank may further limit or prohibit you from pledging the same collateral for any other business debts or loans.

While this sounds reasonable, you should recognize that such restrictions may seriously hamper your ability to borrow additional funds should the need arise. For example, where inventory is used as collateral, you must find out exactly how much of your inventory is involved. A bank may ask for only a percentage of the total inventory to secure the loan. More likely, the bank's security interest will extend to the company's entire inventory on hand at any given time, as well as any later-acquired inventory. Here lies the potential problem. The inventory's value may well exceed the amount of the loan that it secures. Nonetheless, you may find yourself in the position of not being able to use any of the inventory as collateral for additional loans. In cases where this situation is likely to arise, you are well advised to consider alternative sources of collateral.

Periodic Reporting

To protect itself, a lender may require you to supply it with certain financial statements on a regular basis—perhaps quarterly or even monthly. From these, the lender can see if the business is performing up to the expectations projected in the loan application. This type of oversight serves not only to reassure the lender that the loan will be repaid, but also to identify and help solve problems early on before they become insurmountable and threaten the business's viability.

DETAILS OF THE AGREEMENT

The loan agreement itself is a tailor-made document—a contract between the lender and borrower—that spells out in detail all the terms and conditions of the loan. The actual restrictions placed on the borrower will be found in the agreement under a section entitled "Covenants." Negative covenants are things that you may not do without the lender's prior approval, such as incurring additional debt or pledging the loan's collateral or other business assets to another lender as collateral for a second loan. On the other hand, positive covenants spell out those things that you must do, such as carry adequate insurance, provide specified financial reports, and repay the loan according to the terms of the loan agreement.

Note that, with the lender's prior consent, the terms and conditions contained in the loan agreement may be amended, adjusted, or even waived. Remember that you can negotiate the loan terms with the lender before signing. True, the bank is in the superior position, but legitimate lenders are happy to cooperate with qualified borrowers.

COMMUNICATION WHEN PROBLEMS ARISE

Once a loan is approved and disbursed, the borrower must address a new set of obligations and liabilities. Of course, if all goes according to plan, the loan proceeds are invested, the business prospers, the loan is repaid on schedule, and all parties live happily ever after. However, the business world is fraught with uncertainty. If the business falters and revenues tumble, the borrower may not be able to meet the debt obligations. In this unfortunate event, it becomes imperative that the borrower act responsibly. View the lender as a potential ally in solving problems, rather than as an adversary.

At least initially, banks are not eager to exercise their right to foreclose on the collateral securing the loan at the first indication that the debt may not be repaid. They likely have no experience in marketing the types of collateral involved and they do not want to run a distress sale, which, at best, would probably bring in only a fraction of the money owed. Additionally, foreclosing against the business assets further decreases the bank's chance of recovering any of the unpaid balance, since the borrower, having been stripped of the means to carry on the business, is likely to be insolvent and facing bankruptcy. Even if the lender can liquidate the collateral at its current fair market value, that value may be well below the value agreed upon when the loan was made. For these and other reasons, banks foreclose on collateral only as a last resort.

Bear in mind that, in general, lenders prefer to work with a potentially defaulting debtor to help ease the debt burden so that the borrower can overcome the problems, stay in business, and reestablish the enterprise's profitability. To this end, lenders, through their experiences, have learned to identify a variety of red flags as indications that the debtor is experiencing financial difficulty. For example, the alert is sounded when loan payments start to be made later and later each month or when the business account increasingly shows checks being dishonored for insufficient funds.

When the lender sees these signals, the account may be assigned to a separate department set up within the bank to assist borrowers in overcoming problems. The bank may be willing to offer a variety of accommodations to help the borrower. Repayment terms can be extended, the amount of payment due each month can temporarily be reduced, or the bank may accept repayment of interest only until the business has overcome its temporary difficulties. The bank may be in a position to offer advice for ways to help solve the business problems, particularly if poor management is the source of the difficulties.

How far and to what extent the bank will be willing to accommodate a delinquent debtor very often depends on the attitude and degree of cooperation from the debtor. Hard-pressed debtors often fail to understand the importance of establishing a cooperative, rather than an adversarial, relationship with the lender. At the first sign of trouble, the borrower should take the initiative to notify the bank and explain what is being done to remedy the situation. Expecting a bank to be sympathetic to one's plight and to make concessions seems unreasonable in cases where the borrower waits until the debt is long past due before approaching the lender to explain the problems. Additionally, a bank is not likely to be too sympathetic toward a borrower who fails to return phone calls and virtually disappears, or who is always unavailable to discuss the problem with the bank.

The lender is likely to be most cooperative with the hard-pressed debtor who alerts the bank to problems early on. The debtor should explain what efforts are being made to remedy the problems and keep in close contact with the bank, informing it of current developments and the progress made toward solution of the problems.

A favorably impressed lender can be an invaluable asset to your business, not only in granting loans, but also in helping you out in difficult times. Do not underestimate the need for establishing a solid, professional relationship with your lender. The ultimate success and growth of your business may well depend on it.

VENTURE CAPITAL

While some entrepreneurs are able to attract venture capital, this is uncommon for most small businesses. Most venture capitalists typically expect a potential investment return of between four to six times their risk capital within a comparatively short period of time, as well as some form of ownership position in the borrower's business. It is essential to work with an experienced business lawyer when dealing with venture capitalists, since these arrangements are generally hammered out on a case-by-case basis. It has been said that the golden rule in dealing with venture capitalists is—*The one who has the gold is the one who makes the rules.*

CHAPTER 6

Going Public

At some point, you may determine that you wish to obtain capital from investors rather than borrow from lenders. You may, therefore, consider having your business conduct a public securities offering. Each year, many private businesses go public. According to Chris Meyer, analyst for Morgan Stanley, in 2005 there were 1,600 initial public offerings (IPOs) valued at $170 billion, and in the first half of 2006, there were 745 IPOs valued at $103 billion. However, some small companies that went public have become disillusioned and are returning to their former private status. It is worthwhile to look at the pros and cons of going public and some of the factors you should consider before making that crucial decision.

ADVANTAGES OF GOING PUBLIC

Access to capital and increased prestige are some of the motivating forces behind going public. Issuing stock has the advantage of raising capital without obligating the business to repay loans. The additional capital allows for continued growth, even when earnings and bank loans are insufficient to meet expansion objectives. Also, a successful public offering can improve net worth and debt-to-equity ratio, thereby increasing credibility and financing leverage with lenders.

Public offerings also enhance a company's prestige by increasing its visibility within the business community. The prestige of going public can be an effective device for attracting top-rate management executives. In turn, a strong management team is often the key to both increasing profitability and attracting new investors. In fact, during the growth of the high-tech industry bubble, stock options were essential for attracting and keeping employees. Public stock provides its owners with the ability to sell more easily when an exit strategy is desired.

DISADVANTAGES OF GOING PUBLIC

Disadvantages of going public are primarily high costs and diminished control over the company. The costs of going public include printing, attorneys, accountants, filing fees, and underwriter commissions. Businesses contemplating a public offering should expect an initial outlay of $50,000 to $250,000 or more, though small public offerings may be less.

In addition, going public increases a business's administrative costs. Going public has always meant more regulations to adhere to and more paperwork to process. Public corporations undergo extensive auditing and must gather and disseminate information for their shareholders. They must also comply with a host of regulations that have been adopted in an attempt to cure the ills that had surfaced in recent years. These additional administrative functions add to the overall cost of doing business.

Further, the business must be conducted in a "fishbowl"; that is, it will be subject to intense public scrutiny in addition to that of the state and federal regulators, as well as investors.

The *Sarbanes-Oxley Act* was enacted in July 2002 after major accounting frauds were revealed at some of the country's largest corporations. This Act, which mandated a number of reforms to combat corporate and accounting fraud, regulates, among other things, how companies report financial results and disclose executive compensation. The law requires detailed documentation (by companies and their auditors) of procedures for assuring the accuracy of their financial statements—resulting in significantly increased costs for public companies.

IN PLAIN ENGLISH

While shareholders supply much-needed capital to a growing business, they also usurp a degree of control over the company's operations. Suddenly, management is beholden to a large number of investors, whose interest in short-term profits may conflict with what is best for the long-term health of the business.

Shareholders and the general public (including competitors) must also be apprised of previously private information, such as details about management, organization, executives, products, sales, and profit figures. Public divulgence of this information may put a business at a competitive disadvantage.

Furthermore, minority shareholders have certain dissenter and minority rights that give them a voice disproportionate to the size of their ownership interests. These disadvantages—high costs and diminished control over the business— must carefully be weighed before undertaking the rigors of going public.

FEDERAL AND STATE SECURITIES LAWS

Securities laws are promulgated under both state and federal statutes. The *Securities and Exchange Commission* (SEC) is responsible for administering the federal securities laws. Its purpose is to assure equal access to and full disclosure of all material facts about a business. However, the SEC recognizes that the burden of disclosure is often excessive and nonessential as applied to smaller businesses. Consequently, special procedures and exemptions have been established for small businesses to simplify and expedite the registration process. The laws governing securities are very technical. Only experienced securities attorneys are generally in a position to counsel you about the requirements of a particular transaction. Even during the creation of a business entity, the securities law should be considered. Your attorney should determine whether an appropriate exemption from securities compliance is available or whether you must undertake the time-consuming and expensive process of registering the securities you will be issuing.

Compliance with federal law does not end the matter. A securities issuer must also comply with state provisions known as blue sky laws that are sometimes even more stringent than the federal statutes. Consequently, stricter state provisions regarding the registration of small issues may offset the benefits of simplified procedures and exemptions under federal law. Nevertheless, the small business must comply with the stricter state provisions.

Violations of securities laws can result in civil or, in some cases, criminal liability. Sanctions include rescission of the entire offering, money damages, injunction against or voiding of business transactions, and even criminal prosecution. Furthermore, all securities, whether registered or exempt, are subject to strict anti-fraud provisions. Liability of the issuer is unlimited and extends to significant shareholders, as well as to other related persons or entities.

INITIAL PUBLIC OFFERING

Deciding to go public and implementing that decision are time-consuming and complicated tasks. A company must first determine whether it is in an appropriate position to make a public offering, and then must choose the optimal timing. Factors to consider include the availability of other means of financing, the degree of financial need, and the market conditions for the specific product or services being offered. If the amount of capital is $1 million or less, the *Small Corporate Offering Registration* (SCOR) may be used. As of the date of this writing, this streamlined procedure is available in forty-six states.

Since an *initial public offering* (IPO) is highly complex, any business proceeding with an IPO needs to assemble a professional team to assist with the myriad legal and financial considerations that are inherent in the process. This support team typically includes experienced legal counsel, independent accountants, investment bankers, underwriters, and selling agents.

Attorney's Role

The complex nature of securities law makes the experienced securities attorney an indispensable part of any successful public offering. The attorney must ensure adherence to all relevant laws and regulations. The attorney must also make the company aware of possible exemptions, advise on necessary disclosures, and assist in preparing the necessary disclosure documents—such as a prospectus or offering memorandum and a registration statement. Furthermore, an experienced securities attorney can review existing contracts and advise changes, file necessary documents for SEC review, and recommend internal structural changes that will ease the company's transition from private to public.

Accountant's Role

A significant part of any public offering is the accounting required by the SEC. Accountants must provide audits of the company to be sure that its financial data is current, and when appropriate, prepare earnings projections or forecasts. The accountant will work closely with the attorney during the registration process.

Banker's Role

Many companies will need some interim or bridge financing before the offering is completed. The banker may assist with this interim financing. In addition, many companies are funded by a combination of financing vehicles, such as conventional loans, lines of credit secured by inventory or accounts receivable or both, and traditional equity financing (stock). The banker should assist the company in determining its optimum funding mix. The banker will also aid the company in obtaining loans when appropriate.

Underwriter's and Selling Agents' Roles

Rarely will a company be in a position to sell its own securities. It is, therefore, important for an underwriter to be retained for the purpose of placing the investment. Underwriters generally have a network of sales agents who will assist them in selling the company's securities. Generally, there are three kinds of underwriting.

1. *Firm underwriting*—the underwriter purchases the entire offering at a discount and resells it to investors. This is customarily used for very large, established companies with an existing public market.

2. *Standby underwriting*—the underwriter commits to sell a certain amount of the offering and agrees to purchase up to that portion if it is not sold to investors. Again, this form of underwriting is customarily confined to large, established companies with an existing public market in their securities.

3. *Best efforts underwriting*—the underwriter merely agrees to use its best efforts to sell the offering. There is no assurance, however, that any securities will actually be sold and no obligation on the underwriter to purchase unsold securities. This is the most common for IPOs, smaller companies, and private placements.

PRIVATIZATION

While many companies go public in order to satisfy business and other needs, some publicly traded companies have gone private. The process of privatizing a public company is complex, but typically involves a situation whereby an individual company or group offers to purchase the stock or ownership interest from public holders for a price that exceeds the then-trading price of that security. This type of transaction is more likely when it is believed that the publicly traded company's potential value could be enhanced if the individual or group acquiring these securities had more control.

The process of taking a business private is as technical and demanding as the process of taking it public. Compliance with the laws surrounding so-called tender offers and the rules imposed by the SEC also necessitates the skills of experienced securities lawyers, investment bankers, underwriters, and the like.

IN PLAIN ENGLISH

The law surrounding securities is pervasive. It touches every transaction in which businesses obtain investments. Determining whether your business must comply with some or all of the federal and state securities laws is essential. You should work with an experienced securities attorney, accountant, and business advisor in order to make this determination and avoid the undesirable consequences that may result from violating the securities laws.

CHAPTER 7

Contracts

Contracts are an essential part of virtually every business. Clearly, the entire field of contract law cannot be covered here, but by becoming aware of some of the ramifications of contract law, you will see where you need to be cautious.

CONTRACT BASICS

A contract is a legally binding promise or set of promises. The law requires that the parties to a contract perform the promises they have made to each other. In the event of nonperformance—usually called a *breach*—the law provides remedies to the injured party. For the purposes of this discussion, it will be assumed that the contract is between two people, though it frequently involves business organizations as well. It should be noted that when business organizations are involved, there are additional considerations, such as whether the person acting on behalf of the business has appropriate authority, how that authority must be evidenced, and regardless of authority, whether that individual's act will be deemed within the appropriate scope of the business. These issues complicate the analysis. You should discuss these issues with your business attorney.

The three basic elements of every contract are the offer, the acceptance, and the consideration. To illustrate these elements, suppose a salesperson shows a customer a Mustang convertible at an automobile lot and suggests that he or she buy it (the offer). The customer says he or she likes it and wants it (the acceptance). They agree on a price (the consideration). That is the basic framework, but a great many variations can be played on that theme.

TYPES OF CONTRACTS

Contracts may be express or implied. They may be oral or written. There are generally at least two types of contracts that must be in writing if they are to be legally enforceable:

1. any contract that, by its terms, cannot be completed in less than one year, and

2. any contract that involves the sale of goods for over $500.

Express Contracts

An express contract is one in which all the details are spelled out. It can be either oral or written. If you are going to the trouble of expressing contractual terms, you should put your understanding in writing. For example, you might make a contract with a retail store for six dozen gallons of apple cider to be delivered by you on October 1, at a price of $1.75 per gallon, to be paid within thirty days of receipt. This scenario is fairly straightforward. If either party fails to live up to any material part of the contract, a breach has occurred. The other party may withhold performance of his or her obligation until receiving assurance that the breaching party will perform. In the event no such assurance is forthcoming, the aggrieved party may have a cause of action and sue for breach of contract.

If the apple cider is delivered on October 15 and the store had advertised the availability of your special apple cider during the week of October 1, time was an important consideration and the store would not be required to accept the late shipment. If time is not a material consideration, then, even with the slight delay, this probably would be considered substantial performance and the store would have to accept the delivery.

Implied Contracts

Implied contracts are usually not reduced to writing and need not be very complicated. An example might be if you call a supplier to order five boxes of computer paper without making any express statement that you will pay for the paper. The promise to pay is implied in the order and is enforceable when the paper is delivered.

With implied contracts, however, things can often become a lot stickier. Suppose a manufacturer of notepads asks you to send over a supply of a new kind of glue you have just begun marketing to try it out. You deliver a generous amount. The notepad manufacturer likes the glue, uses it up, and is overheard commenting that it is the best glue yet for the manufacture of notepads. Is there an implied contract to purchase in this arrangement? That depends on whether you are normally in the business of giving away large, free samples of new products.

UNDERSTANDING CONTRACT PRINCIPLES

In order to understand the principles of offer, acceptance, and consideration, you should examine them in the context of several potential situations for hypothetical business owner, Pat Smith. Smith is an automobile dealer who has an impressive collection of vintage cars in mint condition. Let us look at the following situations and see whether an enforceable contract comes into existence.

- At a cocktail party, Jones expresses an interest in Smith's cars. "It looks like the market value of your cars keeps going up," Jones tells Smith. "I'm going to buy one while I can still afford it."

  Is this a contract? If so, what are the terms of the offer—the particular car, the specific price? No, this is not really an offer that Smith can accept. It is nothing more than an opinion or a vague expression of intent.

- Brown offers to pay $14,000 for one of Smith's cars that she saw in an auto show several weeks ago. At the show, it was listed at $14,500, but Smith agrees to accept the lower price.

  Is this an enforceable contract? Yes! Brown has offered, in unambiguous terms, to pay a specific amount for a specific car and Smith has accepted the offer. A binding contract exists.

- One day, Jones shows up at Smith's car lot and sees a particular car for which he offers $14,500. Smith accepts and promises to transfer title the next week, at which time Jones will pay for it. An hour later, Brown shows up. She likes the same car and offers Smith $16,000 for it.

  Can Smith accept the later offer? No—a contract exists with Jones. An offer was made and accepted. The fact that the object has not yet been delivered or paid for does not make the contract any less binding.

- Green discusses certain renovations he would like Smith to perform on a particular car Smith has just acquired. He offers to pay $16,000 for the car if the final product is satisfactory to him. Green approves preliminary sketches and Smith completes the work. However, when Green arrives to pick up his car, he refuses to accept it because it does not satisfy him.

  Is there a contract in this case? Green is making the offer in this case, but the offer is conditional upon his satisfaction with the completed work. Smith can only accept the offer by producing something that meets Green's subjective standards—a risky proposition. There is no enforceable contract for payment until such time as Green indicates that the completed work is satisfactory.

  If Green comes to Smith's car lot and says that the car is satisfactory but then, when Smith delivers it, says he has changed his mind, it is too late. The contract became binding at the moment he indicated the work to be satisfactory. If he then refuses to accept it, he would be breaching his contract.

PROVING AN AGREEMENT

Contracts are enforceable only if they can be proven. All the hypothetical examples mentioned could have been oral contracts, but a great amount of detail is often lost in the course of remembering a conversation. The best practice, of course, is to get it in writing. The function of a written contract is not only that of proof, but to make very clear the understanding of the parties regarding the agreement and the terms of the contract.

Some business owners prefer to do business strictly on the basis of a handshake, particularly with their immediate suppliers and retailers. The assumption seems to be that the best business relations are those based upon mutual trust alone. Although there may be some validity to this, business owners really should put all agreements in writing. Far too many trusting people have suffered adverse consequences because of their reliance upon the sanctity of oral contracts.

Under even the best of business relationships, it is still possible that one or both parties might forget the terms of an oral agreement. It is also possible that both parties might have quite different perceptions about the precise terms of the agreement reached. When the agreement is put into writing, however, there is much less doubt as to the terms of the arrangement. Thus, a written contract generally functions as a safeguard against subsequent misunderstandings or forgetful minds.

Perhaps the principal problem with oral contracts lies in the fact that they cannot always be proven or enforced. Proof of oral contracts typically centers around the conflicting testimony of the parties involved. If one of the parties is not able to establish by a *preponderance of evidence* (more likely than not) that his or her version of the contract is the correct one, then the oral contract may be considered nonexistent—as though it had never been made. The same result might occur if the parties cannot remember the precise terms of the agreement.

When Written Contracts Are Necessary

Even if an oral contract is established, it may not always be enforceable. As already noted, there are some agreements that must be in writing in order to be legally enforceable.

An early law that was designed to prevent fraud and perjury, known as the *Statute of Frauds*, provides that any contract, which, by its terms, cannot be fully performed within one year, must be in writing. This rule is narrowly interpreted, so if there is any possibility, no matter how remote, that the contract could be fully performed within one year, the contract need not be reduced to writing.

For example, if a jeweler agreed to submit one piece of custom-designed jewelry to a customer each year for a period of five years, the contract would have to be in writing. By the very terms of the agreement, there is no way the contract could be performed within one year. If, on the other hand, the contract called for the jeweler to deliver five pieces within a period of five years, the contract would not have to be in writing under the Statute of Frauds.

It is possible, though perhaps not probable, that the jeweler could deliver all five pieces within the first year. The fact that the jeweler does not actually complete performance of the contract within one year is immaterial. So long as complete performance within one year is within the realm of possibility, the contract need not be in writing to be enforceable.

The Statute of Frauds further provides that any contract for the sale of goods valued at $500 or more is not enforceable unless it has been put into writing and signed by the party against whom enforcement is being sought. The fact that a contract for a price in excess of $500 is not in writing does not void the agreement or render it illegal. The parties are free to perform the oral arrangement, but if one party refuses to perform, the other will be unable to legally enforce the agreement.

The law defines goods as all things that are movable at the time the contract is made, except for the money used as payment. The real question becomes whether a particular contract involves the sale of goods for a price of $500 or more. Although the answer would generally seem to be fairly clear, ambiguities may arise.

In addition, some states have identified specific contracts that are enforceable only if in writing regardless of the other rules that would otherwise apply. For example, Oregon state law prescribes that a contract for landscape work, regardless of its duration or price, must be in writing.

ESSENTIALS TO PUT IN WRITING

A contract should be written in simple language that both parties can understand and should spell out the terms of the agreement.

A contract should include the following:
- the date of the agreement;
- identification of the parties (i.e., the buyer and seller in the case of sale of goods or services);
- a description of the goods or services sold;
- the price or other consideration; and,
- the signatures of the parties involved.

To supplement these basics, an agreement should spell out whatever other terms might be applicable, such as pricing arrangements, payment schedules, insurance coverage, and consignment details. Many transactions are important enough that additional clauses covering certain contingencies should be added as well.

Finally, it should be noted that a written document that leaves out essential terms of the contract presents many of the same problems of proof and ambiguity as an oral contract.

IN PLAIN ENGLISH

The terms of the contract should be well conceived, clearly drafted, conspicuous (i.e., not in tiny print that no one can read), and in plain English, so everyone can understand them.

NO-COST WRITTEN AGREEMENTS

At this point, owners of small businesses might object, asserting that they do not have the time, energy, or patience to draft contracts. After all, they are in business to make a product or sell a service, not to formulate written contracts steeped in legal jargon.

Fortunately, the businessperson will not always be required to do this, since the supplier or retailer may be willing to draft a satisfactory contract. However, be wary of signing any form contracts—they will almost invariably be one-sided, with all terms in favor of whoever paid to have them drafted.

As a second alternative, the businessperson could employ an attorney to draft contracts. However, this might be cost-effective only for substantial transactions. With respect to smaller transactions, the legal fees may be much larger than the benefits derived from having a written contract.

The *Uniform Commercial Code* (UCC) provides businesses with a third, and perhaps the best, alternative. While the UCC applies only to the sale of goods, in situations where it applies, businesses need not draft contracts or rely on anyone else (a supplier, retailer, or attorney) to do so.

Confirming Memorandum

The UCC provides that, where both parties are merchants and one party sends to the other a written confirmation of an oral contract within a reasonable time after that contract was made, and the recipient does not object to the confirming memorandum within ten days of its receipt, the contract will be deemed enforceable.

A merchant is defined as any person who normally deals in goods of the kind sold or who, because of occupation, represents him or herself as having knowledge or skill peculiar to the practices or goods involved in the transaction. Most businesspeople will be considered merchants.

It should be emphasized that the sole effect of the confirming memorandum is that neither party can use the Statute of Frauds as a defense, assuming that the recipient fails to object within ten days after receipt. The party sending the confirming memorandum must still prove that an oral contract was made prior to or at the same time as the written confirmation. (However, once such proof is offered, neither party can raise the Statute of Frauds to avoid enforcement of the agreement.)

The advantage of the confirming memorandum over a written contract lies in the fact that the confirming memorandum can be used without the active participation of the other contracting party. It would suffice, for example, to simply state—

> *This memorandum is to confirm our oral agreement.*

Since you would then still have to prove the terms of that agreement, it would be useful to provide a bit more detail in the confirming memorandum, such as the subject of the contract, the date it was made, and the price or other consideration to be paid. Thus, you might draft something like the following.

> *This memorandum is to confirm our oral agreement made on July 3, 2007, pursuant to which supplier agreed to deliver to purchaser on or before September 19, 2007, 5,000 sheets of letterhead for the purchase price of $600.*

The advantages of providing some detail in the confirming memorandum are twofold. First, in the event of a dispute, you could introduce the memorandum as proof of the terms of the oral agreement. Second, the recipient of the memorandum will be precluded from offering any proof regarding the terms of the oral contract that contradicts the terms contained in the memorandum. The recipient, or for that matter, the party sending the memorandum, can introduce proof only regarding the terms of the oral contract that are consistent with the terms, if any, found in the memorandum.

Thus, the purchaser in the example would be precluded from claiming that the contract called for delivery of 10,000 sheets of letterhead because the quantity was stated in the written memo and not objected to. On the other hand, the purchaser would be permitted to testify that the oral contract required the supplier to engrave the letterhead in a specific way, since this testimony would not be inconsistent with the terms stated in the memorandum.

IN PLAIN ENGLISH

If drafting a complete written contract proves too burdensome or too costly, the businessperson should submit a memorandum in confirmation of the oral contract. This at least surpasses the initial barrier raised by the Statute of Frauds. Moreover, by recounting the terms in the memorandum, the businessperson is in a much better position to prove the oral contract at a later date.

Additional Terms

One party to a contract can prevent the other from adding or inventing terms that are not spelled out in the confirming memorandum by ending the memorandum with a clause requiring all other provisions to be contained in a written and signed document. Such a clause might read as follows.

This is the entire agreement between the parties and no modification, alteration, or additional terms shall be enforceable unless in writing and signed by both parties.

If you use such a clause, be sure there are no additional agreed-to terms that have not been included in the written document. A court will generally be confined to the four corners of the document when trying to determine what was agreed to between the parties. This means that nothing more than what is on the paper containing the agreement will be allowed as evidence.

An exception to this rule is that a court may allow oral evidence for the purpose of interpreting ambiguities or explaining the meaning of certain technical terms. The court may also permit the other parties to introduce evidence of past practices in connection with the contract in question, in connection with other agreements between the parties, or even in connection with contracts between other parties.

Businesspeople should not rely on oral contracts alone, since they offer little protection in the event of a dispute. The best protection is afforded by a written contract. It is a truism that oral contracts are not worth the paper they are written on.

CONTRACTING ONLINE

In 2000, the *Electronic Signatures in Global and National Commerce Act* (E-SIGN) became effective. This Act was intended, among other things, to encourage online commerce and provide the parties who take advantage of it with the ability to contract in cyberspace.

Where a contract is required to be in writing, parties can decide to contract electronically by affirmatively agreeing to do so. When a company dealing with a consumer is required to provide a contract or notice in writing, that company must both seek the customer's consent to receipt of an electronic document and verify that the document can be accessed and retained by the consumer. For example, the company must notify the customer of the hardware and software requirements for accessing the document.

Once a consumer consents to electronic receipt of documents, the consumer must notify the company of any change in email address. If the customer desires to withdraw his or her consent to electronic receipt, the location where documents can be sent must be disclosed to the company as well.

Online contracting is available only when there is a method for preserving the electronic contracts and other relevant data electronically. This will eliminate the need for warehousing hard copies of the documents for online contracting. No special technology must be used for online contracting and the parties are free to establish their own vehicle for accomplishing the Act's requirements. Electronically signed documents can be encrypted if the parties agree. In fact, this is likely to be the standard procedure, at least at the initial stages of the development of the online process of contracting.

CONSUMER PROTECTION LAWS

The federal government and many states have enacted legislation designed to give consumers the opportunity to change their minds and cancel unwanted sales. The federal law generally applies to any sale, loan, or rental of consumer goods or services at a cost of $25 or more. This applies only when the seller or the seller's representative personally solicits the sale, and the buyer's agreement, or offer to purchase, is made at a place other than the seller's place of business. The seller's place of business is defined as the main or permanent branch office or local address of the seller.

These laws protect the consumer by offering a cooling-off period within which to notify the seller of the consumer's intention to cancel the purchase. The consumer may receive a return of all money paid and rescind any contract signed without further obligation. In effect, the consumer is given a period of time, typically up to midnight of the third business day following the sale, during which to determine whether he or she really wants to go through with the transaction.

The seller's principal obligation under these regulations is to disclose to the potential consumer that such a cooling-off period exists and that it is the consumer's right to take advantage of that escape clause and cancel the sale if desired. The form and content of this disclosure requirement is spelled out in the federal regulations.

To comply with the statute, a seller must furnish the buyer with a fully completed receipt or copy of any agreement pertaining to the sale at the time the sale is made or the agreement is signed. The receipt or agreement must be in the same language that was principally used in the oral sales presentation. For example, if the presentation was made in Spanish, the receipt or agreement must also be in Spanish. The receipt or agreement must also include the seller's name and address, time and date of sale, and a statement on the first page that contains the following language:

> *The buyer may cancel this transaction at any time prior to midnight of the third business day after the date of this transaction. See the attached notice-of-cancellation form for an explanation of this right.*

The notice-of-cancellation form must detail the buyer's rights and obligations in the event the buyer chooses to cancel the sale.

In addition to the federal regulation, many states have enacted similar consumer protection statutes that provide for a cooling-off period and contain a similar disclosure requirement. It is strongly advised that if you engage in consumer sales other than from a permanently established business location, you confer with an attorney who can advise you of the legal requirements in your particular state.

Mail-Order Sales

A popular method of selling is through mail-order services or catalog sales. Here, too, the federal government has established certain guidelines aimed at protecting the consuming public. When a seller solicits a sale through the mail or through a mail-order catalog, the seller must reasonably expect to be able to ship any ordered merchandise to the buyer within the time stated in the solicitation. If no time period is stated, the merchandise must be shipped within thirty days after receiving a properly completed order. If the seller is unable to ship the merchandise within the specified time limit, the seller must offer the buyer the option of either consenting to a delay in shipping or of canceling the order and receiving a prompt refund. The seller is also required to inform the buyer of any anticipated delays in shipping and to explain why the shipping deadline cannot be met.

CHAPTER 8

Consignment

There are many commercial arrangements by which merchandise may be sold. The most common are outright purchase and consignment. In the outright purchase arrangement, merchandise is acquired, title is transferred from the seller to the buyer, and the purchase price is due when the goods are delivered. Under a typical consignment arrangement, the consignor delivers an item to a consignee. The consignee does not make an outright purchase of the goods, but rather, agrees to remit to the consignor the proceeds of sales less the consignment commission as sales are made. Generally, the consignee is under no obligation to sell the goods and may return them to the consignor at any time.

ADVANTAGES

Although it may not be immediately obvious, the consignment arrangement can be beneficial to both parties. For the consignee, consignments eliminate much of the financial risk of carrying goods of questionable market appeal. If the item does not sell or sells poorly, the consignee will generally not lose much money, since it has made no direct investment by purchasing the item. The consignee loses only to the extent that the display space filled by the consigned item could have been filled by other items having greater sales potential, along with whatever amount of money was expended on advertising, overhead, etc.

The advantage to the consignor is that consignment provides an opportunity to get a product into expanded retail networks. Another advantage is that the consignor generally gets a larger share of the retail selling price—around 60% in consignment versus 50% in wholesaling. (That appears to be changing, however, and consignment percentages are getting closer to the 50% wholesale arrangement.)

DISADVANTAGES

Conversely, there are several deterrents to consignment that often make people reluctant to engage in consignment selling. The consignor takes most of the risks in such arrangements, and a number of questions need to be asked and answered.

- How promptly does the consignee pay after the work is sold?
- Is the work insured while it is on the consignee's premises?
- Will unsold work be returned in good condition?

Other deterrents to the consignment arrangement are more complicated. Significant problems can develop if a consignor delivers work to a consignee and the consignee fails to pay debts to a creditor who has a security interest in all the consignee's assets, including the consigned paperwork, or the consignee then goes bankrupt. Other concerns include what happens if the goods are destroyed by fire or stolen while on the consignee's premises. The resolution of these issues depends upon a determination of which party, the consignor on the one hand or the creditor or bankruptcy trustee on the other, has priority over the consigned work. There is no question that all these parties may have valid claims to the work—the question is, rather, which claim is to be given first priority.

Bankruptcy

Before the enactment of the *Uniform Commercial Code* (UCC), the consignor would generally prevail over the consignee's creditors or the consignee's trustee in bankruptcy with respect to a consigned item. Moreover, the consignor would prevail, even if there was no record of the consignment that would give creditors or a trustee in bankruptcy notice of the consignment's existence. In effect, the consignor held a secret lien on the consigned work that was given priority over all other liens.

However, the UCC revised the rule of priority, largely in response to the general consensus that secret liens should not be legally enforceable. Thus, Article 2 of the UCC provides that, where a consignor delivers an item to a business dealing in goods of the kind consigned, the consignor will not have priority over the claims of creditors or a trustee in bankruptcy unless the consignor does one of the following three actions:

1. complies with the applicable state law providing that the consignor's interest be indicated by a sign on the consignee's premises;
2. establishes in court that the consignee is known by its creditors to be substantially engaged in selling goods under consignment; or,
3. complies with the filing requirements in Article 9 of the UCC.

As to the first option, most states do not have sign laws. Even in those states that do, the consignor should not rely on the consignee to place and maintain a sign indicating that items have been consigned, since it may not be in the interests of the consignee to do so. For example, a retailer would generally be in a much better position to obtain loans if a lending institution were led to believe that all the work in the store was owned outright as opposed to being consigned.

The consignor should not expect to prevail under the second option, since it will generally be difficult to prove that the consignee was known by the creditors to be substantially engaged in the business of selling consigned goods.

This leaves the third option. As a general rule, the consignor can best protect a consigned item by complying with the filing provisions contained in Article 9 of the UCC.

Article 9

The purpose of the Article 9 filing requirement is simply to give notice to interested parties that certain property is subject to outstanding interests. The filing requirement gives notice to creditors, lending institutions, and the like that the item in the retail outlet is subject to a consignment agreement between the retailer and the consignor.

That process requires, among other things, the filing of financial statements with the secretary of state in every state where the consigned items are located and paying filing fees each time. This gives constructive notice to the consignee's creditors.

There has been considerable debate as to whether the UCC provisions adequately safeguard the consignor's interests under consignment arrangements. As an initial consideration, there is the problem that the consignor may not even be aware that the protection exists. Many people who are just getting a business started are unaware of certain details of business and law, such as consignor protection.

Moreover, even the consignor who knows that the potential for protection exists may be unable or unwilling to learn how that protection may be secured. In the case of complying with the filing requirements of Article 9, many who know what is required may believe that approach to be too complex and bothersome.

This is not the case. In the past, the form known as a *UCC-1 Financing Statement* had to be signed by the debtor or consignee and varied from state to state. This is no longer true. The process has been greatly simplified in most jurisdictions due to the adoption of a national UCC-1 form that is not required to be signed by the debtor or consignee.

> **NOTE:** The filing requirement still varies from state to state. There may also be a requirement that the document be filed at the county level.

SPECIAL LAWS FOR ARTISTS

As a result of the previously mentioned problems and others, several states have enacted special artist-dealer consignment laws. The first of these laws was enacted by the State of New York in 1966. Thereafter, Alabama, Alaska, Arkansas, California, Colorado, Connecticut, District of Columbia, Florida, Georgia, Idaho, Illinois, Iowa, Kentucky, Maryland, Massachusetts, Michigan, Minnesota, Missouri, Montana, New Hampshire, New Jersey, New Mexico, New York, North Carolina, Ohio, Oregon, Pennsylvania, Tennessee, Texas, Washington, and Wisconsin passed similar legislation. Other states are considering such laws, largely in response to increasing pressures from artists and arts organizations.

Although each state has enacted its own unique version, the basic provisions of artist-dealer consignment laws are essentially the same. Most statutes provide that any works of art and certain specified craft works delivered to any art dealer are presumed to be delivered under a consignment arrangement unless the artist has been paid in full on or before delivery. Thus, the majority of transactions between artists and various art dealers will be deemed consignments for purposes of these statutes.

In addition, most artist-dealer consignment statutes provide that all consigned artwork, as well as the proceeds from sale of the artwork, will be held in trust by the art dealer on behalf of the artist. This basically means that the art dealer will be solely responsible for any loss, theft, or damage occurring to the consigned artwork or the proceeds from the sales thereof that could have been avoided had the art dealer exercised the utmost care and caution.

A few states go further by imposing absolute liability upon the art dealer for loss or damage. In those states, the art dealer will be liable for loss or damage to the consigned artwork even though such loss or damage could not have been avoided, even with the utmost care and caution.

Several of the laws require the artist and dealer to enter into a written agreement containing at least the following information:

- the value of the work;
- the minimum price for which it can be sold; and,
- the percentage to be paid to the dealer.

Of course, the contract can contain more provisions, though an attempt to avoid the protective provisions of the consignment legislation is generally prohibited by the laws.

Finally, and perhaps most importantly, nearly all these statutes provide that the consigned work is protected against all claims made by the art dealer's creditors, including a trustee in bankruptcy. Thus, at least one effect of the consignment legislation is to provide artists with protection similar to that afforded by Article 9 of the UCC without requiring the artist to take any steps to procure that protection.

Definitions

Although art-consignment legislation would seem to solve many of the practical problems with consignments of art, artists should review how the applicable legislation, if any, defines the terms *art dealer* and *artwork*. Fortunately for artists, art dealer has been broadly defined by nearly all states as being any person engaged in the business of selling artwork other than a person exclusively engaged in the business of selling goods at public auction.

On the other hand, artwork has sometimes been given a rather narrow definition. Some statutes have defined artwork as including only the traditional areas of fine art, such as painting, sculpture, and drawing. This means that, under some consignment statutes, functional art—such as pottery, glass, and furniture—may not be deemed to be within the purview of the statutory protection. Other statutes expressly include such items as those made of clay, fiber, wood, metal, plastic, or glass as being within the definition of a work of art protected by the legislation.

• • • • •

Consignment arrangements can provide producers and distributors with expanded sales potential. However, it is necessary to determine what protection is available for the consigned items. Fine artists in many states have been granted automatic protection for their consigned works. Unfortunately for other businesspeople, these laws are not all-encompassing. It is, therefore, prudent to determine what protection is available for your business when engaging in a consignment transaction and to evaluate the costs versus benefits available from complying with the applicable laws.

CHAPTER 9

Collections

There are several ways to deal with collection problems, ranging from preventive action to initiating a lawsuit. If you are fortunate enough to deal with people who always pay their bills on time, the remaining portion of this chapter may be of no interest at all. If, however, you have experienced delays in payment or have some totally uncollectible bills, you should consider the suggestions that follow.

The general rule in a sales transaction is that payment is due upon delivery of the item being sold. While this rule may be subject to technical complications that are beyond the scope of this discussion, it basically means that upon delivery of merchandise to a customer or completion of a project for the customer, the seller has the legal right to demand payment in full at that moment. This assumes that no arrangement has been made between the buyer and the seller allowing the purchaser to delay payment.

While payment upon delivery is common in retail transactions, it is unusual when selling on consignment or in transactions between manufacturers and distributors. In addition, the purchase of a rather expensive item may be subject to an installment-payment arrangement.

POINT-OF-SALE PAYMENTS

Manufacturers who deal directly with the public at shows, fairs, or their own shops customarily expect to be paid at the moment they make the sale, before the item is taken away by the customer. Such payment is made by currency, check, or credit or debit card. Therefore, it is necessary for you to determine whether the currency is authentic and whether the credit or debit card or check is going to be honored by the bank. Obviously, the cash sale is the safest way, though you should be aware that counterfeiting is not a thing of the past.

Currency

Identifying counterfeit currency is usually very technical and difficult. Occasionally, however, it is simple if the counterfeiter has made a glaring error, such as using George Washington on a $5 bill. The federal government is quite diligent in alerting business people to the presence of counterfeit currency in a particular area when it is aware of the problem. The best way to avoid being stuck with a counterfeit bill is to keep your eyes open. Also, it is a good idea not to accept any bill larger than $50.

Credit Cards

With regard to credit card and debit card fraud, the first thing to do is to compare the signature on the back of the card with the signature on the credit card slip. Even more important is to follow the bank's procedures carefully. If the company requires you to get authorization for all credit card sales over $50, then be sure to get that authorization. It may seem time-consuming and troublesome, but the rules are based on bitter experience. If you have made a credit card or debit card sale without following the instructions, and the card turns out to have been stolen or the buyer has exceeded his or her credit limit, you are likely to be stuck with the loss.

It is also an excellent idea to request some form of photo ID to verify that the person with whom you are dealing is the actual card owner, though you should be aware that identity theft is rampant.

You should be very careful when taking credit card numbers over the telephone. Take only numbers of individuals that you know. Otherwise, you run the risk of having someone use a stolen card or number.

Personal Checks

The most frequent problems occur over personal checks. A host of things can prevent a check from being honored or cashed by a bank. To begin with, the person who writes the check may be an impostor using a checkbook that actually belongs to someone else. In order to reduce the likelihood of this occurrence, you should insist upon seeing at least two pieces of identification, one of which should, ideally, contain a photograph of the person. A current credit card or a check guarantee card with a photograph and signature facsimile or any other photo ID should serve this purpose. Do not accept as identification such items as Social Security cards, library cards, or any ID that can be easily obtained or forged.

Watch while the person signs the check (otherwise, the signature may have been previously traced from a valid signature) and compare the signature with that of the other identification. While only an expert can identify a good forgery, most people can recognize a clumsy attempt by an amateur.

Accept checks only if they are made out to you and only if they are written for the exact amount of the sale. In other words, do not take checks made out to someone else and endorsed to you. Never cash a check. Do not take checks for more than the sale amount—that is, when you have to give change in cash.

Assuming that the individual writing the check is legitimate, there are still more potential problems. One of the most common difficulties is the problem of insufficient funds to cover the check. If the amount of your sale is substantial, it is prudent to request a certified or bank-guaranteed check. However, the inconvenience of requiring the purchaser to have a check certified may interfere with impulse sales, and is thus not practical for many retailers.

If the person writing the check is known to you, it is less likely the person will give you a bad check. Even if the buyer is a stranger, the risk of receiving a bad check and not being able to locate the buyer afterward can be reduced if the buyer's address and phone number are copied onto the check from the supporting pieces of identification if they are different from those printed on the face of the check.

Despite all these precautions, some bad checks do slip through. It is a crime in most states to pay for something with a check that the signer knows will be dishonored. A lawsuit can be brought against a buyer to recover the amount of the check. If you win such a suit, most states will allow the recovery of reasonable costs of litigation, including the attorney's fees incurred.

IN PLAIN ENGLISH

A check returned for insufficient funds can be redeposited in the hope that the check will be covered the second time through. Some bad checks are simply the result of a miscalculation of account balance or of the buyer having received a bad check. It is always a good idea to make a phone call before filing a lawsuit.

CONSIGNMENT

If you sell manufactured goods through a retailer, at least two payment arrangements are possible. First, the goods may be consigned, and payment is due only after the actual sale of the item. Unfortunately, it is not uncommon for a retailer to neglect to inform a manufacturer of sales or to delay notification for an unreasonably long period of time. Furthermore, when retail outlets are forced into bankruptcy, you can lose your consigned goods. As discussed in Chapter 8, a consignor is well advised to take steps to protect consigned goods from the consignee's creditors. These measures are covered under the Uniform Commercial Code and are particularly important in states where specific consignment-protection legislation does not exist.

INVOICING

The other method of payment is to submit an invoice to a wholesale buyer. Invoices are commonly paid within a specified time, usually thirty days after they have been tendered. This system virtually guarantees that you will not receive payment until the invoice is due. Indeed, unless some inducement for early payment is offered, you may wait interminably to be paid.

WAYS OF ENCOURAGING PAYMENT

While the law provides vehicles for obtaining payment of legal obligations, it is always preferable for business people to establish benefits that encourage debtors to pay their obligations.

Cash Discounts

By offering a cash discount, you can encourage early payment in a simple way. The offer of a 5% cash discount for early or even on-time payment may be all the encouragement some purchasers need. If the buyers earn more interest on their cash reserves than is offered as a discount, however, buyers will likely ignore the cash discount.

Charging Interest on Overdue Payments

The other option that can be combined with the incentive of cash discounts is to charge interest on payments received after the invoice due date. However, this method involves two possible traps. First, many states still have usury laws limiting the percentage of interest that can be charged. A lender who exceeds the legal interest ceiling may find that the entire debt is forfeited, that all interest is forfeited, or that a usury penalty is imposed.

The second possible problem is the necessity to comply with the federal *Truth in Lending Act* and the various equivalent state laws. The Truth in Lending Act requires certain terms be included on any contract or billing if (1) credit is offered to consumers, (2) credit is offered on a regular basis, (3) the credit is subject to interest or is payable by a written agreement in more than four installments, and

(4) the credit is primarily for personal, family, or household purposes. The task of compliance is eased by the availability of preprinted forms containing the required disclosures.

While many of the required terms may seem inapplicable to a simple sales transaction, you are well advised if you want to charge interest to use a form that contains all the disclosures. Even though they may not be required, omitting them when they are could expose you to significant liability. These forms are available from legal publishers and private attorneys.

WHEN PAYMENT NEVER COMES

If your efforts to obtain payment prove ineffective, you have several other options.

Do Nothing

The first possibility is to do nothing. If the amount is small enough, you may simply decide not to pursue collection. Needless to say, if this alternative is selected, you should refrain from doing any future business with that customer.

Collection Agencies

A second option might be to hire a collection agency to attempt to collect the debt. Collection agencies generally charge a commission of up to 50% of the recovered amount, though some agencies require an up-front fee and take a lower percentage. Others charge a fixed fee. Care should be taken in selecting a collection agency, since it could get you into trouble. That is, if the collection agency violates the law regarding lawful debt collection practices and improper reporting requirements, your business may also be rendered liable for those improper actions.

Lawsuits

A third option is the instigation of a full-scale lawsuit to force payment. In many states, a formal demand for payment must be made prior to commencing a lawsuit. Moreover, this option is practical only if the outstanding debt is relatively large, since an attorney must be hired and will likely be quite expensive, particularly if the case proceeds all the way to trial.

The court fees charged for filing a case can be rather high, ranging from $40 in some states and courts to over $175 in others. The defendant (the debtor) must be personally served with court papers, which can easily cost $50 or more per defendant, depending on the difficulty of service. Lastly, if the case is won and the buyer still refuses to pay, further proceedings must be initiated at additional cost to execute or force payment on the judgment received. All in all, on a moderate debt, the expense involved in a civil trial may amount to more than the debt itself.

Small Claims Court

A simpler and less expensive solution on small debts is to bring an action in small claims court. While the rules vary from state to state, all the systems are geared toward making the process as swift, accessible, and inexpensive as possible. Moreover, most courts have staff members who help guide people through pleadings in small claims court.

The major cost savings in a small claims court proceeding results from the fact that attorneys are not customarily permitted in such courts. Unless they represent themselves or a corporation, attorneys generally may not prepare required documents or appear in court. Even in states where attorneys are not specifically barred by statute, the court rules are set up in such a clear, comprehensible way that an attorney is usually not needed.

A small claims action has other advantages over a conventional lawsuit. However, not all actions can be brought in small claims court. As the name implies, only claims for small amounts can be brought. For example, *small* is defined as $5,000 or less in many states, though some states allow suits for up to $10,000 to be brought in small claims court. Moreover, only actions seeking monetary damages are appropriate in small claims court. Other forms of relief, such as an injunction, cannot be granted.

The small claims process is comparatively swift and inexpensive. Filing fees are generally between $50 and $100. In addition, in most courts, the creditor is not responsible for informing the debtor that a suit has been brought. The clerk of the court customarily mails the notice to the defendant by certified or registered mail. A small fee is generally charged to cover mailing costs.

The hearing itself is kept simple. The technical rules of evidence and of legal procedure are not followed. The judge simply hears both sides of the case and allows any evidence or the testimony of any witnesses either party has to offer. Jury trials are never permitted in small claims court, although the defendant may be able to have the case moved to a conventional court by demanding a jury trial.

An action in small claims court also has disadvantages. The judgment is often absolutely binding, which means neither party may appeal. The judgment may be uncollectible. In many states, the usual methods of enforcing a judgment—garnishment of wages or liens against property—are unavailable to the holder of a judgment from small claims court. Some jurisdictions permit a small claims court judgment to be converted into a traditional judgment, but this often requires the help of an attorney to assist with the process.

For the most part, care in selecting those with whom you do business will minimize the need to use legal means to collect payment for sales. However, if all other methods fail, small claims court is by far the least expensive and easiest way to obtain legal redress for a small outstanding debt.

BANKRUPTCIES

When a bankruptcy petition is filed, the debtor and his or her lawyer are responsible for filing an accurate list of creditors with the court. The court sends a notice of the filing to the listed creditors and gives additional notices to all parties who are listed with the court or who make an appearance in the case.

Even if the amount at stake in the bankruptcy is small, and it seems that it may not be economically practical to pursue the matter, you should file a claim if the court gives notice to do so. Many creditors fail to file claims, often increasing the payment to those who do.

There are three general categories of bankruptcies.

Straight Bankruptcy—Chapter 7

The first, referred to as *straight bankruptcy* in Chapter 7 of the bankruptcy law, contemplates the prompt conversion of all the bankrupt's nonexempt property to cash and the payment of creditors to the extent possible. This type is available to both individuals and business entities. The bankruptcy law establishes a pecking order of creditors, giving some creditors priority for payment. Such creditors would be the U.S. government for taxes and secured parties for the amount of their security interests. Each category of creditor must be paid in full before a lower-priority creditor may be paid at all. If there is not sufficient money to satisfy all creditors in a particular class, the members of that group will receive a pro rata portion of their claim.

Not all of the bankrupt's assets are available for creditors. There are some things that may be retained, such as a modest house, a holy book, clothing, and the like, even after bankruptcy. The list of exempt property varies from state to state, though there are federal exemptions, too. In some states, the debtor can choose whether to use the state or federal exemptions. There are also certain exemptions, such as Social Security, that are not part of the bankruptcy laws but may nevertheless apply.

If no party objects to the debtor's discharge or to the discharge of certain types of debt before the deadline set by the court (usually sixty days after the meeting of creditors), the court will enter an order of discharge preventing creditors from pursuing their claims against the debtor. Certain claims cannot be discharged in bankruptcy. Certain types of claims remain intact with no action on the part of the creditor (such as certain categories of tax debts and clear support obligations).

Some claims require the filing of a complaint with the bankruptcy court before the discharge deadline.

Reorganization—Chapter 11

The second type of bankruptcy proceeding is called *Chapter 11*, or *reorganization*. It is available only to business entities, not to individuals. It contemplates a somewhat different process. Rather than terminating the business, Chapter 11 is designed to facilitate an orderly payment to creditors so that the business may survive.

After the Chapter 11 petition is filed and the creditors meet, a reorganization plan is proposed by the debtor, though after a prescribed period of time, any party can propose a plan. Once a plan is prepared, it is presented to the bankruptcy judge. If it is determined that the plan meets the requirements of the Bankruptcy Code and the creditors have had an opportunity to vote on the plan, the court may confirm the plan. This is true in some circumstances even if certain creditors vote no, and if the court determines that the plan is fair and equitable, and does not discriminate unfairly.

Creditors customarily receive more under Chapter 11 than they do under straight bankruptcy, although reorganization is feasible only for a healthy business suffering a temporary economic reversal. Creditors who have a secured position, such as those who have filed UCC documents to establish their security interests (discussed in Chapter 7), may participate in drafting the Chapter 11 plan. Generally, these creditors would be those who sold on consignment or those who retain a security interest for the purchase price of some goods. The plan will be "fair and equitable" insofar as the secured creditors are concerned, and they may be forced to agree if it provides that they do any one of the following:

- retain their liens and receive future cash payments equal to the value of the security;
- retain a lien on the proceeds from the sale of their collateral; or,
- receive the equivalent of their interests, such as cash up front or substituted collateral.

In a Chapter 11 proceeding, a secured creditor may be forced to accept a less favorable position than the UCC would allow in order to have the plan accepted by all the creditors. Even though this may happen on occasion, someone with a security interest is still far better off than one who is unsecured.

Individuals—Chapter 13

Individuals may file a *Chapter 13* bankruptcy. In this type of arrangement, a plan is worked out so that the individual may pay ordinary and necessary living expenses. Any amounts earned over and above the amounts required for daily existence will be paid to a trustee for ultimate distribution to creditors.

In 2005, Congress enacted significant revisions to the Bankruptcy Code. Highlights of these revisions include adding a means test limiting eligibility for bankruptcy protection under Chapter 7 of the Code, modifications to exemptions and restrictions on discharge, and a reduction in the ability of individuals to file Chapter 7 bankruptcy to discharge their debts. The changes are expected to move more debtors into reorganization, primarily Chapter 13 bankruptcies, with required payments for five years.

IN PLAIN ENGLISH

Common sense, diligence, and attention to detail are always important attributes for any businessperson. When the economy is weak and money is tight, they become essential. There will probably always be some uncollectible bills. With proper care and some preventive attention, you can keep these to a minimum.

CHAPTER **10**

Expanding Your Market

Most successful businesses begin with a novel idea that is nurtured and grows into a profitable enterprise. The entrepreneur invests time, money, and energy into developing the concept, manufacturing a product, or marketing a service. The entrepreneur may have also worked on expanding the business when and where appropriate.

FRANCHISING

An alternative for some businesses is the franchise. A *franchise* is a right or license to follow an established, successful pattern. It also allows the business to use the trademarks, recipes, advertising, and training provided through the franchisor. Those who purchase franchise opportunities are more often likely to succeed than those who start from scratch, since many of the mistakes that dissipate resources can be avoided. The purchaser of a franchise is literally acquiring the goodwill, know-how, and intellectual property of an established business.

The best source for researching franchises today is the Internet. Attending franchise expos, where a number of companies offering franchises present opportunities, is another method of gathering information. There are also a number of books on franchising available at public libraries and bookstores.

The *Federal Trade Commission* (FTC) has adopted specific rules for all companies offering the sale of franchise opportunities. In addition, some states have adopted some sort of franchise regulation. For example, fourteen states require franchise opportunities to be registered prior to sale of a franchise to residents of that state. A typical franchise statute defines a franchise as an agreement by which:

- a franchisee is granted the right to engage in the business of offering, selling, or distributing goods or services under a marketing plan or system formulated by a franchisor;

- the operation of the franchisee's business pursuant to such a plan or system is substantially associated with the franchisor's trademark, service mark, trade name, logo, advertising, or other commercial symbol designating a franchisor; and,

- the franchisee is required to give to the franchisor a payment or something of value (in legal terms, a valuable consideration) for the right to transact business in accordance with the marketing plan. This typically consists of an initial franchise fee and ongoing royalty payments.

Uniform Offering Circular

All companies that offer franchise opportunities are required to comply with the requirements of the FTC rule. They must also prepare extensive disclosure statements for publication in the FTC's *Uniform Franchise Offering Circular* (UFOC). By obtaining a copy of the Uniform Offering Circular, those interested in a franchise will find a wealth of material, including the following:

- information identifying the franchisor, its affiliates, and the affiliates' business experience since joining the franchise;

- information describing the business experience of each of the franchisor's officers, directors, and those management personnel responsible for franchise services, training, and other aspects of the franchise program;

- a description of any lawsuits in which the franchisor or its officers, directors, and management personnel have been involved;

- information about any bankruptcies in which the franchisor or its officers, directors, and management personnel have been involved;

- information about the initial franchise fee and other payments that are required to obtain the franchise;
- a description of the continuing payments franchisees are required to make after a franchise is acquired;
- information about any restrictions on the quality of goods and services used in the franchise, where those goods and services can be purchased, and any restrictions requiring that purchases be made from the franchisor or its affiliates;
- a description of any assistance available from the franchisor or its affiliates in financing the purchase of the franchise;
- a list of restrictions on the goods or services franchisees are permitted to market;
- a description of any restrictions on the customers with whom franchisees may deal;
- a description of any territorial limitations affecting the franchisee;
- a list of the conditions under which the franchise may be repurchased or refused renewal by the franchisor, transferred to a third party by the franchisee, or terminated or modified by either party;
- a description of the training programs available to franchisees;
- a statement regarding the involvement of any celebrities or public figures in the franchise;
- a description of any assistance the franchisor will provide in selecting a site for the franchise;
- statistical information about the present number of franchises, the number of franchises projected for the future, the number of franchises terminated, the number the franchisor has decided not to renew, and the number repurchased in the past;
- the financial statements of the franchisor;
- a description of the extent to which franchisees must personally participate in the operation of a franchise;
- a complete statement of the basis for any earnings claims made to the franchisee, including the percentage of existing franchises that have actually achieved the results that are claimed; and,
- a list of the names and addresses of all franchisees and company-owned stores.

After reviewing the information in the UFOC, the potential franchisee should ask some hard questions about the opportunity. Those questions include the following.

- What sort of controls will the franchisor require of the franchisee with respect to sale of product, territory, etc.?
- What controls over advertising or promises regarding advertising does the franchisor make?
- Has the franchisor appropriately protected the trademark and has the franchisor secured the appropriate domain name?
- Is the franchise for an indefinite term or must it be renewed on a periodic basis?
- What are the terms of renewal?
- Does the franchisor's system seem to be workable, understandable, and able to provide benefits necessary to justify the expense of paying a franchise fee?

Advantages and Disadvantages

There is a cost involved in acquiring a franchise and you must determine whether you are willing to pay that cost to acquire a franchise rather than creating your own business identity. There are pros and cons to both approaches, and it is important for you to consider the costs, benefits, risks, and rewards before undertaking either course.

One of the major sacrifices to be made when acquiring a franchise opportunity is that of creating your own business identity and perhaps franchising it to others. By acquiring a franchise, you are purchasing some degree of security in exchange for the potential that might be realized from your own creation.

You should also be aware of some franchise abuses that have surfaced. Many franchisees have been injured when the franchisor permits competition within a comparatively small geographic area or establishes an owned and operated location in close proximity to an existing franchise operation. This is known in the trade as *cannibalizing*. If the franchisor fails to honor its commitment, a franchisee must be in a position to redress these wrongs.

It is quite clear that the purchase of a franchise ranks as a significant investment. Before you make that investment, check out the pertinent information exhaustively. Consult a franchise attorney and accountant and contact other franchisees to learn about their experiences with the franchisor.

MULTILEVEL MARKETING

Another method of doing business is known as *multilevel marketing* (MLM). The leading companies in this field have surpassed billion-dollar sales marks and their stocks are traded on the New York Stock Exchange. Amway, Mary Kay, and Shaklee are MLMs that have become household names. Many MLM companies advertise through infomercials and websites. In recent years, product lines have expanded dramatically. The corporations involved market everything from computers and video equipment to healthcare products, art, and long-distance telephone services.

Simply stated, multilevel marketing is a form of marketing in which distributors or sales representatives sell products directly to the consumer. In most cases, distributors purchase the company product at wholesale and profit from the difference between the wholesale and retail prices. In other cases, a distributor functions as a sales representative who takes orders for company products or services—for example, long-distance discount telephone services—and receives a commission for whatever is sold.

Distributors are entitled to sponsor other distributors or sales representatives and receive commissions on the sales of the sponsored reps as well as on the sales of any further representatives sponsored in a continuous down line. For a successful distributor, the rewards can be substantial.

Any system that offers dramatic rewards and carries with it a low cost of entry will obviously tend to attract some of the best and some of the worst individuals. The system has not always thrived. Over the years it has come perilously close to extinction as a result of prosecution by regulators who claimed the method promoted pyramid schemes under the guise of legitimate marketing. In many cases, the prosecutors were actually chasing and eradicating unlawful pyramids.

Other programs that were legitimate have survived. In a landmark legal decision in 1979, the Amway Corporation prevailed in such a prosecution and in fact received a stamp of approval for its marketing program by the FTC. This particular decision opened the door to many other legitimate multilevel marketing companies.

Protective Regulations

Because of the abuses in the industry, multilevel marketing is closely scrutinized. Regulations regarding multilevel marketing companies in the United States are a constantly changing patchwork of overlapping laws that vary from state to state. The basic thrust of these statutes is to prohibit marketing plans that require sales representatives to invest in the company or purchase the right to recruit others for economic gain. The statutes are designed to ensure that multilevel marketing companies are bona fide retail organizations that market bona fide products to the consumer. Inventory loading, such as requiring distributors to purchase a minimum amount of the product, and head-hunting (remuneration for the mere act of recruiting others) are prohibited. Sales or sample kits and other marketing materials must be sold to sales representatives at actual company cost or provided free of charge.

What to Look For

In determining whether or not a program is a legitimate multilevel marketing opportunity, the would-be participant or the entrepreneur who is considering starting a multilevel marketing program should keep in mind several important points.

- *Product.* The company should offer a high-quality product in which consumer satisfaction is guaranteed. It must have a demand in the marketplace. If the product is one consumed by distributors themselves, it must be one that distributors would want to buy on its own merits, irrespective of participation in the marketing plan.

- *Price.* The price of the product must be fair and competitive. Distributors should be able to purchase the product at wholesale or at a substantial discount from prices found in retail stores.
- *Investment requirement.* There should be no investment requirement at all except for a sales or sample kit or demonstration materials sold at company cost.
- *Purchase and inventory requirements.* A legitimate marketing program should have no minimum-purchase requirement or any inventory requirement for someone to become or remain a qualified distributor or sales representative.
- *Sales commission.* Sales commissions should not be paid for the mere act of sponsoring other distributors.
- *Buyback policy.* A legitimate multilevel marketing company will agree to buy back inventory and sales materials in resalable condition from distributors who cancel participation in the program.
- *Retail sales.* The focus of the marketing program should be to promote retail sales to nonparticipants.
- *Distributor activity.* Many of the statutes regarding multilevel distribution companies require that distributors perform a bona fide, supervisory, distributive selling or soliciting function in moving the product to the consumer.
- *Earnings statements.* The basic rule is that a legitimate marketing program should not make any earnings representations unless those statements are based on a verifiable track record of average earnings of distributors in a particular geographic area.

Multilevel marketing is an established marketing process. Whether it is right for you is an important consideration. You must be willing to actively promote sales of the product while continuing to recruit individuals to augment your down line. It is only through both activities that you are likely to earn significant returns.

IN PLAIN ENGLISH

Before agreeing to become a distributor for an MLM company, you should be sold on the product itself and not merely the prospect of getting rich from the activities of others. Multilevel marketing distributing is hard work! The time devoted to this activity can be considerable and may preclude you from developing other business opportunities.

Abuses

If you are considering working with an MLM company, be aware of the following types of abuses that have been targeted as potential elements of illegal marketing plans:

- products that have no real-world marketplace;
- products that are sold at inflated prices;
- plans that result in inventory loading by distributors;
- substantial cash investment requirements;
- mandatory purchases of peripheral or accessory products or services;
- plans in which distributors are left with substantial unsold inventory upon cancellation of participation;
- plans in which fees are paid to distributors for headhunting and emphasis is on recruitment rather than the sale of product; and,
- misrepresentations or inflated representations of earnings.

The Web is riddled with bogus MLM opportunities, and emails about the incredible earnings potential are ubiquitous. The FTC has attempted to identify these schemes, but the rate at which they emerge appears to be such as to continue to outpace the regulators' resources. Particular care should be paid to Web-based MLM offerings and email MLM spam since it is often impossible to determine the location of the offeror and to obtain any relief when problems arise.

• • • • •

There are numerous other business opportunities that may be available to an energetic entrepreneur. These include, among many others, the ability to acquire an existing business, buy into a partnership or other business, or invest in someone else's business dream. Many states have laws regulating the promotion, advertisement, and sale of business opportunities. Some of these laws are broad enough to include multilevel marketing and franchises. Before advertising your business opportunity or buying into someone else's, consult with an attorney experienced in this field of law.

CHAPTER 11

Patents and Trade Secrets

Ordinarily, before a product can achieve a market edge, something must distinguish it from other items in the same general category. Of course, you will want to protect the something that sets your product apart so that others cannot exploit its uniqueness. Several bodies of law help you obtain this protection. This chapter and the following two chapters discuss some of these protections.

PATENTS

Patent laws allow an inventor the right to prevent others from exploiting a patented invention. Generally speaking, a patent is available for any new and useful process, machine, composition of matter, or any new, useful improvement thereof.

An invention cannot be patented unless it is new and not obvious. An inventor's invention is not new if, before it was invented, it was known or used by someone else in this country, or if it was patented or described in a printed publication anywhere in the world. In addition, an invention is not new if, more than one year before an application for the patent is filed, the invention was patented or described in a printed publication anywhere in the world, it was in public use, or it was placed on sale in this country.

The one-year period is intended to function as a grace period that allows the inventor or the inventor's company to market the invention to see whether it is worthwhile to incur the expense of seeking patent protection. A consequence of failing to file a patent application during this one-year period, however, is that the inventor (or the inventor's business entity) is absolutely barred from obtaining a patent.

Unfortunately, patents are quite costly and difficult to obtain. It often takes an inordinate period of time for the patent document to be issued, and the period of protection is comparatively short (only twenty years from the date of application).

International Patents

Generally speaking, each country administers its own patent system. The businessperson who wishes to obtain a patent in a foreign country must, therefore, file for a patent in that country. One exception to this general rule is the *European Patent Regime*. A European patent application, which is filed at the European Patent Office in Munich, can designate almost any country in Europe. Once a European patent is obtained, the patent can be translated into the language of any other designated European country. By filing it in a particular country, the European patent may be registered in that country without going through another examination process. The official languages of the European Patent Office include English, so U.S. companies can prosecute their patents in the English language.

There is a movement to adopt legislation that would harmonize the patent laws throughout much of the world in order to have a multinational patent treaty. As of the date of this writing, it is still in the "talking stage," and ultimate adoption is not anticipated in the foreseeable future.

TRADE SECRETS

Another form of protection, known as *trade secret law*, allows exploitation of a particular innovation and may afford even greater protection than copyright (see Chapter 13) or patent laws. A trade secret may be loosely defined as anything that has not been revealed and could give you a competitive advantage. The secret should cover something that you actually use in your business and that you take some reasonable steps to protect. A trade secret may be lost if the owner fails to either identify it or take reasonable steps to protect it. Otherwise, the trade secret protection is perpetual. In fact, one of the most famous trade secrets is the recipe for Coca-Cola®, which is more than one hundred years old.

Patent or Padlock Dilemma

The determination of whether patent or trade secret protection is most appropriate is sometimes referred to as the *patent or padlock dilemma*. You cannot obtain both kinds of protection, since achieving one will render the other impossible. The patent-versus-padlock decision must be made within one year after disclosure. This is because, as previously discussed, the patent laws provide that a patent can be obtained only when the invention in question has not been in public use or on sale for more than one year before application is made. Furthermore, use by the inventor for commercial purposes, even in secret, is considered a disclosure within the meaning of the patent law. Thus, during the first year, the inventor must decide how the innovation will be protected. If trade secret protection is selected and no patent application is filed, then patent protection is probably lost forever.

Selecting a patent will destroy trade secret protection once the patent is issued since the patent application must contain a full description of precisely what was invented. Thus, it is impossible to get both a patent and to keep some aspect of the invention secret. In order to determine which of these methods of protection should be elected, consult an attorney or patent agent who specializes in intellectual property.

Trade Secret Protection

All that is necessary for something to be protectable as a trade secret is that:

- it gives you a competitive advantage;
- it will, in fact, be treated as a secret by you; and,
- it is not generally known in your industry or business.

The fundamental question of trade secret law is—what is protectable? The way you use knowledge and information, the specific portions of information you have grouped together, and the mere assembly of information itself may all be trade secrets even if everything you consider important for your secrets is publicly available information. For example, if there are numerous methods for producing a particular dye and you have selected one of them, the mere fact that you have selected this method may itself be a trade secret. The identity of your suppliers may be a trade secret, even if they are all listed in the Yellow Pages. The fact that you have done business with these people and found them to be reputable and responsive to you may make the list of their names a trade secret.

Many trade secrets will be embodied in some form of document. One of the first things you should do is to mark any paper, photograph, or the like, "confidential." You should also take steps to prevent demonstrations of your trade secret, such as manufacturing methods. Taking these steps will not create trade secret protection. However, the fact that an effort has been made to identify the materials and methods you consider secret will aid you in establishing that you treated them as a trade secret should litigation ever occur.

Protecting a Trade Secret

In this area, a little thought and cleverness will go a long way toward giving you the protection of the trade secret laws.

Physical Security

First, you should have some degree of physical security. It has been said that physical security is 90% common sense and 10% true protection. You should restrict the access to the area in which the trade secret is used. Some precaution should be taken to prevent visitors from peering into the manufacturing area where the secret process, formula, or technique is employed. The credentials of delivery and service persons should be examined. Employee access to trade secret information should be on a need-to-know basis. Employees should not be granted automatic free access to the material you desire to keep as a trade secret. Extra care should be taken with laptops, PDAs, and the like, since if they are lost or stolen, a tremendous amount of data is at risk of disclosure.

Employee Access

As noted, documents, pictures, or sketches containing trade secrets should be clearly labeled. A procedure should be established for controlling employee access to the documents. For instance, one person could be responsible for granting access to them and a sign-in/sign-out process could be instituted for those permitted access to the documents.

Fragmenting Information

If possible, the information that you consider to be a trade secret should be fragmented. This means no one employee should have possession of the entire secret. Thus, no one person will have sufficient information to hurt you.

Confidentiality Agreements

It is also a good idea to have employees sign a confidentiality or nondisclosure agreement when hired. An attorney who deals with intellectual property can prepare agreements for use within your business.

If it ever becomes important for you to reveal a secret to an outsider, such as when someone desires to purchase the right to exploit your innovation through a licensing arrangement, a different form of confidentiality agreement is in order. These agreements generally provide that in exchange for disclosure of the confidential trade secret information, the party receiving such information will keep it in confidence and will not use or disclose it without the express written permission of the person making the disclosure. Again, your intellectual property lawyer can prepare such an agreement for you.

Vague Labeling

Another method of protecting your trade secret is to engage in some vague labeling. For example, if your trade secret consists of a unique mixture for a glaze, then instead of having the components of the glaze bear their true names, you should label them "Ingredient A," "Ingredient B," "Ingredient C," etc. Then, if an employee quits or if a stranger happens into your office, all they will learn is that by mixing some portion of A with some portion of B, combined with some portion of C, the desired result will be achieved. This will not be very useful information. Similarly, if the trade secret is the temperature at which a glaze is fired, instead of actually marking the thermometer, you may wish to have the original temperature marks removed and replaced by colored zones.

IN PLAIN ENGLISH

If you are publishing in or contributing to industry or trade journals, take care not to reveal trade secrets. Occasionally, manufacturers or their employees inadvertently disclose valuable information in an attempt to impress their colleagues.

Misappropriating Trade Secrets

In order to avoid the charge that you are stealing someone else's trade secret, you should question employees who come to work for you from a competitor. If there is any possibility of a new employee using the competitor's trade secret information, the new employee should meet with the former employer and get written permission to use the information while working for you.

Trade secrets have been deemed so important that in the mid-1990s, the U.S. Congress passed a federal law making it a crime to misappropriate another's trade secret. It was felt that if the United States is to retain its technological competitive edge, the government must assist industry with this form of protection. Since its enactment, there have been several high-profile cases underscoring both the importance of trade secrets and the federal government's efforts in helping to protect them.

Trade secret laws may be the only protection available for your business secrets. Care should therefore be taken to restrict access to the information and to treat the information as truly secret. Contractual arrangements both with employees and outsiders are quite useful. These, coupled with your common sense in the day-to-day operation of your business, will go a long way toward protecting your intellectual property.

CHAPTER 12

Trademarks

Branding has become a part of the lexicon of business terms. In fact, today, virtually every business strives to develop its brand and the awareness that results from this process. One of the most important aspects of branding is the establishment of a means of identifying a product or service by use of a name, symbol, logo, device, or combination of these items, commonly known as *trademarks* or *service marks*. A trademark is used to define marks that are affixed to goods. Service marks are used to define marks that are used in connection with services. Both are commonly referred to simply as *trademarks* or just *marks*. There are, as of the date of this writing, thirty-four international classifications for goods and twelve classifications for services.

Although modern trademark law has broadened the protection available for trademark owners, its historical antecedents date back to medieval England. In those days, certain craft guilds often required members to place their individual marks on the products they produced, so that, in the event a product proved defective, the guild could trace its origins to a particular craftsman and impose appropriate sanctions. Thus, the use of marks enabled the guild to maintain the integrity of its name. Moreover, merchants would often affix marks to their products for purposes of identification. Should the product be stolen or misplaced, the merchant could prove ownership by reason of the mark.

The use of marks for purposes of identification would no doubt have worked quite well in an ideal society where all the citizens led principled and moral lives. But such was not the case. It is not particularly surprising that unscrupulous merchants quickly realized that there was easy money to be made from the use of another's mark or one confusingly similar. The shoddy merchants could more readily sell their products by affixing to them the marks belonging to quality manufacturers.

It was in response to this problem of consumer fraud that the first trademark laws developed. Initially, the emphasis was on prevention of one person passing off products as that of another. In contrast, modern American law focuses upon whether one mark is sufficiently similar to another to cause confusion in the minds of the buying public. The emphasis has, therefore, shifted from the sub-jective intent of a dishonest manufacturer or merchant passing off goods as those of another to the objective determination of consumer confusion.

Despite this shift, the essential purpose of trademarks and trademark laws has changed little since the days of the craft guilds. Trademarks still function pri-marily as a means of identifying the source of a particular product. Trademark laws are also designed to enable the trademark proprietor to develop goodwill for the product as well as to prevent another party from exploiting that good-will—regardless of whether that exploitation is intentional or innocent.

DEFINITION

A simplification of the federal definition of a trademark is—

> *any word, name, symbol, device, or any combination thereof, adopted and used by a person, or which a person has a bona fide intention to use in commerce and subsequently does use, which identifies and dis-tinguishes his or her goods or services, including a unique product, from those manufactured or sold by others, and indicates the source of those goods or services, even if that source is unknown.*

A trademark owner may be a licensee, broker, or distributor. The term, used in commerce, means the bona fide use of a mark in the ordinary course of trade—not a use made merely to reserve a right in the mark. Reservation of a mark prior to its use can be achieved by filing an intent-to-use application with the *Patent and Trademark Office* (PTO).

The key concept of trademark law is that the trademark must be distinguishable. In order to secure trademark protection, one must develop a distinctive mark. The most distinctive trademarks are those that are purely arbitrary or fanciful (i.e., those that have no meaning or connotation other than identifying the source of a particular product). For example, the trademark Kodak to identify a brand of cameras is purely arbitrary. Less distinctive are trademarks that have another meaning, such as the trademark Shell to identify gasoline. Although such trademarks as Shell are not purely arbitrary, they are nevertheless afforded substantial protection since the other meaning bears no resemblance to the product identified.

PROHIBITED TRADEMARKS

Generic and descriptive names are not considered distinctive enough to be granted trademark status. A generic word merely identifies the product for what it is. Thus, the use of the name "Beer" to identify a brand of beer is generic and would not be accepted as a trademark. Similarly, a descriptive name only characterizes the attributes or qualities of the product. For example, using the name "Raisin Bran" to identify a cereal is merely descriptive of the product's ingredients and might have difficulty gaining trademark status.

Generic words are never afforded trademark protection. Descriptive trademarks, however, may be protected in limited circumstances. A descriptive mark may be protected if the proprietor of the mark can prove that it has acquired a secondary meaning. Secondary meaning will exist when the public no longer connects the words of the trademark with the literal, dictionary meaning, but rather with a unique product. For example, the descriptive term "TV Guide" also has a secondary meaning as the (registered) trademark of a particular publication that contains television program listings and topical articles about the industry.

Some trademarks, even though they are considered distinctive, are nevertheless prohibited by statute or public policy. Obscene or scandalous trademarks are generally denied trademark protection. Trademarks that are deemed deceptive and misleading, such as the mark "Idaho Potatoes" to identify potatoes produced in some area other than Idaho, are also denied protection.

PROTECTING A TRADEMARK

In order to secure trademark protection, it is not sufficient merely to adopt a distinctive mark. The trademark must be used in the ordinary course of trade or used in commerce. The use requirement is fundamental to trademark law and is necessary for common-law protection, as well as federal and state registration.

Common law is the body of law developed from court decisions rather than from state or federal statutes. Federal or state registration of a trademark has certain advantages, but is not necessary. Common-law protection will suffice and has the benefit of not requiring any interaction with governmental agencies.

A trademark is deemed to be used when it has been placed in any manner on the product, its containers or displays associated with it, or on any of the tags or labels affixed to the product. Thus, it is not always necessary that the trademark actually be physically affixed to the goods. As long as the trademark is associated with the product at the point of sale and in such a way that the product can be readily identified as coming from a particular manufacturer or source, the trademark may be protected. It should be noted, however, that the mere listing of a trademark in a catalog, the ordering of labels bearing the trademark, the use of the trademark on invoices, or the exhibition of trademarked goods at a trade show alone may not be sufficient in and of themselves to constitute use, since the use of the trademark was not associated with the point of sale.

IN PLAIN ENGLISH

To ensure trademark protection, the trademark proprietor is well advised to physically affix the trademark to the product. In this way, the product is certain to bear the trademark when it is sold. Proper use of a service mark is accomplished by identifying the service by the mark in advertising, signs, brochures, and the like.

CONFUSINGLY SIMILAR

Common law protects the trademark proprietor against someone else subsequently using a trademark that is confusingly similar. This raises the question of when trademarks are considered confusingly similar. Generally, trademarks will be confusing if they are similar in sound or appearance, particularly if the trademarks are affixed to similar products or if products are marketed throughout the same or similar geographic areas.

On the other hand, if two products bearing similar trademarks are not related or are marketed in different geographic areas, there may not be any infringement. Thus, a business that distributes its products solely in the Northwest could probably adopt and use a trademark already used by a business distributing its product solely in the state of Maine, provided the mark of the Northwest business does not adversely affect the value of the trademark used by the Maine company.

Moreover, a Northwest toy manufacturer could probably adopt and use a trademark used by a Northwest chainsaw manufacturer. In these situations, there may be no infringement since it is not likely that the use of the mark by the toy manufacturer would confuse chainsaw purchasers. Here again, appropriation of another's trademark may be wrongful if the use, even by a noncompeting business, would dilute the value of the mark to the original owner. (Remedies for trademark infringement will be discussed later in this chapter.)

FEDERAL REGISTRATION

The trademark proprietor can procure greater protection under federal or state statutes than under the common law. The federal statute governing trademarks is known as the *Lanham Act of 1946*. It is not the function of the Lanham Act to grant trademark rights since those are secured by the common-law principles discussed above, but rather to provide a central clearinghouse for existing trademarks via registrations.

In 1989, the *Trademark Law Revision Act of 1988* (TLRA) became effective and made substantive changes to the previous trademark laws. In addition, the trademark law was amended in 1996 to add a federal antidilution provision and again in 2006 to strengthen the antidilution provision. Though the Lanham Act provides much of the skeleton of trademark law, these amendments add the needed detail to make trademark law a more complete body of law.

Prior to enactment of the TLRA, a mark could be registered only upon actual use in interstate commerce. This requirement was satisfied when an applicant sold a few units of the product bearing the trademark in an interstate transaction. A mark could essentially be reserved for later use by making a token use at the time of application. The minimum token use requirement allowed the registering of trademarks that might never be used and possibly prevented other proprietors from legitimately using the mark. This judicially sanctioned practice also clogged the federal register with unused marks.

Under the TLRA, token use is no longer permitted. Actual use of the mark is required in order for a trademark to be registered. In addition, the revised law allows for the filing of an application for a trademark based on a bona fide intention to use that mark in the future. This reserves and protects a mark for a limited time and to a limited extent prior to its being used in commerce. If the mark is not actually used within a certain time period, the trademark registration will be denied.

There are two official registers for trademarks: the *Principal Register* and the *Supplemental Register*. Marks registered on the Principal Register enjoy all of the benefits of the trademark law. Marks registered on the Supplemental Register do not enjoy all of those benefits. The following sections on how to register a trademark apply to the Principal Register. (A separate section included later in this chapter describes what the Supplemental Register covers and how it may be used.)

APPLICATIONS BASED ON ACTUAL USE

The use requirement is met if the mark is protected as a common-law trademark. Once the proprietor has established a mark's actual use in commerce, the mark can be registered by filing an application with the Patent and Trademark Office (PTO). This process entails filling out an application, sending in a drawing of the mark, including specimens of the mark used in commerce, and paying the required fee. (The filing fee is constantly changing, though there is a reduced fee for those who file online and agree to prosecute the entire registration through an online procedure. For current information, see **www.uspto.gov**. As of the date of publication, the fee is $275 for fully electronic registrations and $335 for nonelectronic registrations.)

If the examining officer at the PTO accepts the application, the trademark will appear shortly thereafter in the Official Gazette. Anyone who believes that he or she would be injured by the issuance of the registration has thirty days to file a written notice stating the reasons for opposition. If nobody objects or if the objections are found to be without merit, a certificate of registration will be issued.

APPLICATIONS BASED ON INTENT-TO-USE

Under the TLRA, a right to a particular mark can be preserved for future use through an intent-to-use provision. This does not remove the requirement of actual use in commerce, which is still necessary for registration of the mark.

Protection of a mark for future use can be accomplished by filing an application based on the applicant's bona fide intent-to-use the mark in commerce. An intent-to-use registration should not be requested merely for the purpose of attempting to reserve a mark. The statute does not explicitly define bona fide intent, but the good faith of the applicant will be determined from the circumstances surrounding the application and the applicant's conduct with respect to the mark. The history behind the statute's enactment suggests that the applicant's conduct concerning the intent-to-use the mark will be measured against standards accepted in the trade or business.

Opposition

If the intent-to-use application satisfies the requirements of the PTO regulations, it will receive approval for publication in the Official Gazette. Upon such publication, a thirty-day period for opposition to registration of the mark begins to run. This period is similar to that accorded applications for registration of marks that are in actual use. Those applications that go unopposed receive a notice of allowance. The date the notice is issued is very important because the reservation of the mark is limited to a period of six months from the date of allowance, during which time actual use of the mark in commerce must begin or the trademark application will lapse.

Extensions

If an applicant fails to commence using the mark in commerce within the allowable six-month period, it is possible to obtain an extension for another six months. This extension is automatic upon application and payment of fee only if submitted before the original six-month period expires. Four additional six-month extensions are also possible, but require, in addition to application and fee submission before expiration of the then current six-month period, approval by the PTO upon a showing of good cause why such extension should be granted. In no event shall the period between the date of allowance and the commencement of use of the mark in commerce be permitted to exceed thirty-six months.

In making a request for extension, the applicant must include the following:

- a verified statement of continued bona fide intent to use the mark in commerce;
- the specification as to which classification(s) of goods and services the intent continues to apply; and,
- the required fee (currently $150 per extension per classification of goods or services).

Application forms may be obtained by calling the PTO at 800-786-9199 or from its website at **www.uspto.gov**.

Statement of Use

Once actual use of the mark in commerce has occurred, the applicant must file a verified statement of use. If everything is in order, the mark will be registered for the goods or services that the statement of use indicates. The Commissioner for Trademarks shall notify an applicant as to whether a statement of use has been accepted or refused. An applicant will be allowed to amend the statement of use if the mark was not used on all the goods initially identified.

CONSTRUCTIVE USE

An important concept found in the Lanham Act and improved by later amendments is that of *constructive use*. This concept, which has been called the cornerstone of the intent-to-use method, also applies to use-based applications as well. When an application to register a mark is filed under the doctrine of constructive use, filing constitutes use of the mark as of the filing date. Thus, when the application to register is filed, a right of priority to exclusive use of the mark is created throughout the United States. This is true only if the mark is filed for registration on the Principal Register. The constructive use doctrine does not apply to domestic (or foreign) applications on the Supplemental Register.

This doctrine gives applicants a strong incentive to file for registration as early as possible. The constructive use statute provides priority filing protection, and thereby prevents others from acquiring the mark by simply using it before the intent-to-use applicant does. Constructive use greatly reduces disputes as to which party has priority, thus saving costs and limiting uncertainty in infringement or opposition proceedings.

Exceptions

Exceptions to the priority right of use are marks used prior to the applicant's filing date, intent-to-use applications filed prior to the applicant's filing date, and use-based applications registered prior to the applicant's filing date. Applications for registration filed by foreign applicants are also excepted if the foreign application was filed prior to the constructive use application.

Assignments

The current law generally prohibits assignment of intent-to-use applications, thereby preventing applications for marks being filed by individuals for the sole purpose of selling them. However, an intent-to-use application may be assigned to the applicant's business.

BENEFITS OF REGISTRATION

Registering your mark provides you many benefits. First, registration enables a proprietor to use the "®" symbol or the phrase "registered trademark" in conjunction with the mark. This may well deter others from using the mark. Proprietors of marks that have not been registered are prohibited from using the above symbols with their marks. Commonly, "™" for trademark or "SM" for service mark is used in conjunction with an unregistered mark during the application period. These designations have no official status, but they do provide notice to others that the user is claiming a property right in the mark.

Second, registration on the Principal Register is evidence of the validity of the registration, the registrant's ownership of the mark, and the exclusive right to use the mark on identified goods in commerce.

Finally, a registered trademark that has been in continuous use for a period of five consecutive years may become incontestable. By registering the trademark, the proprietor may secure rights superior to those of a prior but unregistered user, but only if the original user does not object to the registrant's use within five years.

DURATION

Under the trademark law, registration remains in effect for a period of ten years. It may be renewed in additional ten-year increments by filing an application for renewal during the six months prior to the expiration of the existing ten-year term. Registrations issued prior to November 16, 1989, received a first-term registration of twenty years. All subsequent registrations are for ten-year renewals. Those registrations that issue from applications filed with the PTO and that were pending as of the effective date of the 1989 amendment have a first term of only ten years, even though filed under the prior law.

SUPPLEMENTAL REGISTER

Supplemental Register applications may be made directly if the applicant is sure that registration on the Principal Register is unlikely or in response to the PTO's final refusal to register the mark on the Principal Register. This registration provides protection for individuals capable of distinguishing their marks from those of others, but whose marks do not comply with the requirements for registration on the Principal Register. Marks for the Supplemental Register are not published for, or subject to, opposition. They are, however, published as registered in the Official Gazette. If a person believes that he or she will be damaged by the registration of another's mark on the Supplemental Register, that person may, at any time, petition for cancellation of the registration.

Applications filed on the Supplemental Register cannot be based on intent-to-use and do not enjoy the benefits of constructive use. Under the Lanham Act, an application filed on the Supplemental Register had to be in lawful use for a year prior to the filing of the application. For a mark to be eligible for registration on the Supplemental Register under the 1989 amendment, the domestic applicant's mark merely must be in lawful use in commerce, meaning a bona fide use in the ordinary course of trade.

LOSS OF PROTECTION

A use or intent-to-use is a prerequisite to trademark protection. It should be noted that some forms of use might result in the loss of a trademark. A number of well-known trademarks such as Aspirin, Thermos, and Escalator have been lost as a result of improper usage. Trademark protection is lost because the mark is used in some capacity other than as an adjective modifying a noun. When a trademark is used as a noun or a verb, it no longer functions to identify the source of the product, but rather becomes the name of the product itself. At that point, the mark becomes generic and is not subject to protection.

Abandonment of a mark will also result in loss of protection. A trademark is deemed abandoned when it has not been used for two years and there is no intent to resume its use. Token use will not be sufficient to avoid abandonment. To avoid abandonment, the proprietor does not have to use the mark in interstate commerce in the ordinary course of trade or business, but the mark should be used in intrastate commerce.

INFRINGEMENT

A trademark that is in use and has been infringed allows the trademark proprietor to sue the infringing party either for monetary damages or for an injunction prohibiting the infringing use, or sometimes for both. Monetary damages may be measured either by the plaintiff's losses resulting from the infringement or by the defendant's profits. In certain exceptional circumstances where the defendant's conduct is willful and flagrant, the plaintiff might also be entitled to exemplary damages equal to three times the actual damages and/or attorney's fees.

The relevant sections under the Lanham Act provide for remedies for infringement on marks that actually are in use. This effectively precludes an intent-to-use applicant from suing for infringement because use has not been made of the mark. The law permits anyone who feels that he or she will be damaged by acts that are likely to cause confusion, mistake, or deception as to the origin, sponsorship, or approval of the complainant's goods or services with those of another to sue for unfair competition. Under the Act, all remedies available for infringement actions are also available for actions of unfair competition.

ANTIDILUTION

In 1996, the federal trademark law was amended to provide special protection to famous marks. The statute does not define *famous mark*, though case law has adopted much of the legislative history that suggests a famous mark is a mark that has been around for a long time and enjoys extensive notoriety.

In the past, it was possible to appropriate a mark for use on goods or services that do not compete with those of the mark's owner, so long as there was no likelihood of confusion. As a result, it was possible, for example, to call a dog food "Cadillac," intending to suggest that it was the elite form of canine fare, despite the fact that the automobile manufacturer of Cadillacs did not have anything to do with the dog food. The likely intent of the dog food company was to suggest that it was the "Cadillac" of dog foods and thus the top of the line. Under the 1996 amendment, this type of use would probably not be permitted since the dog food manufacturer's use of the mark "Cadillac" would likely be considered a dilution of the General Motors trademark.

While antidilution statutes had been in effect in several states, they were not universal. The federal statute now provides protection, at least for famous marks. The remedies available for violations of the antidilution statute are comparable to those that are provided for trademark infringements. As a result of the Supreme Court's interpretation of the federal antidilution statutes as requiring actual confusion, legislation to clarify and strengthen the antidilution protection for famous marks was passed in 2006. The new legislation prohibits use of marks similar to famous marks if the use would dilute or undermine the protected mark either by blurring or tarnishing the protected mark—even if the products or services are in different categories and even if there is no likelihood of confusion.

INTERNATIONAL PROTECTION

As of the date of this writing, there is no multinational treaty to which the United States belongs providing international trademark protection. The European Union has established a pan-European trademark registration for its member nations, but the United States is not a party to that treaty.

In 2003, the United States became a party to the *Madrid Accord*, which is the closest that this country has come to providing its citizens with international trademark protection. Under the Madrid Accord, Americans can apply for trademark protection in up to seventy countries as of the date of this writing by filing the appropriate application and paying the required fees to the United States Patent and Trademark Office. It is, thus, no longer necessary for U.S. companies to hire specialists in every country in which trademark registration is desired. Under this new arrangement, the application filed with the U.S. Patent and Trademark Office can identify the member countries in which registration is sought and the class of goods or services to be covered. The cost savings for using this process is significant and the convenience will provide U.S. businesses with a more efficient method of obtaining foreign trademark registrations in the Madrid Accord member nations. It should be noted that the countries party to the Madrid Accord continue to increase. The fees required for registration are set by each country, in its own currency, and as a result, are constantly in flux. In order to determine the actual fee at any time, an applicant should check the online registry, which contains a fee meter based on the number of countries, the classes in which a mark is to be registered, and the countries' currency exchange rates. For a current listing of participating countries, as well as the fees charged and application process, see **www.wipo.int/madrid**.

STATE REGISTRATION

Trademarks can also be registered under state law. The trademark proprietor may file with the appropriate state officer a trademark application, along with documentation similar to that required by the Lanham Act. State law protection of a trademark does not extend beyond the borders of the state. The number of specimens of the mark needed to complete registration may vary from state to state, and the registration fee may also be different. Protection under state law can be broader than that found under federal laws. Remedies available under state law are also very likely to be different from those found under the federal statute. If a conflict arises between federal and state trademark law, it is important to remember that under the supremacy clause of the U.S. Constitution, federal law will supersede state law.

USING AN ATTORNEY

Registration can be quite beneficial to a manufacturer who has invested time, money, and energy in developing a reputation for quality work. Procuring trademark protection on either the state or federal level may require a considerable amount of time and skill. In this regard, an attorney may prove invaluable. An attorney can, first of all, determine if the benefits to be derived from registration justify the expenses. The total cost of trademark registration usually runs about $1,500, not counting any artist's fees for drawings. Second, an attorney can research trademark databases to determine if there are any conflicting marks. Finally, an attorney can complete the application and deal with any problems that may occur while it is being processed for registration.

If you are interested in contacting attorneys who specialize in trademark work, you can consult the Yellow Pages (look under intellectual property lawyers or patent attorneys) or ask your state bar association for some recommendations.

CHAPTER 13

Copyrights

It is quite common for start-up companies to use literature, computer software, videotapes, artwork, and similar material created by others. This material may be protected by copyright law and its unauthorized use may subject the user to liability for copyright infringement. There are, however, some situations in which you may be able to use another's work without obtaining permission. The guidelines for this use are found in the federal copyright law.

Some businesses develop their own copyrightable brochures, advertising copy, catalogs, posters, and the like. Since businesspeople tend to take a proprietary view of their creations, they may wish to prevent others from using their work without permission. Again, copyright law provides the vehicle by which these works may be protected. This chapter discusses some significant portions of the copyright law and their possible application to your business.

COPYRIGHT LAW FOUNDATION

Copyright law in the United States has its foundation in the Constitution, which provides in Article I, Section 8 that Congress shall have the power to promote the progress of science and useful arts, by securing for limited time to authors and inventors the exclusive right to their respective writings and discoveries. The first

Congress exercised this power and enacted a copyright law. The legislation was periodically revised, but no major changes were made in the law from 1909 until the *Copyright Revision Act of 1976* became effective on January 1, 1978.

Prior to enactment of the 1976 law, unpublished works were protected by common law copyright governed by state laws. This protection could vary considerably from state to state. Federal protection under the 1909 Act began by protecting a published work to which a copyright notice was attached. The Copyright Revision Act of 1976 preempts the field of copyright law—in other words, it is now the only legislation governing copyright. This law was significantly amended once again in 1989, when the United States became a party to the international copyright treaty known as the *Berne Convention*.

Publication

Publication, within the context of copyright law, is a technical term that applies to all copyrightable material. Under the old law, it meant an unrestricted public display. Today, publication is defined as the distribution of copies of a work to the public by sale or other transfer of ownership, or by rental, lease, or loan.

COPYRIGHTABLE MATERIAL

An author, from the point of view of copyright law, is a creator—be it a photographer, sculptor, writer, computer programmer, or musician. An author is granted copyright protection to original works of authorship fixed in any tangible medium of expression.

IN PLAIN ENGLISH

There have been debates over what constitutes a writing, but it is now clear that the term author includes the creator of computer software programs.

The 1976 Act expressly exempts from copyright protection any idea, procedure, process, system, method of operation, concept, principle, or discovery. In short, a copyright extends only to the expression of creations of the mind, not to the ideas themselves. Frequently, no clear line of division between an idea and its expression exists. For now, it is sufficient to note that a pure idea, such as a plan to create an innovative advertising program, cannot be copyrighted—no matter how original or creative that idea is.

The law and the courts generally avoid using copyright law to arbitrate the public's taste. Thus, a work can be copyrighted even if it makes no pretense to aesthetic or academic merit. The only requirements are that a work be original and show some creativity.

Originality—as distinguished from *uniqueness*—requires that a work be created independently. Originality, however, does not require that it be the only one of its kind. For example, cartographers who independently create identical maps are each entitled to copyright protection. Because their works often look similar to untrained observers, many cartographers will include an intentional minor error on a map so that if the identical error appears on another map alleged to have been independently created, this minor error will provide obvious evidence of copying.

SCOPE OF PROTECTION

A copyright is actually a collection of five exclusive rights. First is the right to reproduce a work by any means. The scope of this right can be hard to define, especially when it involves works such as microfilm or videotape. Under the Copyright Revision Act of 1976, someone may reproduce protected works without permission only if such reproduction involves either a fair or an exempted use as defined by the Act (explained later in this chapter).

Second is the right to prepare derivative works based on a copyrighted work. A derivative work is one that transforms or adapts the subject matter of one or more preexisting works.

Third is the right to distribute copies to the public for sale or lease. However, once a person sells a copyrighted work or permits uncontrolled distribution, the right to control further uses of that work usually ends. This is known as the *first sale doctrine*. It is superseded in a situation where the work is merely in the possession of someone else temporarily by virtue of bailment, rental, lease, license, or loan. In these instances, the copyright owner retains the right to control the further sale or other disposition of the work. Moreover, the first sale doctrine does not apply if the copyright owner has a contract with the purchaser restricting the purchaser's freedom to use the work, as is the case with many software programs. In such a case, if the purchaser exceeds the restrictions, he or she may incur liability. In this situation, however, the copyright owner's remedy will be governed by contract law rather than by copyright law.

One should distinguish between the sale of a work and the sale of the copyright in that work. If nothing is said about the copyright when the work is sold by the copyright owner, the seller retains the copyright. Since the purchaser of the work may not be aware of this, a seller may wish to call it to the purchaser's attention, either in the sales memorandum or on the work itself. If a license is granted, it should be in writing and should be very specific in the scope of rights being granted. For example, a person who has purchased a license to videotapes of a lecture may not generally market the copyrighted instruction manual used in conjunction with the lecture. The drafter of the license should be clear in defining the boundaries of permissible uses.

Fourth is the right to perform the work publicly, such as to broadcast a film on television or to show it in a lecture room or meeting room.

Fifth is the right to display the work publicly. Once the copyright owner has sold a copy of the work, however, the purchaser has the right to display that copy, but is generally still prohibited from reproducing it.

These rights are divisible. This means they can be transferred in whole or in part. If the copyright owner takes no special action upon selling the work, he or she is presumed to have retained all rights. If desired, the copyright owner may explicitly transfer any one or more of these rights.

OWNERSHIP

As a general rule, the creator of a work owns the copyright. The person who owns the copyright also automatically owns the exclusive rights. Under the old law, when a work was sold, ownership of a common-law (prepublication) copyright passed to the purchaser unless the creator reserved the copyright in a written agreement. In other words, there was a presumption in the law that a sale included the work itself plus all rights in that work.

The Copyright Revision Act of 1976, as amended, reversed the presumption that the sale of a work carries the copyright with it. Today, unless there is a written agreement to the contrary, the creator retains the copyright when the work is sold.

Joint Works

The creators of a joint work are co-owners of the copyright in the work. A *joint work* is defined as a work prepared by two or more authors with the intention that their contributions be merged into inseparable or interdependent parts of a unitary whole. Thus, whatever profit one creator makes from use of the work must be shared equally with the others, unless they have a written agreement that states otherwise.

The key point is the intent that the parts be absorbed or combined into an integrated unit at the time the work is created. Although such intent must exist at the time the work is created, not at a later date, the authors do not necessarily have to work together, work during the same period, or even know each other. However, the joint works definition does not include the situation where an artist creates a work such as a piano solo, without intending that the work involve another artist, and later commissions lyrics. If there is no intention to create a unitary or indivisible work, each creator may own the copyright to that creator's individual contribution.

In *Ashton-Tate Corp. v. Ross*, the Ninth Circuit Court of Appeals held that joint authorship was not established by the mere contribution of ideas and guidance for the user interface of a computer spreadsheet. Joint authorship requires each author to make an independently copyrightable contribution.

WORKS MADE FOR HIRE

Works considered to be works made for hire are an important exception to the general rule that a person owns the copyright in a work he or she has created. If a work was created by an employee on the job, the law considers the product a work made for hire, and the employer will own the copyright. However, the parties can avoid the application of this rule with a well-written contract. If the employment contract states that creating the copyrightable material in question is not part of the scope of employment, the employee retains the copyright, and the creation is not a work made for hire.

A work made for hire is defined as a work made by an employee within the scope of his or her employment. The principle is based on the following grounds.

- The work is produced on behalf of and under the direction of the employer.
- The employee is paid for the work.
- The employer, having paid all the costs and bearing all the risks of loss, should reap any gain.

Courts may also consider the amount of an employer's artistic advice before, during, and after the work was created.

Independent Contractors

Some courts developed a doctrine whereby an independent contractor was considered to be a special employee for copyright purposes when a commissioning party had the right to exercise control over the work. This resulted in the commissioning party, rather than the independent contractor, owning the copyright. In 1989, the U.S. Supreme Court, in *Community for Creative Non-Violence v. Reid*, held that unless the party creating the work is an actual employee as that term is defined in the law, the copyright would belong to the creator rather than to the commissioning party. The court left open the question of whether the work could be considered a joint work by virtue of the party's intent.

If the creator is an independent contractor, the works will only be considered works for hire when:

- the parties have signed a written agreement to that effect and
- the work is specially ordered or commissioned as a contribution to a collective work, a supplementary work (one that introduces, revises, comments upon, or assists a work by another), a compilation, an instructional text, answer material for a test or the test itself, an atlas, motion picture, or an audiovisual work.

Thus, unless there is a contractual agreement to the contrary, the independent contractor owns the copyright. It has been held in some jurisdictions that, in order to be valid, the written contract must predate the performance of the work.

DERIVATIVE WORKS

In the case of a derivative work, the contributing author owns only what that person contributed. A *derivative work* is defined as—

> *a work based upon one or more preexisting works, such as translation, fictionalization, motion picture version, sound recording, art reproduction, abridgment, condensation, or any other form in which*

> *a work may be recast, transformed, or adapted, or a work consisting*
> *of editorial revisions, annotations, elaborations, or other modifica-*
> *tions which, as a whole, represent an original work of authorship.*

Thus, any work based completely or substantially upon a preexisting work, if it satisfies the originality requirement and is not itself an infringing work, will be separately copyrightable. The distinction between a derivative work and a joint work lies in the intent of each contributor at the time the contribution is created. If the work is created with the intention that the contributions be merged into inseparable or interdependent parts of a unitary whole, then the merger creates a joint work. If such intention occurs only after the work has been created, then the merger results in a derivative or collective work.

COLLECTIVE WORKS

A *collective work* is defined as—

> *a work, such as a periodical issue, anthology, or encyclopedia, in*
> *which a number of contributions, constituting separate and inde-*
> *pendent works in themselves, are assembled into a collective whole.*

The originality involved in a collective work is the collection and assembling of preexisting works that may themselves be copyrightable, without any changes in such material. This assemblage of works is copyrightable.

COPYRIGHT PROTECTION FOR UTILITARIAN OBJECTS

Because copyright law was originally intended to protect literary works, earlier versions of the law omitted protection for three-dimensional designs. These designs were not given copyright protection until 1870.

The Copyright Act of 1909 did not contain any protection for utilitarian objects, but the regulations adopted to interpret the law extended copyright protection to the artistic elements of a utilitarian piece. The regulation stated that the aesthetic, but not mechanical or utilitarian, aspects of the item would be protected.

Despite the lack of specific legislation, some protection is available for manufacturers of utilitarian objects. The copyright law may be relied on to a limited extent. For example, if an individual draws a copyrightable picture and obtains copyright protection for that design, then the copyrighted picture could be used or incorporated into any utilitarian item and be protected. Similarly, architectural drawings are entitled to copyright protection.

NOTICE REQUIREMENT

The requirement that original works and all copies have a copyright notice affixed to them on publication is basic to both the Copyright Act of 1909 and the Copyright Revision Act of 1976. The notice consists of the international symbol "©" or the word "copyright" or its abbreviation "Copr.," the name of the author (in the case of works for hire, this is usually the employer), and the year of first publication. For example:

Copyright 2007 by John Doe

or

© John Doe, 2007

The order of the words is unimportant.

Under the Copyright Act of 1909, a publication without notice caused the work to fall into the public domain. Once the rights were lost, they could not be retrieved. It was publication with notice that created a federal copyright under this law.

Under the Copyright Revision Act of 1976, a federal copyright is created as soon as an original work is made in tangible form. Until 1989, however, the proper notice had to be attached at publication if you wished to retain a copyright after publication. However, a savings clause provided methods for saving a copyright when notice was omitted.

Due to the 1989 amendment to the 1976 Act, notice is not required on works created or first published after March 1, 1989. Although notice is not required, notice should still be used to make others aware of your rights. One who copies a work, believing it to be in the public domain because there is no notice, may be considered an innocent infringer. In this situation, the author whose work is copied will likely not recover significant damages. In fact, the court might even allow the copier to continue using the work.

APPLICATION PROCESS

To register a copyright you must file an application form with the Copyright Register, Library of Congress, Washington, D.C. 20559. The forms can be downloaded from the Copyright Office's website at **www.copyright.gov**. You must also deposit two copies of the work. Remember, if you have a copyright notice on your work, or if your work was published after March 1, 1989, even without a notice, you already have a copyright. Under the Copyright Revision Act of 1976, as amended, registration is necessary only:

- as a prerequisite to commencing an infringement action;
- when the copyright owner wishes to take advantage of the savings provision of Section 405; or,
- if the Register of Copyrights demands registration of published works bearing a copyright notice (which is not likely to happen unless you have been in correspondence with that office).

The law separates registration from the deposit requirements. Under the 1909 Act, registration involved filing a copyright application, paying a $6 fee and depositing two copies of the work itself or two photographs of the original.

However, fine prints came within the requirements of actual copies, making it necessary to deposit two actual prints. Congress recognized the economic hardship this caused artists and the fact that many of them intentionally failed to take advantage of copyright protection because of the burdensome deposit requirement and, therefore, modified it. Now, the Register of Copyrights is allowed to exempt certain categories from the deposit requirement or provide for alternative forms of deposit. This has been done in the case of computer software, films, videotapes, and other items.

IN PLAIN ENGLISH

Under the present law, you should deposit two of the best copies of the work with the Library of Congress within three months of publication. If the objects are bulky, fragile, or valuable, photographs may be deposited instead of the actual work. The same photograph privilege applies to fine prints in editions of three hundred or fewer. Filing the application (which includes a $45 fee as of the date of this writing) need not be done at the time of deposit. When you feel depositing two copies is a hardship, you may apply for a waiver of the two-copy deposit requirement.

Delaying Registration

Although you can delay registration, there are at least two reasons why you should deposit the work and register the copyright (i.e., file the application) within three months of publication. First, the copyright law prohibits the awarding of attorney's fees and statutory damages for infringements that occur before registration, unless registration took place within three months of publication. Second, if you deposit the required two copies of the work within three months but postpone sending the registration form and fee, the Copyright Office will require two more copies of the work when you eventually do send in the form and money. Finally, if the two copies are not deposited within the requisite three-month period, the Register of Copyrights may demand them. If the copies are not submitted within three months after demand, the person upon whom demand was made may be subject to a fine for each unsubmitted work.

In addition, such person or persons may be required to pay the Library of Congress an amount equal to the retail cost of the work. If no retail cost has been established, the costs incurred by the library in acquiring the work, provided such costs are reasonable, will be substituted. The copyright proprietor who willfully and repeatedly refuses to comply with such a demand may be liable for additional fines.

PERIOD OF PROTECTION

The Copyright Act of 1909 granted copyright protection in a work for a twenty-eight-year period that could be renewed for one additional twenty-eight-year period. Under the revised law, a work created on or after January 1, 1978, has copyright protection from the instant it is fixed in tangible form until seventy years after the creator's death. If the work was created jointly, the copyright expires seventy years after the last author dies. There are no renewals for copyrights created under the 1976 Act. Copyrights granted under the 1909 Act that were in effect on January 1, 1978, automatically received an extension to create a term of ninety-five years from the date the copyright was first obtained. It is important to note that this automatic extension applies only to copyrights that were in effect on January 1, 1978. Thus, if the copyright on a work had lapsed prior to January 1, 1978, the copyright would not have been revived. In all cases, copyright terms end on December 31 of the given year.

The copyright period of life plus seventy years applies only to works created by human beings using their own names. In other cases, for example, a corporation that obtains a copyright in accordance with the doctrine of works made for hire, or for works created anonymously or pseudonymously, the period of protection is either 120 years from creation or ninety-five years from first publication, whichever expires first.

INFRINGEMENT

The federal courts have exclusive jurisdiction over copyright infringement litigation. Under both the 1909 and 1976 Acts, the trial judge has wide discretion in setting damages. Under the 1909 Act, a judge could award either actual damages (plaintiff's out-of-pocket losses or defendant's profit) or statutory damages. Under the 1976 Act, as amended in 1989, a judge may also award actual damages and the range of statutory damages is greater: as little as $200 for innocent infringement, between $750 and $30,000 for the typical case, and up to $150,000 for willful infringement. Both Acts allow the awarding of reasonable attorney's fees to the prevailing party. Both Acts also provide for injunctions against continued infringement, and in some cases, impoundment. The statute of limitations for both Acts allows a plaintiff three years to file a lawsuit after the infringement occurs. This time frame refers to the date the infringement was committed, not the date the infringement was discovered.

In the case of willful infringement for commercial gain, criminal sanctions may also be imposed. The law was amended in 1982 to provide more severe penalties for those who unlawfully reproduce and sell sound recordings, motion pictures, audiovisual works, or phonorecords. Under these provisions, a criminal infringer may be imprisoned and/or fined.

Fair Use

Not every copying of a protected work is an infringement. There are two basic types of noninfringing use—fair use and exempted use.

The Copyright Act of 1976 recognizes that copies of a protected work for purposes such as criticism, comment, news reporting, teaching (including multiple copies for classroom use), scholarship, or research can be considered fair use, and therefore, not an infringement. However, this is not a complete list, and it is not intended as a definition of fair use.

In addition, the Act cites four criteria to be considered in determining whether a particular use is or is not fair:

1. the purpose and character of the use, including whether it is for commercial use or nonprofit educational purposes;
2. the nature of the copyrighted work;
3. the amount and substantiality of the portion used in relation to the copyrighted work as a whole; and,
4. the effect of the use upon the potential market for, or value of, the copyrighted work.

The Act does not rank these four criteria, nor does it exclude other factors in determining the question of fair use. In effect, all that the Act does is leave the doctrine of fair use to be developed by the courts.

The U.S. Supreme Court has interpreted the scope of the fair use doctrine in connection with motion pictures. In *Universal Studios, et al. v. Sony Corporation, et al.*, decided in 1984, the plaintiff movie producers claimed that the defendant, Sony Corporation, was enabling consumers to violate the plaintiff's copyright by selling a machine that could make off-the-air copies of the plaintiff's copyrighted works. This activity, it was alleged, should subject the defendants to liability for copyright infringement as both facilitator and conspirator. The Supreme Court rejected this contention and held that the copying of copyrighted works in one's own home for noncommercial purposes was fair use, at least when applied to audiovisual works. The majority of the justices expressly refrained from considering the applicability of this doctrine to any other forms of copyrighted works.

In *American Geophysical Union v. Texaco, Inc.*, the U.S. Court of Appeals for the Second Circuit held that making even one copy of a copyrighted professional journal for purposes of retaining an article in one's file for reference purposes was an infringement. The court pointed out that if the employees of the Texaco research lab desired additional copies of articles in the copyrighted journals, reprints could have been purchased. The making of an unauthorized copy deprived the copyright owner of a sale, and was therefore, an infringement.

It has also been held that the mere fact that permission to quote from a copyrighted work has been requested and denied does not necessarily mean that a use will be infringing. In *Maxtone-Graham v. Burtchaell*, the defendant, a Catholic priest, requested permission to quote from the plaintiff's book of interviews with women who were, as the title suggests, *Pregnant by Mistake*. Since the priest's intended use of the quoted material was to support his pro-life publication, permission was denied. He, nevertheless, used the excerpts. In the resulting litigation, the court held that the use was fair since the priest's unauthorized use of the copyrighted material was a productive use and the plaintiff was not necessarily deprived of sales. It is, therefore, still relatively unclear how broad or narrow the scope of the fair use doctrine really is.

Exemptions

In many instances, the ambiguities of the fair use doctrine are resolved by statutory exemptions. The exempted uses apply to situations where the public interest in making a copy outweighs the potential harm to the copyright proprietor. For example, the library and archives exemption allows libraries and archives to reproduce and distribute a single copy of a work provided that certain requirements are met. However, this exemption in no way affects the applicability of fair use, and it does not apply where such copying is prohibited in contractual arrangements agreed to by the library or archive when it acquired the work.

INTERNATIONAL PROTECTION

The United States is a party to three multinational copyright treaties. The *Buenos Aires Convention*, in effect in the Southern Hemisphere, provides international protection within member countries provided the words "all rights reserved" are added to the copyright notice. Those words must appear in the official language of the country in which the copyright is initially protected; i.e., Spanish, English, or Portuguese. The United States is also a party to the *Universal Copyright Convention*, which requires a copyright owner to comply with the copyright laws of the copyright owner's country, provided that country is also a party to the Universal Copyright Convention. It also requires the copyright owner to use the international copyright symbol "©" as part of the copyright notice.

As previously noted, the oldest multinational copyright treaty is the Berne Copyright Convention, though the United States did not become a party to it until 1989. This treaty mandates the relaxation of copyright formalities and requires greater protection be afforded copyright owners. For a list of the countries that are parties to these treaties and have reciprocal rights with the United States, see **www.copyright.gov**.

The protection afforded copyright owners under these treaties is automatic so long as the aforementioned minimal compliance standards are met. In this respect, international protection of copyrights is usually more available than international protection of other forms of intellectual property.

• • • • •

If you desire more information, write to the Copyright Office, Library of Congress, Washington, D.C. 20559, and ask for a free copyright information packet, or visit the Copyright Office's website at **www.copyright.gov**.

CHAPTER 14

Advertising

There is a host of different issues that arise in the context of advertising. When preparing an advertising program, it is essential for you to take care not to violate the rights of other businesses or individuals. Care should be taken to work with an attorney skilled in advertising law in order to be assured of having an effective program that will enable you to sell your product or service without exposing your business to potential liability. A poorly planned advertising program is likely to be more harmful than none at all. This chapter covers several important legal considerations that may arise when planning an advertising program.

GOVERNMENT REGULATION

To begin with, a business may always tout the qualities of its products or services, but those representations must be true. If there are any misrepresentations contained in ads or promotions, the state or federal government may file a lawsuit to redress this wrong.

Most states have consumer protection laws that, among other things, impose fines and other legal sanctions on businesses that engage in misleading advertising. The state attorney general can cause an offending advertisement to be withdrawn and may even require corrective advertising. Similarly, the Federal Trade

Commission (FTC) is involved in policing businesses that are engaged in interstate commerce. If your business activity extends beyond your state boundaries and either touches or affects another state, then the Federal Trade Commission has jurisdiction over your company. This is also true if you advertise over the Web. Indeed, advertising online may subject your advertising to regulation throughout the world, and the laws of other countries may be quite different from those in the United States.

If the product or service that your business provides has any medicinal benefits, then it must first be approved by the *Food and Drug Administration* (FDA). The approval process is quite technical and will require you to work closely with a lawyer specializing in this area of practice. Failure to comply with the requirements of the Food and Drug Administration could subject you to fines and, in some instances, imprisonment.

COMPARATIVE ADVERTISING

It has become quite common for businesses to tout the merits of their products and services by comparing them with those of their competitors. This form of comparative advertising is permissible in the United States provided that the statements made are true. Other countries, for example, South Africa, have different rules with respect to advertising. Thus, a business advertising in the United States would be permitted to use the name of a competitor and describe the competitor's products in an advertisement, even though the comparison will likely point out the competing product's or service's inferiority. This is true as long as there is no likelihood that a consumer would believe the advertiser is also selling the competing product or service and as long as the statements made are accurate.

> **EXAMPLE:** In a leading case, it was held permissible to use the names of famous perfumes in an advertisement that stated that those who like the famous perfume will also like the advertiser's less expensive product. The court felt that there was no possibility of a consumer being confused into believing

that the expensive perfume manufacturer was advertising for the cheaper knockoff scent. In addition, since the perfume smelled the same, the statements made were felt to be accurate.

A closely related situation arises when one makes disparaging remarks about the product of another. In this situation, the one who intentionally or negligently makes untrue disparaging remarks about the product or service of another business may be held legally accountable to the injured party.

It should be noted that for a disparaging remark to be actionable, it must be both untrue and believable by a reasonable person. If the statement made was so outlandish as to be unbelievable, it is unlikely the owner whose product was disparaged will be able to prove any injury. Thus, if a car manufacturer claimed its competitor's vehicle was so poorly constructed that it literally fell apart within the first week of use, the likelihood is that this gross exaggeration would not be believed and, therefore, would not be actionable.

PUBLICITY AND PRIVACY

A company may use a celebrity to endorse its product, provided the celebrity consents to the endorsement. If not, the company may be liable to the celebrity for violating his or her right of publicity. This right is granted by the majority of states in the United States to those who commercially exploit their names, voices, or images, such as actors or singers. The use of a look-alike for commercial purposes may also be actionable. Thus, when manufacturers used look-alikes for Jackie Onassis, Woody Allen, and the rap group the Fat Boys, liability was imposed.

People who have not achieved notoriety because of their commercial activities may have a right of privacy, and thus, may have a claim if their names or likenesses are used in an advertisement without their permission. This applies even to employees. They must grant permission for their names, voices, or likenesses to be used for advertising purposes.

If an individual's photograph is not the focal point of the ad, but rather is merely an incidental part, such as a head in a crowd or a member of an audience, then an individual's permission may not be essential for the photograph to be used commercially.

Even though you may not be required to have permission from an individual before using his or her photograph, it is a good idea to get a signed photo release whenever possible. The release should be worded in such a way as to give your business permission to use the name and likeness, or where relevant, the person's voice, for any and all purposes, including advertising your business. This will protect you if, for example, the individual ultimately becomes popular and you wish to use the photos you obtained at an earlier date before the individual became a celebrity.

UNAUTHORIZED USE OF TRADEMARK

An advertiser may be permitted to use the name or logo of another business in its ad as long as there is no likelihood that the average viewer would believe that the ad was sponsored by the company whose name or logo you are using. For example, it would be permissible for you to have an ad for a baseball team contain a photo of individuals incidentally holding a distinctively shaped Coca-Cola bottle, as long as it is clear from the advertisement that the soft drink manufacturer is not sponsoring the ad.

Geographic Locations

Geographic locations may also be used in advertisements without obtaining the owner's consent. It would be permissible for a company to advertise its product by having someone stand in front of a famous building, such as the Empire State Building or the Sears Tower. Similarly, an automobile advertisement may show its vehicle streaking through a metropolitan area and passing several famous businesses.

This is so because items of utility are not copyrightable. Buildings, parks, and other landmarks may incidentally be used in advertising programs without the owner's permission. (However, it was held that a building that was architecturally unique, identifiable, and famous could enjoy the protection of the trade dress laws when it was prominently featured on a poster.)

TRADE DRESS

A form of advertising that has been given special protection is package design. While it is true that the copyright laws do not protect functional items, such as product packaging, the courts have developed a form of protection known as trade dress. This means that the design elements of a particular packaging design are protectable as long as they are not otherwise functional, i.e., a hanger or a lid. The trade dress form of protection may be automatic and has been extended beyond traditional packaging.

> **EXAMPLE:** A leading case involved Blue Mountain Greeting Card Co. It had developed a distinct and very identifiable line of greeting cards. The cards had become quite well known and commercially successful. The Hallmark Greeting Card Company realized this fact and designed a line of cards that were not identical to those of Blue Mountain but, in essence, appropriated the Blue Mountain look and feel. Consumers seeing the Hallmark cards would reasonably believe that they were merely an extension by Blue Mountain of its popular line. For this reason, the court held Hallmark liable for infringing Blue Mountain's trade dress in the cards.

The U.S. Supreme Court, in 1992, endorsed the expansion of the trade dress doctrine in *Two Pesos v. Taco Cabana*. In this case, the court stated that the nonfunctional aspects of a business might be protectable trade dress provided they are distinctive and identifiable. A restaurant's architectural features, décor, and menu may be protected so long as they have a distinctive look and feel, are not functional, and have achieved notoriety. Thus, it is likely that McDonald's golden arches would be considered protectable trade dress. The trade dress doctrine has been used to prevent copying of a business's distinctive theme, a food company's packaging, and a jewelry manufacturer's earring backers.

In 2000, the U.S. Supreme Court clarified the trade dress doctrine by providing that product design trade dress can be established only by conducting an extensive survey of consumers in order to determine that they recognize the unique look and feel of the item involved. As of this writing, the court has not applied the same requirement to package design trade dress.

IN PLAIN ENGLISH

Many businesses have begun to register their trade dress. This is accomplished by registering the distinctive look and feel, as discussed in Chapter 12. By doing this, the proprietor gains the presumption of validity under the Lanham Act and the presumption that the trade dress has been established.

CELEBRITY TRADE DRESS

Individuals can also have distinctive styles. For example, when an advertiser hired one of Bette Midler's backup singers to replicate Ms. Midler's distinctive vocal rendition of a song for a commercial, Ms. Midler sued and recovered for the knockoff. It was held that the intentional copying of the singer's famous, distinctive style and voice was a form of infringement and actionable. When, however, a manufacturer hired a group that looked and sounded like the group known as the Fat Boys, the federal court in New York held the manufacturer liable only for violating the celebrities' publicity rights. The court refused to impose liability for the unauthorized use of the Fat Boys' sound, since the New York publicity statute extends protection merely to one's name, portrait, or picture, and not to one's sound. The Midler case relied on a California statute that, among other things, protects a celebrity's voice.

CONCLUSION

The benefits of advertising are clear, yet if not done properly, the detriments can be significant. This is particularly true today with the advent of inexpensive online advertising. Care must be taken to comply with the laws of every jurisdiction into which an advertisement may be launched. By working with an experienced business lawyer, you will reduce your business's potential exposure.

CHAPTER 15

Licensing

Once you have protected your intellectual property through trademark, trade dress, patent, or copyright, you may want to exploit your creations and prevent others from interfering with your rights. For instance, you may convert pictures from your copyrighted catalog into posters and sell them. If another company likes your work and wishes to duplicate it, you can exploit your own intellectual property by granting the other person a license.

IN PLAIN ENGLISH

Licensing has become so important that entire trade shows devoted to this field have emerged. One of the most prominent is the *International Licensing Show* held in early June at the Javits Center in New York City. For more information, check the website at **www.javitscenter.com**.

GENERAL CONSIDERATIONS

A license to use your copyright, trademark, trade dress, or patent should be in writing. It should describe the scope of the user's permission, such as how long the license will last, whether the user can market copies throughout the world or only in specific locations, and whether the license allows exploitation of the entire intellectual property or only a portion of it (i.e., use of a copyrighted photo on T-shirts, but not on anything else). Care should be taken when defining these boundaries. If a U.S. license permits sales or other exploitation of the licensed products or technology in, for example, Canada, then Canadian sales to a business that ships the goods to the United States may be within the scope of permitted use, resulting in the U.S. licensees competing with Canadian licensees for sales within the U.S. This situation is known as a *gray market*, which can be controlled by using care in drafting the license agreement.

Lawyers who specialize in intellectual property can be helpful in explaining the numerous possibilities available to you through the licensing process. They can be helpful in drafting a document that will afford you maximum protection while another person exploits your intellectual property. A skilled lawyer can also determine whether the licensing arrangement you are proposing could be subject to franchising laws. (see Chapter 10.)

> **NOTE:** Skilled drafters will avoid ambiguity in language, such as using the term *American* when intending the United States, since all countries in the North and South Americas may be considered American.

It is also important to record your license in the appropriate place—the Copyright Office or the office of the Commissioner of Patents and Trademarks—when such recording is available. An intellectual property lawyer should be able to assist you with this process.

LICENSING HAZARDS

Several issues should be considered before deciding whether to grant a license. While the factors that follow may influence your decision to license or not to license, by no means is it intended to be an exhaustive list.

Nature of the Work

First, the nature of the work, technology, etc., must be considered. If the property rights to be licensed are in a new technology that is susceptible to rapid change (i.e., a new development in the computer or electronic industry) or a product that is simply one of many alternatives on the market, then the value of the license to the potential licensee will be decreased. The licensee may then require that updated product enhancements be provided as part of the license agreement. On the other hand, if the product is a new development that exists without alternatives, and is thereby likely to afford the licensee a greater period of exploitation, the licensor is in a much stronger negotiating position to demand a higher price.

Sublicensing

Another issue to consider is whether or not the licensee will be permitted to sublicense. When permitted, the right to sublicense can affect the price paid for a license. In the area of computer software, for instance, sublicense rights are often part of the licensee's comprehensive business plan. Sublicense provisions should be carefully drafted and tied directly to the terms of the original license agreement. All ownership of the licensor's technology should be retained by the licensor via specific provisions in the original license agreement. Provisions should be made for quality control checks of the licensed property. All provisions in the original license agreement should be drafted to apply to any sublicense agreements negotiated by the licensee.

Patented Technology

If the licensor is considering licensing a patented technology, the safety of the technology and potential for liability arising from its use should be evaluated. Licenses can be drafted with *exculpatory clauses* in which the licensee agrees to assume all liability arising from the use of the licensed technology.

Exculpatory clauses that deal with latent design defects (i.e., defects not readily discoverable), however, may not entirely insulate the licensor from liability. Careful testing of the technology to ensure removal of defects will reduce the risk of such a situation occurring.

The exculpatory clause itself, by careful enumeration of what liabilities the licensee assumes, can also provide extra protection to the licensor. The exculpatory clause should be written by an attorney experienced in drafting this type of provision.

International Concerns

Care should also be taken to avoid allowing your intellectual property to be exploited in countries that do not honor U.S. intellectual property laws, that have laws that are less protective than ours, or that have no intellectual property law at all. The U.S. State Department has a watch list of countries that do not honor their intellectual property treaty obligations and of countries that have a poor record of enforcement with respect to intellectual property.

The advent of the World Wide Web has presented a myriad of new challenges. Since material may be captured anywhere in the world, even in areas that may not be desirable, care should be taken in determining what is placed on the Web and whether your license permits or prohibits Web postings.

METHOD OF PAYMENT

Once the decision to license has been made, the price of the license must be negotiated. Payment for the license should be spelled out in the license document. You can demand a flat fee in exchange for permission to use your copyright material, trademark, or patent, or you may prefer to receive some portion of the income as a royalty. This payment can either be a fixed amount per item or a percentage, perhaps 5%, of the money received by the person exploiting the right. Care should be taken to specifically define the sum upon which the percentage will be based. Specify, for example, if it will be a percentage of the net or gross receipts from the sale of items covered by the license, and carefully define the term used.

Royalties

Payments based on sales are referred to as *royalties*. One should be very careful to define when they are due and payable and on what basis they are to be calculated. Unfortunately, numerous unscrupulous individuals have used creative accounting to reduce their obligations.

> **EXAMPLE:** In the case of *Buchwald v. Paramount Studios*, Art Buchwald established that he, and not Eddie Murphy, was responsible for the treatment that ultimately became the movie *Coming to America*. Pursuant to his contract with Paramount, Buchwald was to receive a share of net profits. As of the date of trial, the movie had grossed $350 million, but by the use of creative accounting, Paramount alleged a net loss of $18 million on the picture. The poorly drafted, one-sided contract deprived Buchwald of his fair share of the movie's earnings.

Currency

If international transactions are involved, be sure to specify which country's currency is to be used. The value of U.S. dollars, Canadian dollars, and Australian dollars for example, typically differ. There is also a cost involved in currency conversion.

Accounting Report

It is also important to include in a licensing agreement a provision whereby you can verify the accuracy of the records showing what is due you. This can be accomplished by requiring the person to whom the license is granted to have an accounting report preceding or accompanying any royalty checks. There should be an agreed-upon right to have an independent party audit the books in the event that you dispute the validity of the report.

ACKNOWLEDGMENT OF OWNERSHIP

In order to retain the protection afforded by the patent, trademark, or copyright laws, you must require any person who uses your creation to acknowledge your ownership and include the appropriate notice on the work. It is common to see a legend that states, for example, "Reproduced with permission of J. Jones, the copyright owner."

QUALITY CONTROL

Since the work marketed after you have granted a license will bear your name or trademark, it will usually be difficult, if not impossible, for consumers to distinguish between your work and those works reproduced by the person to whom you have granted a license. For this reason, it is important for you to retain some degree of quality control over the licensed product. In fact, trademark law requires quality control. It has been held that a naked license (one without quality control measures) is void. A provision in the license should, therefore, require the licensee to demonstrate the method by which the item will be reproduced and some means by which you can evaluate the quality of the final products.

SIGNATURE

In order for the license to be valid and enforceable, both parties should sign it. You should make it clear that the license is personal and may not be assigned or exploited by anyone but the person to whom it is given unless you give your written permission. If you are dealing with a business entity, then you should make it clear that a transfer of a large percentage ownership in that entity will be deemed an assignment even though the entity still retains the license. In this way, you will not be surprised by having the business entity to which you granted a license under new management. It is also wise to provide that the license is void and no longer in effect if any of its terms, including payment of royalties, are violated.

CHAPTER **16**

The Internet

It has become commonplace for individuals and businesses to establish a presence on the World Wide Web. Elaborate websites have appeared with regularity not only for large, multinational corporations, but also for smaller companies and individuals. While there are no decisive studies on the extent of commerce that actually occurs on the Web, marketing on and surfing the Web is very common. The vast majority of brick-and-mortar businesses have established websites.

Most U.S. households own or have access to a computer and the Internet. More and more homes have direct Internet connections and multiple computers. Many even have their own networks. New home construction is incorporating computer and network wiring as standard.

Recent surveys have established the Web as a significant retail marketplace, and the use of websites for commercial activities is continuously expanding. Websites exist for bill-paying, securities sales, travel bookings, and for virtually every form of commercial activity. Many businesses encourage Web commerce by providing discounts and exclusive offers for Web-based transactions.

Technology allows even the smallest businesses to create elaborate interactive sites that attract a good deal of positive attention. Theories abound on what makes a website appealing. For some, interactive graphics are the key; others feel it is important to provide browsers with something of value to take with them, such as information or the opportunity to obtain souvenirs of the visit. Some music publishers provide samples of the music they handle, while visual artists may encourage visitors to download images displayed on their sites. Many businesses give discounts or coupons online. With these new technologies, businesses are faced with additional concerns and considerations for their daily operations.

PROTECTING BUSINESS PROPERTY

The World Wide Web's popularity has raised significant questions regarding the extent of legal and intellectual property protection in cyberspace. One of the earliest cases involved the Church of Scientology and raised the question of whether U.S. copyright laws and state trade secret laws are enforceable in cyberspace. In that case, several former church members were sued for posting copyrighted material on the World Wide Web that they had received in confidence.

The court held that these traditional forms of intellectual property protection were, indeed, applicable in cyberspace. In addition, it was held that the *Internet Service Provider* (ISP) could also be exposed to liability for merely permitting the infringing material to appear on the Web. As elsewhere, one who facilitates or aids in the commission of an infringing act may be liable as a contributory infringer. Congress later changed this situation for ISPs who do not have control over the content of the material posted.

The Church of Scientology also claimed that the wrongdoers misappropriated the church's trade secrets and sought an injunction to have the offending material removed from the Web. The court rejected this argument, pointing out that once information is posted in cyberspace, it is no longer secret, and the injunction was denied. However, if a protected trade secret is posted on a website in violation of an agreement or in breach of one's duty to the owner of the protected information, then the act of posting would be wrongful and the perpetrator would likely be liable for the improper activity.

IN PLAIN ENGLISH

Cyberspace is the newest communication vehicle and considered to be one of the most dynamic and effective.

PROTECTING CONSUMER INFORMATION

Legislation has been passed in an attempt to control the dissemination of personal information by businesses. It is now required that all businesses provide customers with an opportunity to elect whether their personal information may be disclosed to others through opting out. In addition, California adopted legislation requiring any company doing business in California or affecting California commerce to disclose any breach in security that has potentially compromised personal information. It is expected that this type of legislation will become far more widespread.

DOMAIN NAMES

Characterization of website names has also presented some vexing problems. It is unclear whether a domain name is merely an address (*Uniform Resource Locator* (URL)) used for the purpose of locating the site or whether that name may be characterized as a trademark. In addition, the problem is compounded by the fact that, while there is only one World Wide Web, each trademark is distinguished by the classification of goods or services it covers. There are thirty-four international classes of goods and twelve international classes of services.

EXAMPLE: The American Bar Association, commonly referred to as the ABA, wished to register its acronym as its domain name. It was not able to do so, because the American

Booksellers Association—also commonly known as the ABA, had already registered www.aba.org.

Domain names were originally registered with Network Solutions. Today, there are a number of different registrars. Competition for domain name registration is fierce. Prices for securing a domain name have become far more competitive. Generally, domain names are registered on a first-come, first-served basis. Many computer businesses can assist you in obtaining a domain name.

Initially, there were five top-level domain name categories for U.S.-based registrants: .com for commerce; .org for organizations; .gov for government; .mil for military; and, .edu for educational institutions. These suffixes were supposed to be made available only to those who qualified for their use. As the availability of popular domain names shrank, it became necessary to create additional opportunities by creating new suffixes—such as .pro for professionals, .biz for businesses, .fm for radio—and the process continues. In fact, the number of suffixes is becoming rather large, though the initial five are still the most popular. In addition to all of the U.S. designators, many other countries have distinctive suffixes as well, such as .uk for the United Kingdom and .ru for Russia.

Disputes

There are several methods for resolving domain name disputes. These include litigation in federal district court, reliance on the anti-cybersquatting legislation, and the online arbitration process using the procedure established by ICANN. (The *Internet Corporation for Assigned Names and Numbers* offers numerous resources at its website **www.icann.org**.) The anti-cybersquatting legislation is intended to prevent so-called cybersquatters from obtaining an inventory of domain name registrations for the purpose of reselling them to those who are likely to have a better right to that name as a URL. A lawyer specializing in online intellectual property issues should be consulted when these issues arise.

Trademarked Business Names

Generally speaking, obtaining a trademark registration for your business name will also provide you with leverage in both obtaining and keeping the business name as a domain name. Thus, for example, Nike would likely have success in either obtaining the URL nike.com or in defending that URL against another potential registrant of that domain name, because the Nike business name is a registered trademark. As noted in the chapter on trademarks, it is possible today to register trademarks in seventy countries throughout the world pursuant to the *Madrid Protocol* through the United States Patent and Trademark Office. One of the principal reasons for this expanded opportunity to obtain international trademark protection was the expanded use of trademarks in commerce on the World Wide Web.

Under some circumstances, using your business name as a domain name may be considered adequate for purposes of trademark registration. A number of cases have dealt with trademark issues in cyberspace. In those cases, the applicability of federal trademark law and the question as to which jurisdiction was proper for purposes of litigating the wrongdoing were considered. While the issues have not been definitively resolved, the trend appears to be in favor of extending trademark laws to cyberspace and holding infringers liable wherever their infringing activity can be accessed.

In a landmark case, an enterprising individual residing in Illinois decided to register a number of popular business names as website domain names. When the business owners who had previously registered those names as trademarks attempted to register their company names as domain names, they were told that they were too late. The entrepreneuring registrant then offered to sell these companies the domain names for their own registered trademarks. The companies filed suit in federal court in California, alleging that the appropriation of the protected trademarks as domain names by one who lacks authority from the trademark owner is an infringement. The court agreed and stated that this outrageous conduct would result in liability.

The defendant in this case objected to being sued in California, stating that he was located in another state and that all his activity actually occurred within his home state. The court made it clear that, since the infringing site could be accessed in California and since the infringer was trying to extort money for sale of the marks from California, the case could properly be brought there.

At least one case appears to have taken a different stance regarding jurisdiction. In that situation, a European restaurant bearing the same name as a restaurant in the United States established a website. The American company sued, alleging trademark infringement, and the court held that it was unlikely the European restaurant would cause the kind of market confusion necessary to establish trademark infringement by advertising on the Web and having those advertisements viewed in the United States. This is consistent with intellectual property law in general, since it would appear that, even in cyberspace, it will be necessary to establish a likelihood of confusion and that the infringer somehow appropriates business from the owner of the protected trademark before liability will be imposed.

Framing

A number of other issues have generated Web-based litigation. When Total News, Inc., decided to provide Web surfers with the ability to compare data from several news sources, such as the *Washington Post* and CNN, problems arose. The other services filed suit, complaining that the visual presentation of their material was framed within the host's name and that their protected material was, thereby, being retransmitted without their permission. The case was settled, with Total News agreeing to refrain from framing the protected material and the plaintiffs agreeing to grant Total News licenses to link directly to their sites. Later cases have judicially established that framing is unlawful and can be legally redressed.

Linking

In the Total News case, the question of linking, where one may jump from one site to another by simply clicking on an identifying icon or phrase, was raised but not resolved. More recently, the question has been reconsidered and it has been held that linking is unlawful when the link is established without the consent of the proprietor of the linked site, though other cases have held that such linking is permissible.

INTERNET ADVERTISING

One of the most important distinctions of advertising on the Internet is the way cyberspace advertising reaches consumers. Ads in traditional advertising forums, such as magazines, newspapers, radio, and television, are intended to affect conduct in the future. It is hoped that the consumer will purchase the product next time he or she goes shopping. Internet shoppers, on the other hand, can instantaneously make a purchase.

Key Words

One of the more controversial practices that has occurred in recent years is the sale by search engines, such as Google, of the right to use the name of a competitor for the purpose of deflecting business. Some courts have held that this practice is unlawful passing off, whereas others have condoned it. Thus far the cases have been primarily against the search engines themselves, but it is likely that disgruntled business owners will seek to hold the advertiser liable as well.

Disclosures

Cyberspace has become a significant marketplace and laws adopted for purposes of preventing deceptive advertising do apply in cyberspace. The Federal Trade Commission (FTC) periodically conducts Internet surf days in conjunction with state attorneys general. The FTC requires certain disclosures in connection with traditional forms of advertising. These disclosures are easily lost in cyberspace. A disclosure can be bypassed when linking from one site to another and required legends can be buried in text that users may just scroll through. In contrast, when a disclosure appears in a more traditional advertisement, the viewer sees the entire composite—and required disclosures are unlikely to be bypassed.

IN PLAIN ENGLISH

According to the FTC, it is a good idea to require website visitors to click through required disclosures whenever an advertising site is visited.

The FTC has announced that it will sue a website designer if that designer knows or should have known that the site he or she created violates the law. However, thus far, users have not uniformly been pressed into having to read disclosures if they do not want to.

AUDITS

Some intellectual property practitioners suggest that an attorney who has expertise in working with websites be requested to conduct a so-called Internet traffic and Web-content audit. This would include evaluating whether the appropriate permissions to display material have been obtained. For example, if copyrighted material is to be used, has the copyright owner granted permission for the work to be displayed on the Web? If testimonials are to be displayed, then it is important to get written permission from the individual providing the testimonial.

Liability Insurance

Internet advertisers also need to determine whether their existing liability insurance covers their activity in cyberspace. Losses resulting from a crashed website are probably not covered in a traditional policy. Similarly, errors and omissions insurance should be considered for situations where your Web designer creates a site that contains infringing work or defames someone.

International Concerns

Since websites are, by definition, worldwide, it is important to determine whether your site, the content of which is legal in the United States, may subject you to liability elsewhere. For example, as noted in Chapter 14, comparative advertising is generally permissible and fairly common in the United States. Other countries, such as South Africa, are far more restrictive in what they permit in a comparative advertising spread.

In addition, activities that are legal in the United States can nonetheless subject a website owner to liability abroad.

> **EXAMPLE:** When eBay permitted auction sales of Nazi memorabilia, it was sued in France by Holocaust survivors for violating French law that prohibits such activities. The court was not sympathetic to eBay's position that it could not technologically isolate France from the rest of the world with respect to its online auctions. In fact, the judge believed the plaintiffs' expert, who said that technology was available to create such a block. The online auction house was found guilty and fined for its activities in France. eBay then filed suit in the United States for the purpose of preventing enforcement of the judgment.

The problem is clear—one who engages in Internet activity has, by definition, established a worldwide presence and must, therefore, comply with worldwide laws—a difficult process even for multimillion-dollar companies like eBay.

COPYRIGHT CONCERNS

The extent of litigation that has resulted from activity on the World Wide Web suggests that care must be taken when establishing your presence in cyberspace. This new dimension gives rise to increased and often desired exposure, but the ramifications of problems can be devastating for a small business.

Permissions

Even the simple act of advertising a product for retail sale could have serious consequences if you are not careful. For instance, if you market or sell a copyrighted item—even if you have obtained permission to advertise this item for sale—you may still not have the right to scan an image of that item into your computer and post it on your website. It may be necessary for you to obtain specific permission to replicate the work in two dimensions before engaging in cyberspace promotional activities.

Downloading and reusing material from other websites may also expose a business to liability. Some business, including *Playboy* magazine, have developed invisible electronic watermarks to place on the images they post on their websites in order to discourage anyone from attempting to capture and reuse those images without permission. *Playboy* also announced its intention to use a device to police cyberspace in order to locate any of its marked images.

International Concerns

Similarly, you have to recognize the fact that the Web is worldwide and that your material may find its way into jurisdictions and geographical regions that do not have copyright treaty relations with the United States. In this event, you may find that you have lost control of protected work.

While the *World Intellectual Property Organization* (WIPO) has expanded the extent of protection available for intellectual property with the WIPO Treaty of 1996, not all countries have adopted or implemented it. As of the date of this writing, 183 countries belong to WIPO, yet few have ratified the treaty to expand protection for sound recordings, motion pictures, computer software, and other digitally transmitted literary works. Even where the treaty is in force, there is still some risk, since it is limited in scope. Additionally, not all countries can be expected to participate and enact this treaty without reservation. Some countries will certainly remain on the U.S. watch list, since they continue to disregard their current treaty obligations, and there is no reason to believe these countries will adopt or respect the WIPO treaty.

Peer-to-Peer Problems

Online music and video streaming have presented a host of problems. Many individuals have been involved in peer-to-peer activities whereby copyrighted music, videos, and films are made available to anyone who wishes to download them without the copyright owner's permission. The situation has been so ubiquitous that drastic steps have been taken. The music industry announced that it would be filing suit against individuals who were felt to be involved in the practice of music and video swapping.

In fact, in the fall of 2003, lawsuits were filed and the companies announced that amnesty would be available only to those who voluntarily agreed to cease the unauthorized practice. It is expected that the threat of litigation, coupled with the actual enforcement activity, will effectively discourage the continued violation of the copyright laws. Only time will tell.

SERVER PROTECTION

One significant risk in maintaining a website is that it may serve as a window to your company's computer system. There are some safeguards that should be taken in order to prevent improper access and protect your business's valuable trade secrets.

IN PLAIN ENGLISH

If your business hosts its site on its own server that is networked with your other business computers, hackers could gain access to your entire system and all of your data.

Information you deem to be confidential and sensitive should be encrypted. That is, it should be available only through use of special software. Similarly, your system should always be protected by a password, and that word should not be obvious or simple. In addition, it should be changed frequently. More and more systems are using firewalls, which are electronic blocks preventing access to all but those who have the proper key. Many businesses have been created for the purpose of developing and installing computer security devices or software. You should consult with an expert when designing your website in order to take advantage of the latest technology.

EMAIL

The popularity of the World Wide Web has been paralleled by the expanded use of email. Communications within a business are commonplace and efficient. Internal, paperless transmissions of important messages throughout an office or plant help facilitate the day-to-day operations in many businesses. In addition, more and more businesses are developing intranets. These are websites available only to a defined network, such as a company's employees.

Because of the widespread use of internal email, business handbooks and policy statements should deal with the proper use of email, as well as other related computer issues. For instance, it has been held that repeated transmission of sexually or racially explicit email messages by one employee to another may be deemed harassment, and if not controlled by the employer, may render the employer liable as well.

External use of email is also quite common, enabling business users to communicate quickly with customers, clients, suppliers, and the like. Here, too, security is an issue to consider to make sure that the transmission is safe from uninvited inquisitors. Once again, there are a variety of vehicles available for security, such as encryption.

SPAM

Internet email is often abused. The advertisements and other uninvited literature that tend to clutter the traditional, or snail mail, mailbox has now found its way into the email system. This persistent transmission of undesired electronic junk mail, commonly called *spam*, continued after a request to stop, is an actionable wrong.

In response to this problem, most of the major ISPs have developed spam filters and pop-up blockers. Similarly, software can be purchased to serve the same function.

Interestingly enough, the very word *spam*, which has been used to describe bulk email, usually advertising, itself became the subject of litigation. Hormel, the meat company that first developed the name Spam for its canned meat, filed suit for trademark infringement against a software manufacturer for using the word as part of the name of its spam-filtering product.

VIRUSES, WORMS, AND TRAPS

One of the most serious problems to arise in cyberspace is the prevalence of computer viruses, worms, and traps. These parasites are intended to interfere with computer use, and in some cases, to damage software and/or hardware. Briefly, viruses and worms are computer programs, usually transmitted via email, contaminated floppy disks, or CDs, often designed to damage a computer or computer system by compromising or destroying the computer's hard drive. Many have been created with the ability to invade a computer's address book and resend itself to all of the addressees, unbeknownst to the computer owner. The purpose of the retransmission is to invade the recipient's computer and repeat the process in a never-ending progression. Others do not leave the recipient's computer but destroy some or all of the computer's software or hardware.

Traps, on the other hand, are website-based programs that automatically spring on a user. They may be as simple as opening dozens of websites within a few seconds to downloading and installing automatic dialers and resetting various computer settings. They also may embed other unwanted software in the victim's computer. These are easy to remove, but difficult to identify and locate.

Cyber-terrorism

As a result of the breakup of the Soviet Union, the burst of the so-called technology bubble, and widespread unemployment of computer-savvy individuals, cyber-terrorism has become epidemic. In fact, the Department of Homeland Security has identified computer hacking and the infiltration of worms and viruses as one of the more significant problems to be faced by the free world today.

Sadly, no computer system is immune from these unwanted intrusions and the havoc they wreak. Even software giants such as Microsoft have been forced to announce the discovery of vulnerabilities in their systems that have been exploited by hackers and those who produce worms and viruses. While hackers typically invade government sites and those computers belonging to large business operations, worms, viruses, and traps can interfere with and cause significant damage to even a small business's computer system or an individual's home computer. As quickly as they are identified and software developed or modified to block them, new ones appear. (A number of companies, including notably McAfee and Symantec, specialize in antivirus/antiworm protection software.)

Security for Online Commerce

Another reason for ensuring cybersecurity is the expanded use of online commerce. As discussed in Chapter 7, it is now possible to contract online and to engage in other forms of commercial activity, such as credit card purchasing. In the early days of cybercommerce, there was a great deal of fear among consumers with respect to the security of their credit card information being compromised on the Web. Today, secure sites are the norm and companies such as Visa have established certification programs for ensuring customers of a website's security.

By proceeding with good judgment and consulting with experienced intellectual property lawyers who have been involved with new technology and computer system specialists, you can remain on the cutting edge of cyberspace. For more information, you may wish to visit the author's firm's website at **www.dubofflaw.com**.

CHAPTER 17

Warranties

You may be warranting certain attributes of your business's products or services whether you realize it or not. The rules that govern warranties for products are set forth in the Uniform Commercial Code (UCC), some form of which has been adopted in every state.

A warranty is, in essence, a guarantee that an item will be of a certain quality or have particular attributes. Giving a warranty involves certain obligations, so you should be aware of what those obligations are.

EXPRESS WARRANTIES

Any statement of fact or promise that describes the characteristics of an item will create an express warranty. In general, you do not need to use the words *warranty* or *guarantee* to create an express warranty. However, the more explicit your statement, the more likely it is that you, perhaps unwittingly, have given an express warranty.

In order to determine whether statements are the type that will give rise to an express warranty—as opposed to mere expressions of opinion, which will not—the courts have developed a test. If the seller makes a statement to the buyer relating to goods about which the buyer is uninformed, that statement is probably an express warranty. On the other hand, if the seller merely expresses a judgment about something on which each party would be expected to have an opinion, no express warranty is given.

> **EXAMPLE:** If a manufacturer were to state that a ceramic bowl was oven-safe, this statement would likely be considered an express warranty since most buyers do not know much about pottery and only the seller would know about this bowl in particular.

Making an Express Warranty

In order to determine whether a statement will be considered an express warranty, a number of factors are relevant. A written statement, particularly if it is part of a contract or bill of sale, is more likely to be considered an express warranty than an oral statement. How much the seller qualifies the statement is also an indication of whether an express warranty is created.

Basis of the Bargain

Another way an express warranty can be created is by giving a description of the item that becomes part of the basis of the bargain. The description does not need to be the sole inducement to purchase the goods in order for it to constitute a warranty. If a contract is involved, any statements must have been part of the contract negotiations. The precise time a statement is made is irrelevant. The buyer could already have paid for an item and the seller could then make a statement that could be considered part of the basis of the bargain. This is so since, theoretically, the buyer could still decide to return the goods to the seller and get the money back. However, post-purchase statements must be made within a reasonable period of time to be considered part of the bargain and they probably only apply to face-to-face dealings.

An additional problem presents itself if you sell your goods both through a catalog or ads and in person. Catalogs or ads, and any statements made in them, could be considered part of the basis of the bargain for those making purchases in person. Buyers would probably have to prove that they relied on those statements in making the decision to purchase.

Samples and Models

An express warranty can also be created by the use of samples or models. This type of warranty will arise if you sell from a catalog or ship items from your stock after the buyer has viewed samples at a trade show. There is a distinction between a sample and a model. A sample is drawn from the actual goods that are the subject of the sale. Therefore, the sample describes the qualities of the goods being purchased unless the seller specifically states otherwise.

IN PLAIN ENGLISH

If you show a customer one placemat from a group of eight and the customer does not investigate the other seven, an express warranty is created that the remaining seven are of similar color, size, and composition as the one examined.

On the other hand, a new model may not be drawn from the exact group of goods that are the subject of the sale. Therefore, a model is not quite as descriptive as a sample, but an express warranty can still be created.

Services

While the UCC does not expressly deal with services, still most of the rules discussed should apply by analogy. Some state statutes, other than the UCC, may have more specific laws dealing with services, though, they are not common.

IMPLIED WARRANTIES

In addition to express warranties, the UCC imposes a number of implied warranties to the sale of goods. Such warranties are presumed to be part of the sales transaction.

Merchantability

The implied warranty of merchantability applies whenever the seller is a merchant. Merchants are defined as people who deal with goods of the kind involved in the sale or who, by their occupation, hold themselves out as having particular knowledge or skill. Merchants can also be those to whom this knowledge or skill can be attributed because they are acting as agents or intermediaries for a merchant.

Various tests for merchantability have been developed, including the following.

- Does the item pass without objection in the trade under the description given in the contract between the buyer and seller?
- Is the item at least fit for the ordinary purposes for which such goods are used?
- Is the item adequately contained, packaged, and labeled as the contract or usage of trade may require?
- Is the item of average quality based on the description given?
- Does the item run within the variations permitted by the agreement between the buyer and seller?
- Are the items of a consistent kind, quality, and quantity within each unit and among units?
- Does the item conform to any promises made on its container or label?

To be merchantable, an item need not be perfect. Trade usage, that is, the norms of a particular trade, will also establish the particular qualities that will be acceptable for items produced by members of that trade. Generally, the higher an item is priced, the more justifiable is the buyer's expectation of high quality.

Particular Purpose

When a seller knows of a particular purpose for which the buyer is purchasing the goods and knows the buyer is relying on the seller's skill or judgment to choose something suitable, there is an implied warranty that the goods will fit such a purpose. The usual way this warranty is created is when the buyer asks the seller for assistance.

EXAMPLE: If an individual comes to you and requests assistance in choosing a bedspread for a baby's crib, an implied warranty is created. The implied warranty would probably include at least two specific attributes: (1) that the bedspread is not made out of any toxic materials so that the baby can safely put it in his or her mouth and (2) that it can be washed without running or shrinking, unless you specifically tell the buyer it must be dry cleaned or hand washed.

A particular purpose means a specific purpose for a specific buyer's use. Therefore, purchasing an item because it aesthetically pleases the buyer probably is not a particular purpose. It is an ordinary purpose. A particular purpose must be reasonably specific and explicit in order to assume that the seller has been informed of the buyer's purpose. In this regard, if the buyer is knowledgeable about what you sell, it is less likely that this implied warranty is created.

The one exception to this warranty is when a buyer asks for a particular brand or a particular company's product. In that case, the buyer is not relying on the seller's skill and judgment, so no implied warranty is created.

Title

A warranty of title is implied in every contract for the sale of goods. It simply means that the seller has good title, or the right to sell the item, and that the seller is unaware of any outstanding lien against the item. The seller does not need to be a merchant, as defined above, and is not saved from liability by ignorance of a defect in the title. This warranty is based on the commonsense idea that a buyer should not have to defend ownership of goods against the claims of a third party.

Infringement

The most modern of the implied warranties is the implied warranty against infringement. When an item is sold, the seller warrants that the item is not infringing any rights protected by patent, trademark, copyright, or trade dress.

If it appears that the object was created in violation of a third person's intellectual property rights, this warranty is breached.

IN PLAIN ENGLISH

At one time, there may have been some technical legal defenses available to a defendant who, as a manufacturer, did not sell a defective item directly to a person who was injured. It now appears that the vast majority of states would permit a victim to sue the retailer, wholesaler, manufacturer, or component-part manufacturer for injuries sustained as a result of a defective product.

DISCLAIMERS

Disclaimers can be used when you do not want to give one or more of the express or implied warranties mentioned. They must be given in certain specific ways and should be in writing.

Express Warranties

Once you have given an express warranty, it is difficult to disclaim it. It is considered unreasonable to give an express warranty and then turn around and take it away. Therefore, an attempt to disclaim an express warranty will usually not be successful. This includes any express warranties that may be set forth in a description of an item.

Oral Agreements

A common problem results when a customer claims that oral warranties were made before the signing of a written contract. The seller may be shielded from this problem by a rule that sometimes prevents prior oral statements from being considered as part of the contract. However, there are exceptions that you should be aware of. If there is a written agreement and it is not the final agreement, the written agreement will not supersede prior oral express warranties. Also, if the oral terms are consistent with a written disclaimer, they will be considered binding if the writing was not intended as a complete and exclusive statement of the terms. These types of problems tend to arise most often when someone else sells your goods for you. If you often have a salesperson sell your goods, you would be wise to include a limitation of the salesperson's authority on any written receipt.

Implied Warranties

Implied warranties can also be disclaimed. To exclude or modify the implied warranty of merchantability, the word *merchantability* must be specifically mentioned and the disclaimer must be conspicuous. This warranty can be disclaimed orally. The implied warranty of fitness for a particular purpose, however, can be disclaimed only in writing. Meanwhile, the implied warranty of title can be disclaimed only by specific language or by circumstances that give the buyer reason to know that the seller does not have title or that the seller's title is subject to a third party's interest.

IN PLAIN ENGLISH

Consult an attorney regarding the warranties you wish to disclaim and the best method of accomplishing your goal. The rules on disclaimers are technical, and care must be taken in determining how much exposure you may have in a particular situation.

MAGNUSON-MOSS WARRANTY ACT

If you decide to give a written warranty or disclaim warranty protection in writing, you should be aware that there are federal regulations promulgated under the *Magnuson-Moss Warranty Act* to cover consumer products. According to the Act, all of the following must be indicated in a written warranty:

- to whom the warranty is extended;
- exactly what parts of the product are covered;
- what the warrantor will do in case of defect;
- when the warranty begins and ends;
- what the buyer has to do to get warranty coverage;

- any limitations on the duration of implied warranties (this is not allowed in some states); and,
- any exclusions or limitations regarding relief.

In the written warranty, you must also specify what you are promising regarding the material and workmanship, and specify that the item is defect-free or will meet a specific level of performance. You must also clearly indicate whether the warranty is full or limited. Under a full warranty, the warrantor agrees to the following:

- to remedy the problem with the product within a reasonable period of time without charge if the product has a defect, malfunction, or fails to conform to the written warranty;
- not to impose a limitation on implied warranties;
- not to exclude or limit consequential damages unless this is clear on the face of the warranty; and,
- to replace the item or refund the purchase price if the item is unsuccessfully repaired numerous times.

If any one of these qualifications is not met, you have given a limited warranty.

Consumer Remedies

If you breach a warranty and the buyer is damaged by your failure to comply with the warranty obligations, the buyer may sue. You may be ordered to pay damages, court costs, and in some instances reasonable attorney's fees. Since this remedy exists, you should be careful to determine which warranties you are giving and learn how to disclaim them if you do not want to give them.

USING AN ATTORNEY

You should consult with a business lawyer to evaluate the extent of exposure that may be expected as a result of the numerous warranties and consumer protection laws that apply to sales. Where appropriate, warranty disclaimers and notices of right of cancellation, as well as limitations of liability, can be used to reduce your exposure. However, skilled drafting is necessary for effective protection. In addition, product liability insurance (see Chapter 18) may be procured as a means of insulating yourself from extensive liability.

Product Liability

Caveat emptor—let the buyer beware. This maxim has been repeated time and again in both English and American cases until comparatively recent times. Now, however, the pendulum has swung the other way and the rule has become *caveat vendor*—let the seller beware.

DEFECTIVE PRODUCTS

One of the harshest rules of early product liability cases was that people injured by defective products could not sue the manufacturers unless they purchased directly from them. This technical requirement was carried down the distribution lines so that only individuals who dealt directly with each other had rights against each other. Consumers could not sue anyone but the retailers with whom they had traded.

Inherently Dangerous Goods

An exception to this doctrine was recognized if the product was *inherently dangerous*. The courts struggled for some time over just what was and what was not inherently dangerous. Now almost anything can be injurious if defective, resulting in negligence suits for such seemingly innocuous items as a toy top, rubber boots, and a lounge chair.

Component Parts

A manufacturer can also be liable for defects in component parts made by another manufacturer if the assembler did not inspect them. This shift of the burden of responsibility from the buyer to the seller is a natural response to several factors. First, as products became increasingly more complex, it was no longer true that the buyer and seller were equally knowledgeable or uninformed. Second, it was felt that businesses were large enough to bear the immediate losses, and ultimately, could spread the risk over a broad number of consumers. Since the majority of the products on today's market are mass-produced by large manufacturers, the rule reflects present economic reality.

Unfortunately, this is not the economic reality of the small business. It must learn to cope with these laws in a climate of litigious consumers and generous juries. It is better to learn about these problems while you can still protect yourself, rather than when it is too late.

TYPES OF DEFECTS

There are two kinds of defects—*mechanical defects*, such as loose screws and faulty component parts, and *design defects*, such as instability, flammability, toxicity, and tendency to shatter.

Mechanical Defects

Under the current rule of strict liability followed by a majority of the states, you can be held liable even for defects that could not have been discovered or prevented by human skill, knowledge, or foresight. Your only protection is insurance.

However, many defects are detectable before an accident occurs if the right tests are made. The courts have held that manufacturers have a duty to inspect and test their goods. Failure to adequately test has been held reason enough to impose large awards of punitive damages on top of the actual damages awarded.

There is no hard and fast rule as to how much testing is adequate. The more sophisticated the testing the better; however, this is often too expensive for the small business. Some level of testing is necessary.

IN PLAIN ENGLISH

Design the best test you can for whatever you make, even if it is only a good tug here and there. Most importantly, keep a record of it. This may serve to prove that you attempted to fulfill your duty to test the product. While this precaution might not protect you from product liability, it may result in reducing, if not eliminating, punitive damage awards against you.

It is rare for an injured plaintiff to be able to prove that a defect was present when a product was purchased. The plaintiff frequently must rely on inferences drawn from the accident itself. If the jury is convinced that there is better than a 50/50 chance that the defect was there when the product was bought, the plaintiff will probably win. However, if you come into court with a record of tests on your product, the odds might shift in your favor.

Besides keeping records of your tests, you should also keep records of your purchases of materials and devise some method of identifying the components in your product. That way, if you are sued for a defect in a component part, you can pass the liability on to the party really at fault. For example, if a stained glass window collapses because the camming is inferior, you might be able to pass your liability on to the manufacturer of the defective cam.

Design Defects

The category of design defects can be further subdivided into those that violate a statute and those that do not. In defective-design cases where no statute has been violated, the courts have usually adhered to a commonsense criterion. If the product conformed to the state of the art when it was made, it will usually not be held defective.

The state of the art is not the same as industry-wide standards. Industry-wide standards may be introduced in evidence, but it cannot be assumed that these assure due care. This is because the law will not allow an industry to adopt sloppy practices in order to save money or time when better, more protective methods are available. The state of the art, on the other hand, determines the norm for an industry based on how far technology in the relevant field has advanced.

In addition, a design may be defective if it does not meet the standards set forth in a statute. No product should be sold for consumer use before checking to see whether it is covered by a consumer protection law. A violation of these laws may carry criminal sanctions. In some jurisdictions, consumers injured by a product have proven their case merely by proving that a statute was violated in the production or sale of the product. The manufacturer would then have the burden of establishing that the injury was not the result of the statutory violation. That is almost impossible in cases where the law had been enacted to prevent the very type of injury alleged.

FEDERAL LAWS

In addition to laws passed by individual states, there are at least three federal laws that directly affect the manufacturer. The first of these is a group of Acts— the *Hazardous Substance Labeling Act*, as amended by the *Child Protection Act of 1966* and the *Child Protection and Toy Safety Act of 1969*. These laws were passed in response to the staggering number of injuries and poisonings that occur each year to children under the age of 15. They empower the Federal Trade Commission (FTC) to name any potentially dangerous material a hazardous substance. Such substances may not be used in any product that might give a child access to the hazardous substance. That is, no amount of use or abuse by a child should make the product unsafe. (Presently banned under this Act are jaquirty beans used in necklaces, jewelry, and dolls' eyes. For a list of other hazardous substances, consult the FTC's website at **www.ftc.gov**.)

The second statute is the *Flammable Fabrics Act*. This statute empowers the FTC to establish appropriate standards of flammability for the fabrics used in clothing and household products, including children's toys.

Finally, there is the *Consumer Product Safety Act*, a statute that empowers the FTC to regulate the composition, content, and design of any consumer product. The FTC has promulgated regulations for the use of architectural glass in doors, windows, and walls, and has banned the use of surface-coating materials (paints) containing lead. This is a dynamic area and all manufacturers should check with the FTC to determine whether the materials used in their products are subject to regulation.

PRODUCT LIABILITY

In every product liability case, the plaintiff must prove that:

- injury occurred to the plaintiff;
- the injury was caused by some defect in the product; and,
- the defect was present in the product when the defendant had control over it.

Once people are in possession of your product, you will not be able to stop them from injuring themselves. You can control this third element, however, by making sure that any item that leaves your control does not contain a defect.

Under the current law of product liability, a seller held liable for a defective product may, in turn, seek reimbursement from the manufacturer for the amount paid in damages. This may involve another expensive lawsuit. If the manufacturer is broke, the seller is out of luck.

There are two things that a seller might do for protection. First, incorporate or use another business form that offers limited liability. (see Chapter 2.) The second method of self-protection is to obtain insurance.

LIABILITY INSURANCE

In general, the cost of product liability insurance may be high, but it may be essential for a small business. In addition, as discussed in the insurance chapter, there may be ways to reduce its cost. Consult with your insurance broker or agent to ascertain the rates in your area.

IN PLAIN ENGLISH

Determine whether you can obtain this form of insurance from professional trade or business associations with which you are involved. Many trade associations provide product liability insurance to their members for reasonable prices.

When you evaluate the cost of insurance against the risk of a lawsuit, it is a wise investment. Many product liability suits are settled for, or are litigated to a judgment of, over $100,000. You can deduct the cost of this kind of insurance as a business expense for tax purposes. Given these factors, if there is any reasonable expectation that a purchaser of your product could sustain personal injury from it, you should seriously consider obtaining product liability insurance.

The area of product liability has evolved to a point where manufacturers are being held liable for injuries caused by their defective products. The doctrines appear to have evolved with an eye to the large manufacturer of a mass-produced item, but the rules are applied with the same vigor to the small manufacturer. Since a single lawsuit could ruin a small business, it is important to be aware of the potential risks involved and to take the necessary precautions.

CHAPTER 19

Business Insurance

Recent crime statistics show that even in rural areas you may become the victim of burglary. The forces of nature—such as fires, floods, earthquakes—are undiscriminating in their targets. A sale of your products subjects you to virtually unlimited liability to anyone who may be injured by them, no matter how careful you may have been in creating them. Loss of earnings through sickness or accident is a risk common to all small businesses. These risks and others are far too often overlooked, but the potential cost makes even the slightest chance of these occurrences disastrous to a small business. Fortunately, many of these risks can be insured against.

History contains too many gruesome stories of desperate or disturbed people obtaining insurance with an eye toward collecting the proceeds. Because of such insurance frauds, most kinds of insurance, particularly liability insurance, do not cover injuries that are intentionally caused by the policyholder.

BASICS OF INSURANCE LAW

Before analyzing the mechanics of choosing whether or not to insure a particular risk, a brief outline on the law of insurance is in order.

Insurable Interest

Public policy will not permit you to insure something unless you have what is called an *insurable interest*. To have an insurable interest, you must have a property right, a contract right, or a potential liability that would result in a real loss to you if a given event occurs. This is simply to minimize the temptation to cause the calamity against which you are insured.

The Contract

All insurance is based on a contract between the insurer and the insured whereby the insurer assumes a specified risk for a fee called a premium. The insurance contract must contain at least all of the following:

- a definition of whatever is being insured (the subject matter);
- the nature of the risks insured against;
- the maximum possible recovery;
- the duration of the insurance; and,
- the due date and amount of the premiums.

When the amount of recovery has been predetermined in the insurance contract, it is called a *valued policy*. An unvalued or open insurance policy covers the full value of property up to a specified policy limit.

The very documents that a company uses to make insurance contracts are regulated from state to state. Sometimes the state requires a standard form from which the company may not deviate, especially for fire insurance. A growing number of states require that plain English be used in all forms. *Plain English* is measured in reference to the average number of syllables per word and the average number of words per sentence. Because of a federal ruling that all insurance contracts are, per se, fraudulent if they exceed certain maximum averages, the insurance companies are forced to write contracts that an average person can understand.

After Hurricane Katrina and several other catastrophic natural events, many individuals and businesses learned, to their horror, that the insurance coverage they thought they had was being denied. The litigation that resulted from the insurance companies' refusals to pay claims in some cases was even more trau-matic than the disasters that gave rise to the claims. The moral is clear: read your policy—and be sure that you understand it. If you have any doubt, review it with your broker and your business lawyer.

After the insurance contract has been signed, its terms can be *reformed* (revised) only to comply with the original agreement from which the written contract may somehow have deviated.

Ascertaining Risk

The insurance contract does more than merely shift the risk from the insured to the insurance company. The insurance industry is regulated by state law so as to spread the risk among those subject to that same risk. The risk-spreading is accomplished by defining the method used for determining the amount of the premium to be paid by the insured. First, the insurance company obtains data on the actual loss sustained by a defined class within a given period of time. State law regulates just how the company may define the class. An insurance company may not, for example, separate white homeowners and nonwhite homeowners into different classes, but it may separate drivers with many acci-dents from drivers with few.

Next, the company divides the risk equally among the members of the class. Then, the company adds a fee for administrative costs and profits. This amount is regulated from state to state. Finally, the premium is set for each individual in proportion to the likelihood that a loss will occur.

Additional State Regulations

Besides the method of determining premiums, state insurance laws usually specify the training necessary for agents and brokers, the amount of commis-sion payable to them, and the kind of investments the insurance company may make with the premiums.

Expectations vs. Reality

One frequent result of the difficult language used in most insurance contracts is that the signed contract may differ in some respect from what the agent may have led the insured person to expect. If you can prove that an agent actually lied, then the agent will be personally liable to you for the amount of promised coverage. In addition, the insurance company itself may be liable for the wrongful acts of its agents.

Most often, the agent will not lie, but will accidentally neglect to inform the insured of some detail. For instance, if you want insurance for transporting your products, the agent may sell you a policy that covers transport only in public carriers—when you intended to rent a truck and transport the products yourself. In most states, the courts hold that it is the duty of the insured (you) to read the policy before signing. (In the example, if you neglect to read the clause that limits coverage to a public carrier, you would be out of luck.)

In other states, this doctrine has been considered too harsh. These states will allow an insured to challenge specific provisions in the signed contract to the extent they do not conform to reasonable expectations resulting from promises that the agent made. In the example, it might be considered reasonable to expect that you would be insured when transporting your own goods. If the agent did not specifically call your attention to this limitation in the contract, odds are that you would have a good case for getting rid of it. In addition, it is common for the insured to receive the policy only after the premium is paid or only after a specific request is made.

Other states follow a different approach for contract interpretation and attempt to ascertain the intention of the parties. The first step in interpreting an insurance policy is to examine the text and context of the policy as a whole. If, after that examination, two or more conflicting interpretations remain reasonable, the ambiguity is resolved against the insurer. A court in these states will assume that parties to an insurance contract do not create meaningless provisions and will favor the interpretation that lets all provisions have meaning.

IN PLAIN ENGLISH

Read the contract with the agent. If it is unintelligible, ask the agent to list on a separate sheet of paper all of the important aspects before you sign it. Keep that sheet with the policy.

Overinsuring and Underinsuring

If an insured accidentally overvalues his or her goods, the insurance coverage will still apply. However, the recovery will only be for the actual value of the goods. Overinsurance does not entitle you to a recovery beyond the actual value of the goods insured. This is because one does not have an insurable interest beyond the actual value of an item.

Since you can, at best, break even with insurance, you might think it would be profitable to underinsure your goods. You could gain by paying lower premiums and lose only in the event that the damage exceeds the policy maximum. This has been tried and failed.

> **EXAMPLE:** An insured stated the value of her unscheduled property as $9,950 and obtained insurance on that amount. (Unscheduled property means an undetermined collection of goods—for example, all a person's clothes and furniture— that may change from time to time.) A fire occurred causing at least $9,950 damage.
>
> The insurance company investigated the claim and determined that the insured owned at least $36,500 in unscheduled property. The company refused to pay on grounds that the insured obtained the insurance fraudulently. The court agreed with the insurance company, stating that the

intentional failure to communicate the full value of the unscheduled property rendered the entire contract void. Therefore, the insured could not even collect the policy maximum.

Although at first glance this may seem harsh, its ultimate fairness becomes apparent with a little analysis. The chance of losing $9,950 out of $36,500 is greater than the chance of losing $9,950 out of $9,950, simply because most accidents or thefts do not result in total losses.

Various tests are used by the courts to determine whether an omission or misstatement renders such a policy void. In almost all cases, the omission or misstatement must be intentional or obviously reckless and it must be material to the contract. Materiality is typically measured with reference to the degree of importance that the insurance company ascribes to the omitted or misstated fact. If stating the fact correctly would have significantly affected the conditions or premiums that the company would demand, then the fact is likely material. In the above example, had the full value of the unscheduled property been stated, the insurer would either have demanded that the full value be insured or that a higher premium be paid for the limited coverage. Thus, the misstatement was clearly material.

Unintentional Undervaluing

Not all undervaluations will be material. Many insurance contracts do allow some undervaluation where it is unintentional. This provision is designed to protect the insured from inflation, which causes property to increase in replacement value before the policy's renewal date.

A so-called *coinsurance clause* generally provides that the insured may recover 100% of any loss up to the face value of the policy provided the property is insured for at least 80% of its full value. For example, if a house worth $100,000 was insured for $80,000 and suffered a $79,000 loss from a covered casualty, the insured would recover the full amount of the loss, or $79,000. If the property was only insured for $50,000, then a formula would be used to determine the amount of recovery. This formula requires you to establish a ratio between the amount of insurance coverage and the total value of the property and then multiply the resulting fraction by the loss to get the recovery.

IN PLAIN ENGLISH

It is important to carry insurance on at least 80% of the value of your property. Considering inflation, it is wise to reexamine your coverage each year. Some policies automatically increase the coverage annually, based on some fixed percentage.

PROPERTY COVERED

All insurance policies are limited to certain defined subject matter and to losses caused to that subject matter by certain defined risks. Once the risks are recognized, it is a simple matter to decide whether or not to insure against them. However, correctly defining the subject matter of insurance is tricky business. Mistakes here are not uncommon and can result in anyone finding him- or herself uninsured.

Scheduling Property

The typical insurance policy will include various exclusions and exemptions. For example, most homeowner and auto insurance policies cover personal property, but exclude business property. This brings up the question for small business owners who keep certain products at home for personal enjoyment—are they personal or business property? The answer depends on whether the person ever sells or displays any of these goods. If any are sold or displayed, this may convert them all to business property.

In order to avoid the potentially uninsured loss of such property, the owner may schedule the pieces that are held for personal enjoyment. Scheduling is a form of inventorying where the insured submits a list and description of all pieces to be insured with an appraisal of their value. The insurer assumes the risk of loss of all scheduled works without concern as to whether or not they pertain to the business. Insurance on scheduled property is slightly more expensive than that on unscheduled property.

Valuing Scheduled Property

Many battles occur over the value of objects stolen, destroyed, or lost. In anticipation of such battles, you should maintain records of sales to establish the market price of goods and an inventory of all goods on hand. In the case of certain kinds of property (artwork, for example), the value must be determined by an expert in the field. However, this will not avoid all problems, because the insurance company can always contest the scheduled value.

WHEN AND HOW TO INSURE

Three factors should be weighed to determine whether or not to obtain insurance. First, you must set a value on that which is to be insured. Health is of the utmost value and should always be insured. Material goods are valued according to the cost of replacement. If you keep a large inventory of goods or if you own expensive equipment, it probably should be insured. You may also want to consider obtaining business interruption insurance. The most elementary way to determine if the value is sufficiently high to necessitate insurance is to rely on the pain factor —if it would hurt to lose it, insure it.

Second, you must estimate the chances (risk) that a given calamity will occur. An insurance broker can tell you what risks are prevalent in your line of work or in your neighborhood. You should supplement this information with your personal knowledge. For example, you may know that your workshop is virtually fireproof or that only a massive flood would cause any real damage. Although these facts should be weighed in your decision, you should not be guilty of audaciously tempting fate. If the odds are truly slim, but some risk is still present, the premium will be correspondingly smaller in most cases.

The third factor is the cost of the insurance.

IN PLAIN ENGLISH

Bear in mind that insurance purchased to cover your business is tax-deductible. This means that if you pay tax at a 33% rate, Uncle Sam is theoretically paying for 33% of your premium.

Keeping the Cost Down

As already explained, the premiums charged by an insurance company are regulated by the government. Nonetheless, it still pays to shop around. Insurance companies can compete by offering different packages of insurance and by hiring competent agents to assist you in your choice.

If there are enough small-business owners in your area engaged in a similar business of similar size, it may be possible for you to form a co-op insurance fund. To do this, you must estimate the total losses your co-op would sustain in the course of a year. Each member then contributes a pro rata share. The money is put into a bank to collect interest. If a disaster occurs and the losses are greater than the fund, each member must contribute to make up the difference. If there is money left over, it can be used to lessen the following year's premiums. This method is cheaper than conventional insurance because it eliminates insurance agents' commissions and the profit earned by the insurance company. Before you form your co-op, contact an attorney to determine what regulations exist in your state.

CHAPTER 20

People Who Work for You

There comes a time in the life of almost every small business when it is necessary to get help, be it brain or brawn. The help most commonly needed first is the bookkeeper or accountant who can handle taxes, billing, and the like. When things get a little hectic around the shop or office, you might then hire someone to help with the packing or running errands. If selling is not your greatest talent, you may engage the services of a salesperson or a manufacturer's representative. If this salesperson is really good, you will soon have to hire more employees to keep up with the demand.

INDEPENDENT CONTRACTORS

Someone hired on a one-time or job-by-job basis is called an *independent contractor*. Although paid for their services by the hiring firm or individual, contractors remain their own bosses and may even employ others to actually do the work.

If you occasionally give products to a friend to sell on consignment, the friend is probably an independent contractor. If you hire a bookkeeper or accountant once or twice a year to go over your business records, that person, too, is an independent contractor. The fact that the person is independent and not your employee means that you do not have to pay Social Security taxes, withhold income taxes, obtain a workers' compensation policy, or comply with the myriad rules imposed on employers.

More importantly, you are generally not liable for injuries to a third party resulting from the independent contractor's negligence or wrongful acts even while working for you. However, there are situations where, despite your innocence, an independent contractor can render you legally responsible for his or her wrongful acts. Such situations fall into the following three basic categories.

1. If an employer is careless in hiring an independent contractor and a careful investigation would have disclosed facts to indicate that the contractor was not qualified, the employer may be liable when the independent contractor fails to properly perform the job and a third person is injured.

2. If a job is so dangerous as to be characterized as *ultrahazardous* or *inherently dangerous* (both legal terms) and is to be performed for the employer's benefit, then regardless of who performs the work, the employer will remain legally responsible for any injuries that occur during the performance of the work. A fireworks displayer, for example, cannot escape liability by having fuses lit or rockets aimed by independent contractors.

3. An employer may be required by law to perform certain tasks for the health and safety of the community.

These responsibilities are said to be nondelegable—that is, an employer cannot delegate them and escape liability for their improper performance. If, therefore, a nondelegable duty is performed by an independent contractor, the employer will remain responsible for any injury that results.

A good example of a nondelegable duty is the law (common in many states) that homeowners and storekeepers are responsible for keeping their sidewalks free of dangerous obstacles. If a homeowner hires an independent contractor to fulfill this obligation by removing ice during the winter, the homeowner is still legally liable if someone is injured on the slippery sidewalk, even if the accident resulted from the contractor's carelessness.

EMPLOYEES

The second capacity in which someone can work for you is as an *employee*. This category includes anyone over whose work you exercise direct control—helpers, apprentices, salespeople who represent you alone, a bookkeeper who is a full-time member of your staff, and so forth. The formation of this relationship entails nothing more than an agreement on your side to hire someone and an agreement by that person to work. Although a written contract is generally not necessary, it is suggested that employment terms be put down in writing so that there are no misunderstandings later.

Liability

Unlike the situation where you have hired an independent contractor, you are vicariously liable for the negligence, and sometimes even the intentional wrong-doing, of your employee when the employee is acting on your behalf. This means that if your employee is on the job and is involved in an automobile accident that is his or her fault, you, as well as your employee, are legally liable. It would be wise to be extremely careful when hiring and to contact your insurance agent to obtain sufficient insurance coverage for your additional exposure.

EMPLOYMENT CONTRACTS

While there is no prescribed form that an employment contract must take, there are, nevertheless, certain items that should be considered.

Term

The first item of an employment contract is the term of employment. An employment contract may be either terminable at will or for a fixed duration, though if the employment is to be for more than one year, there must be a written contract specifying the period of employment; otherwise, either party may terminate the relationship at any time.

Making the contract for a fixed period gives the employee some job security and creates a moral and contractual obligation for the employee to remain for the term. Of course, if the employee chooses to quit or the employer chooses to fire the employee, the law will not compel fulfillment of the contract. Improper premature termination of a contract for a fixed period, however, will subject the party who is responsible for the wrongful act to liability for damages.

Wage

The second item is the wage. Unless you have gross sales of $500,000 or more or are engaged in *interstate commerce* (which is very broadly defined), you will not have to comply with federal minimum wage laws. Most states, however, have their own minimum wage laws with which you will still have to comply. Above the requirement imposed by this law, the amount of remuneration is open to bargaining.

In the event no salary is specified, the law will presume a reasonable wage for the work performed. Thus, you cannot escape paying your employees fairly by not discussing the amount they will earn. If you hire a mechanic and the accepted salary in your region for a qualified mechanic is $20 per hour, then it will be presumed that the mechanic was hired for this amount unless you and that person have agreed to a different salary.

In addition to an hourly wage or monthly salary, other benefits can be given, such as health and life insurance or retirement pensions. Some legal advice in this area may be necessary in order to take advantage of tax laws.

Duties

Third, it is often wise to spell out your employee's duties in the employment contract. This serves as a form of orientation for the employee and also may limit future conflicts over what is and what is not involved in the job.

Noncompetition

Fourth, you may want your employee to agree not to work for someone else while working for you or, more importantly, not to compete against you at the end of the employment period. The latter agreement must be carefully drawn to be enforceable. Such an agreement must:

- not be overly broad in the kind of work the employee may not do;
- cover a geographic area no broader than that in which you actually operate; and,
- be for a reasonable duration.

Some states impose restrictions on noncompetition agreements. In Oregon, for example, a noncompetition agreement is unenforceable unless it was entered into either prior to or contemporaneously with the beginning of employment— or unless it became effective after a meaningful promotion. Other states refuse to uphold noncompetition agreements. For example, California law states that a noncompetition agreement is void as against public policy unless it is coupled with a business sale of the purchase or sale of stock.

Employers may achieve some form of protection by restricting the use of the business's intellectual property. This should include a prohibition on the use of any company trade secrets, both during the term of employment and thereafter. These restrictions should be in writing. It has been held that trade secrets may include, among other things, customer lists, supplier lists, secret formulas, and know how.

Termination

Finally, grounds for termination of the employment contract should be listed, even if the contract is terminable at will. You should clearly specify that the contract may be terminated either for the specified causes or at the will of the employer.

Employers should take some precautions to avoid being placed in the untenable position of having bound themselves to individuals in their employment when the relationship has soured. This can result from language in employee handbooks that might be construed as giving rise to a contractual right. It is also possible that oral statements made by recruiters or interviewers could give rise to contractual rights. To avoid this problem, an employer should have a legend placed in any employee handbook making it clear that the material is not an employment contract. It has also become common for employers to require prospective employees to sign a statement making it clear that the employment is at will and does not give rise to any contractual right.

If there is a probationary period, the employer should be careful to state that the probationary employee will become a regular or full-time employee rather than a permanent employee. In addition, if there is any evaluation of the employee after the probationary period has ended, it should be conducted fairly. When evaluations become merely pro forma, problems can and do arise. Employees may argue that they have received sparkling evaluations and are being fired for some invalid reason.

OTHER CONSIDERATIONS IN HIRING

There are other issues you should consider when hiring an employee, most of which fall into the realm of accounting or bookkeeping responsibilities. You should, therefore, consult with your accountant or bookkeeper regarding such items as the following.

- A workers' compensation policy for your employees in the event of on-the-job injury or occupational illness. State laws vary on the minimum number of employees that trigger this very important requirement. The workers' compensation laws of many states provide that an employer who has failed to obtain or keep in force required workers' compensation insurance will be strictly liable even in the absence of negligence for on-the-job injury or illness. This includes not only medical expenses, but also damages for pain and suffering, lost earning potential, and other damages that are a consequence of on-the-job injuries or illnesses.
- Withholding taxes (federal, state, and local). Here, too, the laws vary, and you must find out what is required in your locale. Employers are required to withhold employees' federal taxes, and failure to do so will expose the employer to liability for that amount plus interest and penalties.
- Social Security (FICA). There are some exemptions from this body of social legislation. Contact your nearby Social Security office to determine how these exemptions may affect you.

- Unemployment insurance (both federal and state). These also include certain technical requirements for subcontractors and the like.
- Health and safety regulations (both federal and state).
- Municipal taxes for specific programs such as schools or public transportation.
- Employee benefits such as insurance coverage (medical, dental, prepaid legal), retirement benefits, memberships, and parking.
- Union requirements, if you or your employees are subject to union contracts.
- Wage and hour laws (both federal and state). These include minimum wage and overtime requirements. In some states, the law also regulates holidays and vacations, as well as the method of paying employees during employment and upon termination.

As already noted, the requirements of these laws may vary dramatically from state to state. You are well advised to discuss them with your lawyer, accountant, and bookkeeper. In addition, you should find out if any other forms of employment legislation, such as licensing requirements, apply to you, your employees, or your business.

HAZARDS IN THE WORKPLACE

While few manufacturers would intentionally injure a fellow human being, you may nevertheless find yourself in an industry or using a process that involves hazardous activities. It is not uncommon to use toxic materials. Employees are often not aware of the potential hazard that may result from the toxic materials. It is essential to research the potentially toxic effects of all substances used in your process or product. OSHA regulations require that all employers with hazardous chemicals in their workplaces provide labels and *Material Safety Data Sheets* (MSDS) for their exposed workers and train them to handle the chemicals appropriately. (More information on this can be found at the OSHA website at **www.osha.gov/SLTC/hazardcommunications/index.html**.) In other words, there is a regulatory duty to advise and train employees with respect to hazardous substances in the workplace.

Congress and federal administrative agencies are active in the field of regulation of hazardous substances. You should also be aware that your state workers' compensation agency and the *Occupational Safety and Health Administration* (OSHA) may have specific rules regarding your specific type of business. It is critical to obtain a lawyer's assistance in determining whether any of these regulations apply to your particular manufacturing process or other business. Your state's labor department may also be able to give you information regarding applicable workplace regulations.

If an employment contract is used, a paragraph containing the required disclosure regarding hazardous substances and the employee's acknowledgment of the known risks should be incorporated in the contract. A similar statement should also be included in any employment handbook.

While these documents would not provide a defense to a workers' compensation claim, they would sensitize employees to the need for caution in working with the toxic materials. Needless to say, you should take all precautions possible to protect the health and safety of your employees.

DISCRIMINATION

Business owners must comply with numerous antidiscrimination laws, including the Civil Rights Act, the Equal Pay Act, the Age Discrimination in Employment Act (amended by the Older Workers Benefit Protection Act), and the Americans With Disabilities Act. The Equal Employment Opportunity Commission (EEOC) is responsible for enforcement of these laws. Antidiscrimination laws apply not only during the hiring processes, but also during the employment itself, including considerations for transfer, promotion, layoff, and termination, as well as job advertisements, recruitment, testing, use of company facilities, training, benefits, and leave. These laws generally prohibit not only intentional discrimination, but also practices that have the effect of discrimination. Note that many antidiscrimination laws apply to independent contractors as well as to employees.

These laws make it clear that management may not legally retaliate against employees or job applicants who file discrimination charges against them. If a business is found to have unlawfully discriminated, then that business will likely be liable for lost wages, and punitive and other damages, including attorney fees.

Many states, as well as some cities and counties, have also passed laws that reiterate and expand the federal government's protection against discrimination. These laws are often more protective of employees than the federal law. In addition, some categories not covered by federal law, including those with respect to sexual orientation, may be covered by state or local law.

Civil Rights Act

The *Civil Rights Act* prohibits discrimination based on race, color, religion, sex, or national origin.

With regard to religious discrimination, employers generally may not treat employees or applicants less or more favorably because of their religious beliefs or practices. Employees cannot be forced to participate or not participate in a religious activity as a condition of employment. Employers must reasonably accommodate employees' sincerely held religious beliefs and permit employees to engage in religious expression if employees are permitted to engage in other personal expressions at work. This law also requires the employer to take steps to prevent religious harassment of their employees, not only by other employees and management, but also by vendors and customers.

National-origin discrimination includes discrimination based on foreign accents and English fluency, as well as English-only rules, though there are exceptions if they are necessary for the safe or efficient operation of the business.

Race-based discrimination includes discrimination based on skin color, hair texture, and facial features, as well as harassment and segregation. It also includes discrimination based on a person's marriage to or association with those of a different race.

The prohibitions against sex-based discrimination encompass pregnancy, birth, and related medical conditions, as well as sexual harassment.

The Equal Pay Act

The *Equal Pay Act* (part of the *Fair Labor Standards Act of 1938*, as amended) also prohibits sex-based discrimination. It prohibits sex-based wage discrimination among persons in the same establishment who are performing under similar working conditions. Virtually all employers are subject to this Act.

More information about the Civil Rights Act and the Equal Pay Act can be obtained at the EEOC's website at **www.eeoc.gov**.

HARASSMENT

One of the legal obligations of all business owners is to create a nondiscriminatory work environment. A policy should be established prohibiting any discriminatory language (i.e., ethnic jokes or racial slurs) or other offensive language or activities.

Sexual harassment is one form of illegal discrimination, though harassment based on race and certain other characteristics also violates the Civil Rights Act. There are two basic types of sexual harassment: quid pro quo and that of a hostile environment. *Quid pro quo* refers to either a harasser asking for sexual favors in exchange for some advantage in the workplace or a harasser penalizing another person for rejecting his or her sexual advances. A *hostile environment*, on the other hand, is more generalized in that the harasser creates or permits a hostile work environment through language, activities, or conduct.

An employer is subject to vicarious liability for a hostile work environment; that is, the employer will be responsible for the actions and language of a supervisor that results in an employee's injury, harm, or damage. If a supervisor has harassed or permitted harassment of an employee and this situation has led to that employee's termination, relocation, or the like, the employer will be held liable for the discriminatory sexual actions of its supervisor. To avoid this form of liability, the employer must exercise reasonable care to prevent and promptly correct any harassment behaviors that are reported or otherwise become known to it, and the employee who was harassed must have taken advantage of all preventive programs or policies provided by the employer. There is a host of training and other resources available to business owners. Check with your business attorney or state employment division.

Many states have antiharassment policies as well. For example, California requires employers with fifty or more employees to provide certain sexual harassment training and education to supervisory employees. Details of the California sexual harassment laws can be obtained at **www.dfeh.ca.gov**.

More information on sexual harassment is available at the EEOC website (**www.eeoc.gov**).

AGE DISCRIMINATION

Federal age antidiscrimination laws apply to employers of twenty or more employees, as well as to government and union offices. These laws provide that persons 40 years old or older may not be discriminated against due to their age in connection with any term, condition, or privilege of employment, including hiring, firing, layoffs, job compensation, benefits, job training, assignments and tasks, and promotions.

More information on age discrimination is available at **www.eeoc.gov**.

DISABILITIES DISCRIMINATION

The *Americans With Disabilities Act* (ADA) prohibits discrimination against disabled persons in public accommodations, transportation, telecommunications, and employment. This Act applies to those who employ fifteen or more individuals. "An individual with a disability" means a person who has a physical or mental impairment that substantially limits one or more major life activity, has a record of such an impairment, or who is regarded as having such an impairment. A qualified individual with a disability is someone who, with or without reasonable accommodation, can perform the essential functions of the job.

Reasonable accommodation must be made so that that a disabled job applicant or employee can perform the necessary and essential work of the job position. Reasonable accommodations include making existing employee facilities readily accessible to and usable by disabled employees, including the acquisition or modification of equipment or devices, job restructuring, and modifying work schedules.

A business is not required to provide reasonable accommodations if it will result in an undue hardship. "Undue hardship" under the Americans With Disabilities Act refers to an action requiring significant difficulty or expense when considered in light of factors such as the employer's size and financial resources.

Under the ADA, complex rules apply to medical examinations and inquiries, so you should contact an attorney for more information if you plan to make such inquiries or require any physical examinations.

For more information concerning the Americans With Disabilities Act, see **www.ada.gov**. Many states have laws that are comparable to or more restrictive than the ADA. You should check with your business attorney or state employment division to determine whether your state has such legislation.

EMPLOYEE HANDBOOKS

As discussed elsewhere in this chapter, your business should have an employee handbook. It should set forth, among other things, your policies on sexual harassment and nondiscrimination, hours of work, as well as security, overtime, and the like. The handbook should make it clear that it is not an employment contract, and in fact, that employment is at will. It should also cover trade secret protection previously discussed. This document should be drafted or reviewed by a business attorney, since there are numerous requirements for legal notices and other areas that a layperson or even a handbook software program may fail to properly address.

If you plan to monitor your employees' Internet usage, email, computer files, phone calls, voice mail, and the like; use video surveillance; or, conduct searches of employees' personal belongings (such as lockers), you should include a specific written employee privacy policy identifying the types of situations in which employees should not have an expectation of privacy. Note that your employees do have certain privacy rights, such as privacy in the restroom. Any monitoring must be done in a nondiscriminatory manner, to ensure quality and equitably enforced policies and standards.

ZERO TOLERANCE POLICIES

A zero tolerance standard will best protect an employer from discrimination claims. An employee handbook containing policies against sexual harassment, offensive behaviors, and the like is a good starting point. A well-drafted discrimination policy will apply to behavior and oral and written (including electronic) communications. It will include procedures that provide employees with a way to confidentially report problems regarding offensive or harassing behavior and will direct management on how to investigate and resolve the issues. The process should include an employee appeals process for any adverse findings. The complaint and appeals procedures should direct an employee to contact someone other than the employee's immediate supervisor, since that supervisor may be the one responsible for such conduct.

Employees should be advised that both the complaints and appeals need to be put in writing so that there can be no misunderstandings, though the first step is often verbal. A well-drafted policy will state that the employer will, whenever possible, provide complaining employees and witnesses reasonable confidentiality, but it should be made clear that there can be no assurance of confidentiality, since it may become necessary for management to disclose the identity and testimony of relevant parties in any legal proceeding.

It is also essential for employers to provide employees with ongoing education with respect to employment relations, including harassment and discrimination issues.

THE FAMILY AND MEDICAL LEAVE ACT

The *Family and Medical Leave Act of 1993* (FMLA) allows employees to take up to twelve weeks of unpaid leave each year for certain family or medical reasons if they have worked for the employer for a year and meet certain other eligibility requirements. FMLA must be followed by private sector employers who employ fifty or more employees during the current or preceding calendar year and who are engaged in interstate commerce or any activity affecting commerce.

An eligible employee may take his or her twelve-week leave due to the birth and care of his or her newborn; a foster child being placed with the employee; to care for a spouse, child, or parent with a serious health condition; or, to take care of the employee's own serious health condition. The Family and Medical Leave Act defines "serious health condition" as an illness, injury, impairment, or physical or mental condition that brings about a period of incapacity or requires intensive and continual medical treatment, and specifically includes prenatal care.

When the worker returns to the job, the job may be the exact job that the employee left or it may be an equivalent job—with equivalent duties, pay, benefits, and the like. The only employees to which this would not apply are *key* employees whose absence from their positions will cause *substantial and grievous economic injury* to the employer.

There are certain notice requirements, as well as rules for requiring medical certification of the need for leave. Further information can be found at **www.dol.gov**.

Many states have supplemental leave acts. Check with your business attorney or state employment division.

TERMINATION OF EMPLOYMENT

Determining whether someone is an employee or an independent contractor is not always easy. One reason that the characterization is important is that employers are responsible for income tax withholding, Social Security, workers' compensation, and the like, whereas one who hires an independent contractor is not.

Another reason that the characterization may be important regards how the employment relationship may end. If the individual working for you is merely an independent contractor, the contract between you and that person will govern your respective rights of termination. On the other hand, if the individual is an employee, care must be taken not to become responsible for a wrongful termination when dismissing the individual.

Wrongful Termination

Historically, an employee who was not under contract could be terminated for any reason whatsoever. Now an employee's job can be terminated for the right reason or for no reason at all, but cannot be terminated for the wrong reason. For example, an employee whose job was terminated for refusing to commit perjury before a legislative committee was entitled to recover against the employer for wrongful termination. The public policy of having individuals testify honestly was considered more important than the employer's right to control the employment relationship.

Courts have become even more protective of the rights of employees. In a 1983 case, *Novosel v. Nationwide Insurance Company*, the U.S. Circuit Court of Appeals held that the power to hire and fire could not be used to dictate an employee's political activity, and that even a nongovernmental entity is limited by the Constitution in its power to discharge an employee. The court, in essence, held that one's right to exercise constitutionally protected free speech was more important than the employer's right to control an employee's conduct.

Wrongful termination cases generally fall into certain categories. Employers may not legally terminate an employee's job for:

- refusing to commit an unlawful act, such as committing perjury or refusing to participate in illegal price-fixing schemes;
- performing a public obligation, such as serving on a jury or serving in a military reserve unit;
- exercising a statutory right, such as filing a claim for workers' compensation; or,
- discrimination.

Some courts appear to go quite far in holding that an employer cannot discharge an employee unless there is just cause for termination. A number of states have considered the adoption of legislation that would restrict the employer's right to terminate an employee's job to cases in which there was just cause. Most states have laws that contain specific prohibitions on the termination of employment for whistle blowing, (i.e., cases in which employees notify government authorities of wrongful acts by the employer, such as tax evasion).

Progressive Discipline

Perhaps an employer who uses evaluations should employ what has been characterized as progressive discipline. In this procedure, the employer starts by orally warning a problem employee of his or her concern and progressively imposing disciplinary practices until termination becomes the only form of recourse left. Care should be taken not to violate the employee's rights since the liability for wrongful termination can be catastrophic to a small business. When in doubt, an employer should contact an attorney with some experience in the field of employment relations. In this area, as with many others, pre-problem counseling can prevent a good deal of time-consuming and costly litigation.

CHAPTER **21**

Keeping Taxes Low

A business can enhance profitability by increasing sales or by reducing expenses. Careful purchasing will go far in expense reduction, but one of the most profound areas affecting business conduct is tax. Prudent businesspeople are careful to determine the tax consequence of virtually every transaction. Most business planning is tax-driven.

Periodic meetings with your business lawyer and tax accountant in order to determine the most expeditious and cost-effective method of conducting your business are important. At least one year-end planning session for the purpose of evaluating business activities and tax planning is advisable.

After allowing for basic needs through personal exemptions, a narrow list of personal deductions, and one reduced tax rate at the low end of the income scale, our income tax system is essentially a fixed-rate system. There are now six graduated tax rates for individuals: 10% on the lowest taxable income range; 15%, 25%, and 28% on income in the middle taxable income ranges; and 33% and 35% on income in the highest taxable income ranges.

INCOME SPREADING

There are two important means of reducing tax liability. The first is spreading taxable income by the use of several provisions in the tax code. The second is the use of tax deductions.

Installments

One way a business can spread income is to receive payment in installments. The Internal Revenue Code (I.R.C.) enables a taxpayer who sells property with payments received in successive tax years to report the income on an installment basis in some situations if the sale is properly structured. Under this method, tax is imposed only as payments are received.

Care must be taken with the mechanics of this arrangement. If a business sells a product for a negotiable note due in full at some future date or for some other deferred-payment obligation that is essentially equivalent to cash or that has an ascertainable fair market value, the business may have to report the total proceeds of the sale as income realized when the note is received, not when the note is paid off with cash. (A negotiable note is a written and signed promise to pay a specified sum of money either on demand or at a specified time, payable either to an identified party or to the bearer.)

> **EXAMPLE:** Suppose you sell a custom-designed computer software package for $3,000. Ordinarily, the entire $3,000 would be taxable income in the year you received it, but if you use the installment method, with four payments of $750 plus interest received over four years, income from the sale will be taxed as the installments are received. In either case, the amount of income is $3,000, but under the installment method, the amount is spread out over four years and you are taking advantage of being in a lower tax bracket than had you taken the full $3,000 in the year you sold the software package.

In this example, if the product sold was a standard software package that would be characterized as inventory, the installment method would be unavailable. Installment sales are generally not available for the sale of any inventory. Be aware that there are special rules for installment sales that should be discussed with your tax advisor.

Deferred Payments

Someone in a high tax bracket might wish to defer income until the future. For example, a commissioned salesperson could obtain an agreement from the employer that commissions paid would not exceed a certain amount in any one year, with the excess to be carried over and paid in the future. This would result in tax savings if, when the deferred amounts are finally paid, the salesperson were in a lower tax bracket.

There are drawbacks to deferred payments. These include the possibility that the party owing the money may not be willing to pay interest on the deferred sums and the possibility that that party could go broke before the debt is fully paid. One should consider these risks carefully before entering into a contract for deferred payments, because it might be quite difficult to change the arrangement if the need should arise.

SPREADING INCOME AMONG FAMILY MEMBERS

Another strategy for business owners in high tax brackets is to divert some income directly to members of their immediate families who are in lower tax brackets by hiring them as employees. Putting dependent children on the payroll can result in substantial tax savings because their salaries can be deducted as a business expense. If the business is unincorporated, then no Social Security and Medicare taxes have to be withheld or paid relating to these wages. This salary arrangement is permissible so long as the child is under 18 years of age.

Your child, stepchild, or grandchild can earn up to the amount of the standard deduction without any tax liability. You as the taxpayer can still claim a personal dependency exemption for the child if (1) the child is a U.S. citizen, resident, or national, or is a resident of Canada or Mexico; (2) the child has the same principal residence as you for more than one-half the year; (3) the child does not provide over one-half of his or her own support; and (4) the child does not file a joint return. This is true if the child is under 19 years of age at the end of the tax year or if the child is between the ages of 19 and 24 and is a full-time student. The child may not claim a personal exemption if he or she can be claimed by the parents on their tax return.

The following are additional restrictions on such an arrangement.
- The salary must be reasonable in relation to the child's age and the work performed.
- The work performed must be a necessary service to the business.
- The work must actually be performed by the child.

Family Partnerships

A second method of transferring income to members of your family is the creation of a family partnership. Each partner receives an equal share of the overall income, unless the partnership agreement provides otherwise. The income is taxed once as individual income to each partner. Thus, if you are the parent who heads a family business, you can break up and divert your income to your family members so it will be taxed to them according to their respective tax brackets. The income received by children may be taxed at significantly lower rates, resulting in more income reaching the family than if it had all been received by the parent, who is presumably in a higher tax bracket than the children. The law stipulates, however, that if a child is under 18 years of age and receives unearned income from the partnership, any amount over $1,600 will be taxed at the parents' highest marginal rate.

Although the IRS recognizes family partnerships, it may subject them to close scrutiny to ensure that the partnership is not a sham. In addition, because partnership capital produces significant income and partners are reasonably compensated for services performed for the partnership, the IRS may opt to forbid the shift in income, in accordance with the Internal Revenue Code section that deals with distribution of partners' shares and family partnerships. The same section provides that a person owning a capital interest (or ownership interest) in a family partnership will be considered a partner for tax purposes even if he or she received the capital interest as a gift, if the gift is genuine and irrevocable.

FAMILY CORPORATIONS AND LIMITED LIABILITY COMPANIES

Some families have even incorporated or created family-owned limited liability companies. If the IRS questions the motivation for such incorporation, the courts will examine the intent of the family members. If the sole purpose of incorporating was tax avoidance, the scheme will not stand. If the IRS successfully contends that the business entity should be disregarded, the IRS can reallocate income from the corporation or LLC to the individual taxpayer. This will be done, for example, if the corporation or LLC does not engage in substantial business activity, does not observe proper formalities, or if its separate status is not otherwise adhered to by the businessperson.

Tax Advantages and Disadvantages

A *bona fide* (genuine) corporation or limited liability company being taxed as a corporation, however, may provide some tax advantages for the small business owner. As an employee, the owner can control his or her taxable income with a limited salary. Although the corporation or LLC must recognize income whenever a sale is made, the corporation or LLC can deduct the owner's salary as well as other business expenses.

Incorporating or creating an LLC should not be done solely for tax reasons. Further, since individual tax rates are now substantially lower than corporate tax rates, you may actually find that you are paying more tax on any profits left in the corporation than if you had chosen a flow through type of entity such as a partnership or an S corporation.

Additionally, there are some unavoidable legal and accounting expenses that will have to be paid for incorporation. If your business operates on very small margins, you should determine if the possible tax savings to you justify the additional legal and accounting costs associated with incorporating. The cost to the entity for payroll taxes, unemployment taxes, workers' compensation, and legal and accounting fees can be substantial.

IN PLAIN ENGLISH

Use of the corporate form is no longer necessary for setting up a retirement plan. Revisions to the rules for pension plans allow a self-employed person to set aside as much money for retirement as could be done through a corporate retirement plan.

While creating a business entity may not provide tax benefits in some situations and may even result in added expense, it still may afford you a liability shield. Many businesses are incorporated or created as LLCs for the sole purpose of obtaining limited liability for their owners, rather than for the tax treatment accorded business entities.

Moreover, there are several potential business tax problems that the businessperson should carefully consider before incorporating. Making use of a corporate form means that any distribution of profits to shareholders in the form of dividends will be taxed twice—once at the entity level as business income and again at the shareholder level as personal income when profits are distributed to the shareholders or owner.

This double taxation can be avoided through careful tax planning and distribution of profits through means other than dividends, such as wages. Thus, although incorporation allows income to be shifted from the businessperson to other shareholders, such as family members, the shift may occur at the expense of double taxation without the use of careful tax planning. Obviously, it is important to consult with a CPA or tax advisor in order to determine whether the benefit of shifting income to a corporation outweighs the effects of double taxation.

S Corporations

Another alternative for the small enterprise is to organize as an S corporation. Income from an S corporation is taxed only once at the individual level. Although income from a partnership or from being self-employed is also taxed only once at the individual level, the tax rates associated with the incomes are different. In an S corporation, income is not subject to Social Security and Medicare taxes (or *self-employment taxes* as it is sometimes called). (The S corporation is discussed in Chapter 2.)

LLC Tax Election

The tax law allows LLCs to make an election to be taxed like a corporation or to be taxed as if the business were still run as a sole proprietorship (in states allowing one-person LLCs) or a partnership. If no election is made, the default tax treatment will be that of a partnership if there is more than one member, or a sole proprietorship if there is only one member. You should be aware that some states have a gross receipts tax for LLCs that may make an LLC an unattractive option in your state. (LLCs are discussed more fully in Chapter 2.)

Taxes on Accumulated Earnings and Passive Investment Income

If a person incorporates in order to postpone a significant portion of income, the IRS may impose an accumulated-earnings tax. The Internal Revenue Code (I.R.C.) allows a maximum accumulation of $250,000 to not be subject to the accumulated-earnings tax. For corporations whose principal work is in the fields of health, law, engineering, architecture, accounting, actuarial science, performing arts, or consulting, the maximum is $150,000. Accumulated earnings beyond these maximums must be justified as reasonable for the needs of the business. Otherwise, they will be subject to a tax of 15% in addition to the regular corporate tax.

The I.R.C. also imposes an additional tax on most types of passive investment income. This is income retained by the corporation if the business entity is found to be a personal holding company. The current rate is 15%. This may occur if 60% of the corporation's income consists of copyright, book, movie, or other royalties; dividends; rents; or, personal-service contracts. These low rates will sunset along with the reduced capital gains rate.

Also, if the owner sells his or her stock or ownership interest before the corporation has realized any income, the corporation could become a collapsible corporation, causing the gain realized on the sale of the stock to be taxed at ordinary income rates.

QUALIFYING FOR BUSINESS DEDUCTIONS

Another means of reducing tax liability involves making use of various tax deductions. For this, you must keep full and accurate records. Receipts are a necessity. Even if your business is home-based, as are many start-up businesses, you should have a separate checking account and a complete set of books for all the activities of your trade or business. A hobbyist or dilettante is not entitled to trade or business deductions, except in very limited circumstances.

Tax laws presume that a person is engaged in a business or trade, as opposed to a hobby, if a net profit results from the activity in question during three out of the five consecutive years ending with the taxable year in question (or, in the case of horse breeding, training, or racing, two out of the seven consecutive years ending with the taxable year in question). For instance, if a freelance writer, artist, or craftsperson does not have three profitable years in the last five years of working as such, the IRS may contend that the work merely constitutes a hobby. In this case, the taxpayer will have to prove profit motive in order to claim business expenses in excess of income for that year. Proof of a profit motive does not require proof that profit would actually be made. It requires proof only of intention to make a profit. However, if the profit is nominal, the presumption may not be met.

The Treasury regulations call for an objective standard on the profit-motive issue, so statements of the taxpayer as to intent will not suffice as proof. The regulations list the following nine factors to be used in determining profit motive:

1. the manner in which the taxpayer carries on the activity (i.e., effective business routines and bookkeeping procedures);
2. the expertise of the taxpayer or the taxpayer's advisors (i.e., study in an area, awards, prior publication, critical recognition, and membership in professional organizations);
3. the time and effort expended in carrying on the activity (i.e., at least several hours a day devoted to the activity, preferably on a regular basis);
4. expectation that business assets will increase in value;
5. the success of the taxpayer in similar or related activities (i.e., past successes, even if prior to the relevant five-year period);
6. history of income or losses with respect to the activity (i.e., increases in receipts from year to year, unless losses vastly exceed receipts over a long period of time);
7. the amount of occasional profits, if any, that are earned;
8. financial status (wealth sufficient to support a hobby would weigh against the profit motive); and,
9. elements of personal pleasure or recreation (if significant traveling is involved and little work accomplished, the court may be suspicious of profit motive).

No single factor will determine the results.

EXAMPLE: The 1928 case of *Deering v. Blair* provides an example of how the factors are used. Deering was the executor of the estate of Reginald Vanderbilt, whose financial affairs and residence were in New York. Vanderbilt had purchased a farm near Portsmouth, Rhode Island because he was interested in horses, and operated it as a business. The business produced little income, but Vanderbilt claimed business expenses of over $25,000 in each of three years. The fact that Vanderbilt did not rely on the income from the farm for his livelihood was considered by the court in making its decision. The court held that, despite the fact that he had several employees and advertised the farm's horse-boarding and rental services, the purpose for operating the farm was not to produce a profit. Rather, the land was used for pleasure, entertaining, exhibition, and social diversion. Thus, the business deduction was disallowed.

While a new business is not presumed to be engaged in for profit until it shows a profit three out of five years (or, where applicable, two out of seven years), deductions have been allowed in cases where this test is not met.

EXAMPLE 1: In *Allen v. Commissioner*, the tax court decided to allow business deductions for the proprietors of a ski lodge that was rented out during the ski season. The deduction was allowed even though the lodge did not show a profit during the years in question and despite the fact that the proprietors did not depend on the income from the lodge for their livelihood. They did, however, keep accurate records and did not use the lodge for their personal pleasure. Consequently, they were able to show that the lodge was operated as a business.

EXAMPLE 2: In *Engdahl v. Commissioner*, the tax court found a profit motive on the part of the taxpayers who were considering retirement and wanted to supplement their incomes by operating a horse ranch. The court held that, despite a series of losses, the taxpayers had kept complete and accurate records reviewed by an accountant, had advertised the operation, took their horses to shows, and had worked up to fifty-five hours per week on the operation. Additionally, the assets of the ranch had appreciated in value. All these facts showed that the taxpayers had a profit motive and, therefore, the business-expense deductions were allowed.

Once you have established yourself as engaged in a business, all your ordinary and necessary expenditures for that business are deductible business expenses. This would include materials and supplies, workspace, office equipment, research or professional books and magazines, travel for business purposes, certain conference fees, any agent commissions, postage, legal fees, and accountant fees.

In past years, one of the most significant and problematic of these deductible expenses is the workspace deduction. However, as you will see in the next section, the rules for home office deductions have relaxed in recent years. This is very important to the small business owners, as it is not uncommon for new businesses to be based at home for a variety of reasons, the most important of which is probably economic. The cost of renting a separate office is such that many small-business owners, especially in the start-up phase, are unwilling or unable to pay it. Others, of course, choose to work at home because it enables them to juggle work and family.

DEDUCTIONS FOR THE USE OF A HOME IN BUSINESS

Tax law changes have made taking a home office deduction much more attractive than it has been in the recent past. Each small-business owner with a home-based office should consider the benefits of taking a home office deduction carefully, even if they have been told in the past that they would be better served not to take the deduction. The home office deduction allows various home expenses to be deducted against the net business income. Expenses that fall into this category include, but are not limited to:

- mortgage interest;
- real estate taxes;
- home repairs/maintenance;
- rent;
- utilities;
- insurance;
- security system; and,
- depreciation.

Indirect expenses are those that benefit both the business as well as the personal use portions of the home. The business portion of the expense is taken as a percentage of the total spent. The business use percentage is determined by dividing the square footage of business use of the home by the total square footage.

Direct expenses are those that were made to improve only the business use portion of the home. These amounts are allowed in full.

Regularly and Exclusively

In order for an area of your home to be considered business use, it must be used regularly and exclusively. Regularly means that the space is consistently used for business purposes only, meaning that occasional use does not qualify. Exclusively means that the area is used only for the business purpose. (There is an exception for the storage of inventory or by the use of a day care facility. Under these two circumstances, the area does not have to be exclusive.) Generally, an area is used for business if it meets the above tests and is:

- the principal place of business (this includes administrative use). A home office will generally qualify a business use for administrative work if the area is used exclusively and regularly and there is no other location available for the taxpayer to conduct these activities;
- used as a place to meet clients; or,
- used for business purposes and is a separate structure from the taxpayer's personal residence.

Separate Structure

When the office is in a structure separate from the principal residence, the requirements for deductibility have always been more relaxed. The structure must be used exclusively and on a regular basis, just as an office in the home. However, when the office is in a separate structure, it need only be used in connection with the business, not as the principal place of business.

Storage Areas

When taxpayers use a portion of their homes for storage of business materials (as well as for business), the requirements for deductibility of the storage have also been more relaxed than other rules in the recent past. The dwelling must be the sole fixed location of the business and the storage area must be used on a regular basis for the storage of the business equipment or products. The room used for storage need not be used entirely or exclusively for business, but there must be a separately identifiable space suitable for storage of the business-related materials.

> **NOTE:** No home office deductions are allowed when employees rent their homes to their employers in their capacity as employees.

Tax Advantages

The primary tax advantage comes from a deduction for an allocable portion of repairs, utility bills, and depreciation. Otherwise, these would not be deductible at all. The allocable portion is the square footage of the space used for the business, divided by the total square footage of the house, and multiplied by your mortgage interest, property taxes, etc. Determining the amount of allowable depreciation is highly complex, and you should discuss it with your accountant or tax advisor.

The total amount that can be deducted for an office or storage place in the home is artificially limited. The amount that can be deducted is determined by taking the total amount of money earned in the business and subtracting the allocable portion of mortgage interest and property taxes and other deductions allocable to the business. The remainder is the maximum amount that you can deduct for the allocable portion of repairs, utilities, and depreciation. In other words, your total business deductions in this situation cannot be greater than your total business income minus all other business expenses. The office-at-home deduction, therefore, cannot be used to create a net loss, but any disallowed home office expense can be carried forward indefinitely and deducted in future years against profits from the business.

Selling Your Home

Generally, there is an exclusion of gain of up to $250,000 ($500,000 for joint filings) on the sale of your personal residence. However, if you have taken the home office deduction, the gain may be excluded to the extent the house was not used for business purposes. Thus, any business deductions taken for depreciation expense after May 6, 1997 will have to be recaptured and taken into income. If you plan to sell your home any time soon, you should confer with an accountant or tax advisor.

OTHER PROFESSIONAL EXPENSES

As mentioned earlier, deductible business expenses include not only the workspace, but also all the ordinary and necessary expenditures involved in the business. *Current expenses*, items with a useful life of less than one year, are fully deductible in the year incurred. Office supplies, postage, and telephone bills are all examples of current expenses.

Many expenses, however, cannot be fully deducted in the year of purchase, but can be depreciated. These kinds of costs are called *capital expenditures*. For example, the cost of equipment, such as a typewriter, computer, word processor, or pickup truck, all of which have useful lives of more than one year, are capital expenditures and cannot be fully deducted in the year of purchase. Instead, the taxpayer must depreciate, or allocate, the cost of the item over the estimated useful life of the asset. Although the actual useful life of professional equipment will vary, fixed periods have been established in the tax code over which depreciation may be deducted.

In some cases, it may be difficult to decide whether an expense is a capital expenditure or a current expense. Repairs to machinery are one example. If you spend $200 repairing your delivery van, this expense may or may not constitute a capital expenditure. The general test focuses on whether the amount spent restoring the vehicle adds to its value or substantially prolongs its useful life. Since the cost of replacing short-lived parts of a vehicle to keep it in efficient working condition does not substantially add to its useful life, such a cost would be a current cost and would be deductible. The cost of rebuilding your van's engine, on the other hand, significantly extends its useful life. Thus, such a cost is a capital expenditure and must be depreciated.

For most small businesses, an immediate deduction can be taken when equipment is purchased. In 2006, up to $108,000 of such purchases could be expensed for the year and need not be depreciated at all (though this begins to phase out when the cost of your qualifying Section 179 property placed in service in a year is more than $430,000). This was a generous increase as a result of the *Jobs and Growth Tax Relief Reconciliation Act of 2003*. The Act also cut capital gains taxes for most investments held at least twelve months from 20% and 10% to 15% and 5%, respectively. This is a great tax advantage over the higher capital gains rates that were in place over the last decade.

NOTE: Rates for gain on specialty gains, such as depreciation recapture and gain on the sale of collectibles, did not change.

Commissions paid to salespeople, as well as fees paid to lawyers or accountants for business purposes, are generally deductible as current expenses. The same is true of salaries paid to others whose services are necessary for the business.

IN PLAIN ENGLISH

If you need to hire help, it is a good idea to hire people on an individual project basis as independent contractors, rather than as regular employees. This avoids your having to pay Social Security, disability, and withholding-tax payments on their accounts. You should specify the job-by-job basis of the assignments, detail when each project is to be completed, and, if possible, allow the person you are hiring to choose the place to do the work. If there is any doubt about whether an individual is actually an independent contractor, contact a skilled employment-law attorney, since the IRS could characterize the individual as an employee. In that event, you will be responsible for tax withholding and paying FICA taxes.

TRAVEL EXPENSES

On a business trip, whether within the United States or abroad, your ordinary and necessary expenses, including travel and lodging, may be 100% deductible if your travel is solely for business purposes (except for luxury water travel). Business meals and meals consumed while on a business trip are deductible up to 50% of the actual cost. If the trip primarily involves a personal vacation, you can deduct business-related expenses at the destination, but you may not deduct the transportation costs.

If the trip is primarily for business, but part of the time is given to a personal vacation, you must indicate which expenses are for business and which for pleasure. In such cases, a portion of the business-related expenses will be nondeductible. This is not true in the case of foreign trips if one of the following exceptions applies.

- You had no substantial control over arranging the trip.
- Less than 25% of the time was spent in nonbusiness activity.
- The trip outside the United States was for a week or less.
- A personal vacation was not a major consideration in making the trip.

If you are claiming one of these exceptions, you should be careful to have supporting documentation. If you cannot take advantage of one of the exceptions, you must allocate expenses for the trip abroad according to the percentage of the trip devoted to business as opposed to vacation.

Determining Business Stay

The definition of what constitutes a business stay can be very helpful to the taxpayer in determining a trip's deductibility. Travel days, including the day of departure and the day of return, count as business days if travel outside the United States is for more than seven days and business activities occurred on such days. Any day that the taxpayer spends on business counts as a business day, even if only a part of the day is spent on business. A day in which business is canceled through no fault of the taxpayer counts as a business day. Saturdays, Sundays, and holidays count as business days even though no business is conducted, provided that business is conducted on the Friday before and the Monday after the weekend, or on one day on either side of the holiday.

ENTERTAINMENT EXPENSES

Entertainment expenses incurred for the purpose of developing an existing business are also deductible in the amount of 50% of actual cost. However, you must be especially careful about recording entertainment expenses. You should record in your logbook the amount, date, place, type of entertainment, business purpose, substance of the discussion, the participants in the discussion, and the business relationship of the parties who are being entertained. Keep receipts for any expenses over $75. You should also keep in mind the stipulation in the tax code that disallows deductibility for expenses that are lavish or extravagant under the circumstances. No guidelines have yet been developed as to the definition of the term *lavish or extravagant*, but one should be aware of the restriction nevertheless. If tickets to a sporting, cultural, or other entertainment event are purchased, only the face value of the ticket is allowed as a deduction. If a skybox or other luxury box seat is purchased or leased and is used for business entertaining, the maximum deduction now allowed is 50% of the cost of a nonluxury box seat.

CONVENTIONS

The rules for business travel and entertainment expenses are more stringent when incurred while attending conventions and conferences outside the United States. Also, the IRS tends to review very carefully any deductions for attendance at business seminars that also involve a family vacation, whether inside the United States or abroad. In order to deduct the business expense, the taxpayer must be able to show, with documents, that the reason for attending the meeting was to promote production of income. Normally, for a spouse's expenses to be deductible, the spouse must be a co-owner or employee of the business.

IN PLAIN ENGLISH

Seminars often offer special activities for husbands and wives and will provide necessary documentation at a later date.

As a general rule, the business deductions are allowed for conventions and seminars held in North America. The IRS is taking a closer look at cruise ship seminars and is requiring two statements to be attached to the tax return. The first statement substantiates the number of days on the ship, the number of hours spent each day on business, and the activities in the program. The second statement must come from the sponsor of the convention to verify the initial information. In addition, the ship must be registered in the United States and all ports of call must be located in the United States or its possessions. The deduction is also limited to $2,000 per individual per year. Again, the key for the taxpayer taking this sort of deduction is careful documentation and substantiation.

LOGBOOKS

Accurate recordkeeping is crucial for tax preparation. Keeping a logbook or expense diary is probably the best line of defense for the businessperson with respect to business expenses incurred while traveling. If you are on the road, keep the following things in mind.

- With respect to travel expenses—
  - Keep proof of the costs.
  - Record the time of departure.
  - Record the number of days spent on business.
  - List the places visited and the business purposes of your activities.
- With respect to the transportation costs—
  - Keep copies of all receipts in excess of $75.
  - If traveling by car, keep track of mileage.
  - Log all other expenses in your diary.

Similarly, with meals, tips, and lodging, keep receipts for all items over $75 and make sure to record all less expensive items in your logbook.

Businesspersons may also take tax deductions for their attendance at workshops, seminars, retreats, and the like, provided they are careful to document the business nature of the trip. It is, however, no longer possible to deduct for investment seminars or conventions, as opposed to business conventions.

CHARITABLE DEDUCTIONS

The law provides that an individual or business can donate either money or property to qualified charities and take a tax deduction for the donation. Individuals are afforded more favorable deductions for donations of money or property they own than are artists donating their creations or businesspeople who donate property out of their inventories.

The tax law requires independent appraisals of property donated in a form prescribed in the I.R.C. In addition, if the taxpayer receives any benefit from the charity, the amount deducted must be by the fair market value of the benefit received. Benefits could include, for example, attendance at museum openings or merchandise such as books, tapes, or CDs.

Since this area can be quite technical, you should consult with your tax advisor before making any charitable donations. In addition, there have been some abuses on the part of charities that resulted in misappropriations of donated funds. If you have any question about the validity of a particular charity, you should contact your state attorney general's office or the local governmental agency that polices charitable solicitations in your area.

GRANTS, PRIZES, AND AWARDS

Individuals who receive income from grants or fellowships should be aware that this income can be excluded from gross income, and thus represents considerable tax savings. For an individual to qualify for this exclusion, the grant must be for the purpose of furthering his or her education and training. However, amounts received under a grant or fellowship that are specifically designated to cover expenses related to the grant are no longer fully deductible. Furthermore, if the grant is given as compensation for services or is primarily for the benefit of the grant-giving organization, it cannot be excluded.

For scholarships and fellowships granted after August 16, 1986, the deduction is allowed only if the recipient is a degree candidate. The amount of the exclusion from income is limited to the amounts used for tuition, fees, books, supplies, and equipment. Amounts designated for room, board, and other incidental expenses are included in income. No exclusion from income is allowed for recipients who are not degree candidates.

The above rules apply to income from grants and fellowships. Unfortunately, the *Tax Reform Act of 1986* also put tighter restrictions on money, goods, or services received as prizes or awards. Previously, the amounts received for certain awards were excluded from income if the recipient was rewarded for past achievements and had not applied for the award. Examples of this type of award are the Pulitzer Prize and the Nobel Prize. Under the present law, any prizes or awards for religious, charitable, scientific, or artistic achievements are included as income to the recipient unless the prize is assigned to charity.

HEALTH INSURANCE

Self-employed individuals may deduct a percentage of the amount paid for medical insurance for themselves, their spouses, and their dependents. The percentage has worked its way up from being limited in the recent past to 100% deductibility in the year 2003. (Check with your financial advisor or tax professional regarding the current deductible amount.)

IN PLAIN ENGLISH

If you do not know whether a particular activity is deductible, consult with a competent CPA or tax advisor. In any case, consultation with qualified tax professionals is always advisable to ensure maximum benefits.

CHAPTER 22

Zoning

It is not uncommon for the small business owner to have an office or workshop in a home or garage, especially with the increased sophistication of computer systems. Telecommuting has become a viable option for many businesses, and online business activities can also be conducted through home computers.

Problems raised by the multiple use of a dwelling can be divided into two basic areas: whether local zoning regulations legally allow working and living in the same place and whether the income tax laws recognize the realities of home-based businesses. This chapter covers the problem of zoning and similar laws. (See the previous chapter for a full discussion of the income tax considerations of designating a part of your home as an office.)

LOCAL ZONING RESTRICTIONS

For the person who wants to live and work in the same space, local zoning ordinances can be a significant issue. Some city ordinances flatly prohibit using the same space as a business and as a dwelling. In some commercially zoned areas where low-cost spaces are available, it is illegal to maintain a residence in the same space. In residential areas, regulations may require permits and restrict the size and use of the workspace. Since municipal and county ordinances vary, the business owner should check with the appropriate local government agency to determine specific requirements. The fire department, for example, would likely have to approve the use of a kiln.

For the person who wants to maintain an office or workshop in the garage or basement of a residence, several types of restrictions may apply. The space devoted to the work activity may be limited to a certain number of square feet. Outbuildings may or may not be allowed. The type of equipment used may also be restricted. Noise, smoke, and odor restrictions may apply. Approval may be required from all or some of the neighbors. If remodeling is contemplated, building codes must, of course, also be considered.

You also may have to obtain a home-occupation permit or, in many areas, a business license. The application fee for either of these will normally be a flat fee or a percentage of annual receipts from the activity. Depending upon the success of the business, this could become a substantial expense. In addition, your homeowner's or renter's insurance policy will typically contain some restrictions relating to commercial activity. You should contact your insurance broker to find out whether or not your policy contains such limitations and what can be done to deal with them.

In commercially zoned areas, small manufacturers may have more flexibility in the types of activities they conduct, particularly if they produce noise or odors that would be offensive to others in a residentially zoned location. But if you also wish to use the workspace for eating and sleeping, zoning ordinances may prohibit such use.

FEDERAL REGULATIONS

Additional regulations that can adversely affect those who want to work at home are federal laws that inhibit so-called *cottage industries*. The U.S. Department of Labor actively enforces a 1943 regulation that forbids individuals from producing in their homes for profit the following six categories of goods: embroidery, women's apparel, gloves and mittens, buttons and buckles, jewelry, and handkerchiefs.

The regulation was originally enacted many years ago when the Department of Labor found that minimum wage violations were widespread in industries in which working at home predominated. The minimum wage is mandated by the federal *Fair Labor Standards Act* and requires employers to pay their employees no less than a set hourly rate. Overtime, at one-and-one-half times the employee's hourly rate, is also mandated for hours worked over forty hours per week.

In 1981, the Department of Labor proposed repealing all regulations that prohibited cottage industries, but bitter labor union opposition resulted in the continuation of the regulation for all the targeted crafts except knitted outerwear.

The remaining regulations may create serious difficulties for people who want to work at home. In recent years, the disputes between labor unions, principally the International Ladies Garment Workers Union, and women who make their livings from cottage industries have become quite heated. The unions argue that they merely want to prevent sweatshop conditions, but many people believe that the real issue is nonunionized, home labor competing with union members who work in unionized factories.

In order to fall within the scope of the regulation, the worker must be an employee. This does not mean, however, that a person can avoid the effect of the regulation simply by labeling him or herself an independent contractor. Under the Fair Labor Standards Act, the test of employment is the economic reality of the relationship.

At the other end of the spectrum are manufacturers who are self-employed and independent, selling their products on the open market, at wholesale or retail, for whatever price they can command. In this situation, the federal regulations do not apply.

TELECOMMUTING AND WEB-BASED BUSINESSES

As previously noted, telecommuting has become popular for many businesses. It makes it possible for individuals to maintain a traditional employment relationship while working at home and enabling individuals to reside anywhere they wish. Thus, for example, many technology companies based in the high-rent areas of the Silicon Valley have employees who telecommute from rural areas of Oregon, Washington, and Montana. The cost savings to the business in rent is obvious; the lifestyle benefits to the employee are also clear.

The vast majority of tax issues that telecommuters should consider are similar to those that affect employees in general and are discussed in the tax chapter of this text. There is at least one tax issue that has arisen for telecommuters in particular. When a telecommuter is located in Nashville, for example, working for a New York company, which jurisdiction's income tax will apply to the salary earned? The highest court in the State of New York held that since the salary was derived from New York sources and the telecommuter chose to live in Nashville, New York income tax was due on 100% of the income earned by the out-of-state employee. The result might have been different if the employee had been transferred to Nashville rather than voluntarily choosing to live in that state for the employee's own convenience.

Web-based businesses can be run from anywhere. It is quite common for individuals to conduct those businesses from home. All that is needed is a telephone, computer, and Internet connection.

IN PLAIN ENGLISH

A number of individuals have made a good living buying and selling on commercial sites such as eBay, where the activity can be and usually is conducted from home.

Various forms of independent contractors establish their home base at home.

Since the zoning laws that prohibit the operation of home-based businesses were generally enacted for the purpose of preserving a residential quality in residential neighborhoods, including air quality, traffic flow, and noise, it is not clear whether these laws would be violated by the types of home-based businesses described previously. Technically, the laws state that any business activity would be a violation, yet the purpose of the law is not affected by businesses that do not result in increased air pollution, traffic, or noise. Thus, it would seem that a modernization of the legislation would be appropriate, or at the very least, a clear legislative exemption for these types of businesses should be enacted.

Notwithstanding the logic of this position, there is a risk in establishing any home-based business without complying with the laws as they are written or obtaining a proper exemption from them.

CHAPTER 23

Renting Commercial Space

At some point in the life of your business, you will probably find it necessary to evaluate the terms and conditions of a commercial lease. Commercial leases are much more subject to negotiation and pitfalls than residential leases, which are more tightly regulated in most states. You should consult an attorney with experience in negotiating commercial leases before signing one.

Landlords typically employ the services of a broker when attempting to rent commercial space. In addition, many businesspeople hire brokers to assist them with lease negotiations. This discussion is intended to alert you to some of the topics that should arise in your discussion with your lawyer or real estate broker.

PREMISES

To begin with, the exact space to be rented should be spelled out in detail in the lease. Determine whether there is a distinction between the space leased and the actual space that is usable. Often, tenants are required to pay rent on commercial space measured from wall to wall (commonly referred to as a *vanilla shell*) even though, after the area is built out, the resulting usable space may be significantly smaller.

If your space is in a shopping center or office building and you share responsibility for common areas with other tenants, your responsibilities for the common areas should be explained. Such matters as who will be responsible for cleaning and maintaining them; when will the common areas be open or closed; and when other facilities, such as restrooms and storage, are available must be spelled out.

COST

Another important item is the cost of the space. A flat monthly rental or one that will change based on your earnings at the location, as is often the case in shopping centers and office buildings, must be determined. In order to evaluate the cost of the space, you should compare it with other similar spaces in the same locale. Do not be afraid to negotiate for more favorable terms. Care should be taken not to sign a lease that will restrict you from opening another facility close to the one being rented.

TERM

It is also important for you to consider the period of the lease. If, for example, you are merely renting a booth at a trade show, then you are only concerned with a short term. On the other hand, if you intend to rent for a year or two, it is a good idea to get an option to extend the lease, because when you advertise and promote your business, your location is one of the things about which you will be telling people. Moving can cause a lot of problems with mail and telephone numbers. Besides, if you move every year or two, some customers may feel that you are unstable and customers who buy on an irregular basis may not know where to find you after the lease period ends. Worse still, they may find a competitor in your old space. In fact, goodwill is often defined as including a stable location.

Long-term leases are recordable in some states. Recording, where permitted, is generally accomplished by having the lease filed in the same office where a deed to the property would be filed. Check with a local real estate title company or real estate attorney for the particulars in your locale.

IN PLAIN ENGLISH

If you are in a position to record your lease, it is probably a good idea to do so. You will then be entitled to receive notices, legal and otherwise, that are related to the property.

RESTRICTIONS

It is essential for you to determine whether there are any restrictions on the particular activity you wish to perform on the leased premises. For example, the area may be zoned so as to prohibit you from manufacturing. It is a good idea to insist on a provision that puts the burden of obtaining any permit or variances on the landlord or, if you are responsible for them, the inability to obtain them should be grounds for terminating the lease without penalty.

Be sure the lease provides that you are permitted to use any sign or advertising on the premises or spells out any restrictions. It is not uncommon, for example, for historic landmark laws to regulate signs on old buildings. Some zoning laws also prohibit signs.

REMODELING

You should also be aware that extensive remodeling may be necessary for certain spaces to become suitable for your use. If this is the case, then it is important for you to determine who will be responsible for the costs of remodeling, who will determine the contractors to be used, and who owns the tenant improvements. In addition, it is essential to find out whether it will be necessary for you to restore the premises to their original, pre-remodeled condition when the lease ends. This can be expensive, and in some instances, impossible.

Americans With Disabilities Act

The *Americans With Disabilities Act of 1990* (ADA), which was discussed in the context of employment in Chapter 20, also covers real estate. The ADA requires places of public accommodation to be reasonably accessible. The law is broadly interpreted and includes virtually every form of business. The term *reasonable accommodation* is not precise, and thus, it is important to determine what must be done in order to fulfill the requirements of this federal statute. Typically, approximately 25% of the cost of any covered remodel must be allocated to items that aid accessibility. These would include, among other things, levered door openers, Braille signs, larger bathroom stalls, wheelchair ramps, approved disability-accessible doors, and elevators. You should determine whether the cost of complying with the ADA will be imposed on the landlord, the tenant, or shared.

Environmental Laws

Environmental laws will inhibit the use of your space for certain businesses. It is essential for you to determine whether any of the materials used in your business will violate federal, state, or local rules with respect to hazardous materials. In addition, there can be hazardous materials cleanup problems resulting from prior uses of the space to be occupied by you. For example, space previously used by a dry cleaner, chemical company, automotive repair business, or the like may require an expensive cleanup operation prior to any occupation. Other issues, such as whether your building contains any asbestos, lead-based paint, or the like may exist. These present specialized problems in the costs of remodeling and occupation. It is essential for you to spell out who will bear the costs of any environmental compliance in the lease.

UTILITIES

If you need special hookups, such as water or electrical lines, you should determine whether the landlord will provide them or whether you will have to bear the cost. Of course, even if the leased premises already have the necessary facilities, you should question the landlord regarding the cost of these utilities, and whether they are included in the rent or are they to be paid separately.

In some locations, garbage pickup is not a problem, since it is one of the services provided by the municipality. On the other hand, it is common for renters to be responsible for their own trash disposal. In commercial spaces, this can be quite expensive and should be addressed in the lease.

Customarily, the landlord will be responsible for the exterior of the building. It will be the landlord's obligation to make sure that it does not leak during rainstorms and that it is properly ventilated. Notwithstanding this fact, it is important for you to make sure the lease deals with the question of responsibility if, for example, the building is damaged and some of your property is damaged or destroyed.

IN PLAIN ENGLISH

If you have to take out insurance for the building, as well as its contents, your cost will greatly increase. Determine who will be responsible for insuring the building.

Similarly, you should find out whether or not it will be your obligation to obtain liability insurance for injuries that are caused in portions of the building not under your control, such as common hallways and stairwells. You should, of course, have your own liability policy for accidental injuries or accidents that occur on your leased premises.

SECURITY AND ZONING

A good lease will also contain a provision dealing with security. If you are renting indoor space in a shopping center or office building, it is likely that the landlord will be responsible for external security, although this is not universally the case. If you are renting an entire building, it is customarily your responsibility to provide whatever security you deem important. You should address the question of whether the lease permits you to install locks or alarm systems.

If you are dealing with large bulky items and are accepting deliveries or making them, your lease should contain a provision that will give you the flexibility you desire.

If the place you wish to rent will be used as both your personal dwelling and for business, other problems may arise. It is quite common for zoning laws to prohibit certain forms of commercial activities when the area is zoned residential. (see Chapter 22.) You should consult with your attorney before attempting to operate out of your home.

WRITTEN DOCUMENT

Finally, it is essential for you to be sure that every item agreed upon between you and the landlord is stated in writing. This is particularly important when dealing with leases, since many state laws provide that a long-term lease is an interest in land and can be enforced only if in writing.

The relationship between landlord and tenant is an ancient one that is undergoing a good deal of change. Care should be taken when examining a potential business location to determine exactly what you can do on the premises and whether the landlord or municipal rules will allow you to use the location for its intended purpose.

CHAPTER 24

Pension Plans

One of the methods by which a business owner may attract and retain key personnel is to provide certain benefits. Today, one of the most important benefits for employees is the ability to participate in a retirement plan. In addition, any form of succession planning will necessitate the establishment of a method by which the senior generation can step down and hand off control of the business. In order to create an effective succession plan, it is necessary to implement an arrangement that provides an economic incentive for senior workers to retire. This is likely to be a retirement plan.

A *retirement plan* is a written savings program. If the plan meets specific rules and regulations, then it is called a qualified plan. This means contributions are tax deductible for the person or the business making the investments. Income taxes on the investment earnings are delayed until benefits are paid to participants. A qualified plan is one of the last remaining legal tax shelters available to highly compensated individuals. It may be used to set aside funds for retirement and to attract and retain key employees. If properly structured and invested on a prudent basis with a diversified portfolio of investments, the plan should provide financial security for the individual's retirement.

Since 1982, federal tax laws have allowed unincorporated businesses the same status as corporations with regard to qualified retirement plans. Further, this same legislation eliminated the need for a corporate trustee (who was approved by the IRS), thus allowing the self-employed person to be the trustee of his or her own plan.

IN PLAIN ENGLISH

When choosing a plan, select the type that will most satisfactorily meet your needs and those of your employees.

There are essentially two types of qualified plans—defined benefit and defined contribution.

DEFINED BENEFIT PLANS

Contributions to a defined benefit plan are determined by a relatively complex formula and are then monitored by an enrolled actuary. The promised benefit is not to exceed the lesser of 100% of the employee's annual average income for the three highest-salaried consecutive years or a specified amount that is adjusted annually and dependent on changes in the *Consumer Price Index*. For the current permissible amount, see the IRS website at **www.irs.gov**. Excess earnings (investment income greater than the assumptions made by the actuary) are used to reduce the cost of contributions to the plan by the employer.

Advantages

Normally, defined benefit plans are appropriate where the business owner is mature, with less than ten to fifteen working years until retirement. Defined benefit plans are appropriate—and potentially beneficial—for businesses that have enjoyed considerable financial success with limited fluctuations in cash flow. The defined benefit plan can be designed to drain excess funds and allocate them to retirement on behalf of the senior preferred participant (the principal owner). In many instances, this same advantage can be attained through the use of an age-weighted defined contribution plan, such as a profit-sharing or target-benefit plan.

DEFINED CONTRIBUTION PLANS

In a defined contribution plan, the contribution on behalf of the participant is defined and is usually either a discretionary amount or a percentage of his or her annual compensation (ignoring compensation in excess of $220,000). The benefit that will be available to the participant at retirement is not defined. Investment earnings increase the retirement benefit for the plan participants and the longer the period over which investments are accumulated and interest is earned, the greater the amount of benefits that will be available to the participants at retirement.

IN PLAIN ENGLISH

A major difference between a defined contribution plan and a defined benefit plan is who bears the risk of poor investment performance. The employer bears the risk in defined benefit plans, whereas participants bear this risk in defined contribution plans.

Profit-sharing plans, money-purchase plans, and salary savings or reduction plans, such as 401(k)s and SIMPLE plans, are all defined contribution plans, as are Simplified Employee Pension Plans (SEPs) and Employee Stock Ownership Plans (ESOPs).

Profit-Sharing Plans

If the income from your business varies significantly from year to year, a *profit-sharing plan* may be the most appropriate type of plan to offer your employees. Contributions may be determined at or after the end of the tax year. Contributions to the plan can be determined by a vote of your business's management (i.e., managing partners or the board of directors) or by a formula previously designated in the plan's documents. It is no longer required that business entities, such as corporations or certain types of LLCs, actually have a profit in order to make a contribution. The maximum deductible contribution to a profit-sharing plan is now 25% of an employee's annual compensation, with each participant's total annual addition limited to $44,000 per year.

Salary Savings/Reduction Plans

These plans, which include 401(k)s, are a variant of profit-sharing plans. Under this type of plan, the employee elects to have a percentage of his or her gross salary diverted into a qualified plan. Employees can have a choice of saving on a tax-deferred basis or by making after-tax Roth contributions that may eventually qualify for tax-free withdrawal. Depending on the plan, the employer may elect to match all or a portion of the contributions made by the employee. Usually, the amount of the matching contribution has a self-imposed percentage limit.

The main feature of salary savings/reduction plans is that a portion of the cost shifts from the employer to the employee. The business, therefore, makes less of a cash contribution.

A major drawback is the limitation of contributions by highly compensated employees. The maximum contributions allowable continuously change and can be found on the IRS website at **www.irs.gov**. In addition, owners and highly compensated employees may not be allowed to save the maximum amount if the savings rate of the other employees is too low. They are generally allowed to save about 2% of compensation more than the average of the non-highly compensated employees. To avoid being limited by this restriction, you may consider a safe harbor 401(k) plan that requires advance notice to participants and a nonforfeitable employer contribution.

A new approach to dealing with low savings rates of rank-and-file employees is called *automatic enrollment*. Instead of being asked how much they want to save, they are informed that they will be saving at a plan-prescribed rate unless they elect otherwise. A year later, the plan's *automatic escalation* feature kicks in to raise their savings rate unless they act. Studies have proven that this inertia approach increases the overall savings rate substantially.

Simplified Employee Pension Plans

These plans are often viewed incorrectly as an alternative to the more highly structured qualified plans. The maximum contribution that the employer may contribute per participant to a SEP continues to change and can be found on the IRS website at **www.irs.gov**. Contributions are based on an equal percentage of annual salary for all employees 21 years or older who have performed service for the employer during at least three out of five years and have received a salary specified by the tax laws. You should also consult the IRS website for the current salary range. Although its low maintenance cost is an initial attraction, its simplicity results in a significant inflexibility that many employers are not willing to accept. For example, those whose employment has been terminated must share in any contribution and all contributions are 100% vested and nonforfeitable.

SIMPLE IRAs

Salary Reduction Simplified Employee Pension Plans (SAR/SEPs) could no longer be created after December 31, 1996. Existing SAR/SEPs were grandfathered in and are allowed to exist until the employer terminates them. A new salary reduction plan called the SIMPLE IRA was introduced to replace the SAR/SEP. This plan is available to employers with up to one hundred employees. Employees are eligible if they earned at least $5,000 during any of the previous two years and are expected to earn at least $5,000 during the current year. These requirements can be reduced or eliminated if the employer waives them. The maximum employee contribution for 2006 is $10,000 for participants under the age of 50 and $12,500 for participants aged 50 or older. The employer is required to match up to 3% of the employee compensation. Vesting for the employer contributions is 100% and immediate.

Money-Purchase Plans

This type of defined contribution plan has a fixed funding requirement, such as 10% of compensation of all eligible participants. It also requires that participants be offered a qualified joint and survivor annuity as a form of benefit distribution. It has the same tax deduction and annual addition limits that apply to profit-sharing plans. Most new plan sponsors choose the profit-sharing plan instead. Many money-purchase plans have been converted to profit-sharing plans.

Employee Stock Ownership Plans

In an *Employee Stock Ownership Plan* (ESOP), the majority of the assets are shares of stock in the corporate plan sponsor. Generally, ESOPs are not useful for owners of small businesses.

Hybrid Plans

The target-benefit plan is receiving renewed interest as a result of changes in income tax law. This hybrid plan combines the contribution and benefit levels of a defined contribution plan with the recognition for mature employees found in defined benefit plans. Another hybrid, the *age-weighted profit-sharing plan* (AWPSP), is also available. As with the target-benefit plan, the contributions are weighted or skewed toward senior employees.

DESIGNING AND DOCUMENTING A PLAN

The creation of a qualified plan requires the creation and adoption of a written plan document and trust agreement before the end of the first plan year. A summary plan description must also be drafted to inform participants about the plan. Documentation is available in two forms—prototype documents and individually drafted documents. Each form has its own advantages and limitations. It is, therefore, essential to work with an experienced professional when selecting and establishing a plan.

EMPLOYER-SPONSORED PLANS

Many qualified plans of small businesses are top heavy. This is a special status that results from key employees having more than 60% of the plan's benefits. As a result, minimum contribution rules and faster vesting rules apply. The minimum contribution is the lesser of 3% of compensation or the highest rate allocated to a key employee. The vesting schedule options are a three-year cliff of a graded schedule of 20% per year from the second to the sixth year of employment.

Plans may be combined or stacked in order to more specifically meet the needs of the business. However, this creates a need for separate sets of rules and limitations. Stacking also increases the amount of administrative paperwork and forms, thus driving up the cost of operating and maintaining the plan. Fortunately, the need to stack plans was significantly reduced in 2002, when the deduction limit of profit-sharing plans was raised from 15% to 25%.

The design features outlined below can be used to limit or reduce the cost of rank-and-file employees in the employer-sponsored plan.

Vesting

A key element of any qualified plan is rewarding long-term service by employees. One method used to limit benefits for employees who have been employed for a relatively short period of time is by a vesting schedule that forfeits all or some of the participant's employer-provided benefits. Vesting means having rights in, which is to say that the employee has the right to all or part of his or her benefits in the retirement plan.

Currently, there are two primary vesting schedule formulas.

1. *Five-year cliff vesting.* This schedule does not allow vesting for employees with less than five years of service. Upon completion of five years of service, the employee is 100% vested in all employer-provided benefits. When the plan is top heavy, the longest permitted cliff vesting schedule is three years.
2. *Three-to-seven-year graded vesting.* This vesting schedule provides for 20% vesting after three years of employment and an additional 20% for each subsequent year. After completing seven years of employment, the employee is eligible to receive 100% of the employer-provided benefits upon termination of employment. When the plan is top-heavy, the graded schedule must start with the second year of employment, rather than the third year.

Minimum Hours

The plan sponsor may limit the participation of employees by permanently excluding those who work fewer than one thousand hours per year and then by limiting each year's contributions to those who have worked at least five hundred hours during the year. This feature is very important for businesses that use temporary employees.

Minimum Age

The plan sponsor may also limit participation of employees through the use of a minimum-age requirement. Current law allows an employer to postpone participation by employees under 21 years of age. At the time the employee reaches age 21, he or she enters the plan and all of his or her years of employment are counted in the vesting formula.

Unions

Employees that are a part of a collective bargaining unit may be specifically excluded from participation in a qualified plan established by an employer for its nonunion employees, provided that retirement benefits were the subject of good-faith bargaining.

Integration with Social Security

This feature allows the plan sponsor to recognize contributions made on behalf of the employee to Social Security. An integrated plan (also referred to as allowing permitted disparity) has an extra contribution for those whose compensation is greater than the Social Security wage base.

INVESTMENTS IN A QUALIFIED PLAN

The primary governing law regarding investments made by a qualified plan comes from the *Employee Retirement Income Security Act* (ERISA). Under its Prudent Expert Investment Principle, investments should be made with primary consideration given to what an expert, rather than an amateur investor, would do.

There is a plethora of investment opportunities, including stocks, bonds, money market accounts, real estate, and partnership interests. Therefore, it is essential that you confer with a registered investment advisor or certified financial planner to structure your plan investments based on the plan's goals, the economy, and other relevant factors.

CHAPTER 25

Estate Planning

No matter what business you are involved with and no matter how successful you are in that business, the time that you will work with your business is limited by either retirement or death. Prudent businesspeople will make appropriate plans for both. This is commonly known today as *succession planning*. One of the most important aspects of succession planning is estate planning. (Another aspect of succession planning is retirement, discussed in Chapter 24.)

All businesspeople should give some thought to estate planning and take the time to execute a proper will. Without a will, there is simply no way to control the disposition of one's property. Sound estate planning may include transfers outside of the will, since these types of arrangements typically escape the delays and expenses of probate. Certain types of trusts can be valuable will substitutes, but they may be subject to challenge by a surviving spouse.

Proper estate planning will require the assistance of a knowledgeable lawyer and, perhaps, also a life insurance agent, an accountant, a real estate agent, and a bank trust officer. What help will be needed and from whom will depend on the nature and size of the estate. This chapter considers the basic principles of estate planning. This discussion is not a substitute for the aid of a lawyer experienced in estate planning; rather, it is intended to introduce you to the basic principles, alert you to potential problems, and aid in preparing you to work with your estate planner(s).

THE WILL

A will is a legal instrument by which a person directs the distribution of property in his or her estate upon death. The maker of the will is called the testator. Recipients of gifts are known as beneficiaries or legatees. Gifts given by a will are referred to as bequests (personal property) or devises (real estate).

Certain formalities are required by state law to create a valid will. About half the states require formally witnessed wills, that is, that the instrument be in writing and signed by the testator in the presence of two or more witnesses. The other states allow either witnessed or *holographic* wills. A will that is entirely hand-written and signed by the testator is known as a holographic will.

A will is a unique document in two respects. First, if properly drafted, it is ambulatory, meaning it can accommodate change, such as applying to property acquired after the will is made. Second, a will is revocable, meaning that the testator has the power to change or cancel it at any time. Even if a testator makes a valid agreement not to revoke the will, the power to revoke it remains. If the testator uses that power, he or she may be liable for breach of contract.

Generally, courts do not consider a will to have been revoked unless it can be established that the testator either (1) performed a physical act of revocation, such as burning or tearing up a will with intent to revoke it or (2) later executed a valid will that revoked the previous will. Most state statutes also provide for automatic revocation of a will, in whole or in part, if the testator is subsequently divorced or married.

To change a will, the testator must execute a supplement, known as a codicil. It has the same formal requirements as those for creating a will. To the extent that the codicil contradicts the will, the contradicted parts of the will are revoked.

PAYMENT OF TESTATOR'S DEBTS

When the testator's estate is insufficient to satisfy all the bequests in the will after debts and taxes have been paid, some or all of the bequests in the will must be reduced or even eliminated entirely. The process of reducing or eliminating bequests is known as abatement. The priorities for reduction are set by state law according to the category of each bequest. The legally significant categories of gifts are generally as follows:

- specific bequests or devises, meaning gifts of identifiable items (I give to X all the furniture in my home);
- demonstrative bequests or devises, meaning gifts that are to be paid out of a specified source unless that source contains insufficient funds, in which case the gifts will be paid out of the general assets (I give to Y $1,000 to be paid from my shares of stock in ABC Corporation);
- general bequests, meaning gifts to be paid out of the general assets of an estate (I give Z $1,000); and,
- residuary bequests or devises, meaning gifts of whatever is left in the estate after all other gifts and expenses are satisfied (I give the rest, residue, and remainder of my estate to Z).

Intestate property (property not governed by a will but part of the testator's estate) is usually the first to be taken to satisfy claims against the estate. (If the will contains a valid residuary clause, there will be no such property.) Next, residuary bequests will be taken. If more money is needed, general bequests will be taken, and, lastly, specific and demonstrative bequests will be taken together in proportion to their value. Some states, however, provide that all gifts, regardless of type, abate proportionately.

DISPOSITION OF PROPERTY NOT WILLED

If the testator acquires more property during the time between signing the will and death, the disposition of such property will also be governed by the will. If such property falls within the description of an existing category in the will (i.e., I give all my stock to X; I give all my real estate to Y), it will pass along with all similar property. If it does not and the will contains a valid residuary clause, such after-acquired property will go to the residuary legatees. If there is no residuary clause, such property will pass outside the will to the persons specified in the state's law of intestate succession.

Intestate Succession

When a person dies without leaving a valid will, this is known as dying *intestate*. The estate of a person who dies intestate is distributed according to the state law of intestate succession. These laws specify who is entitled to what parts of the estate. In general, intestate property passes to those persons having the nearest degree of kinship to the decedent. An intestate's surviving spouse will always receive a share, generally at least one-third of the estate. An intestate's surviving children generally get a share. If some of the children do not survive the intestate, the grandchildren of the intestate may be entitled to a share by representation.

Representation is a legal principle meaning that if an heir does not survive the intestate but has a child who does survive, that child will represent the non-surviving heir and receive that parent's share in the estate. In other words, the surviving child stands in the shoes of a dead parent in order to inherit from a grandparent who dies intestate.

If there are no direct descendants surviving, the intestate's surviving spouse will take the entire estate or share it with the intestate's parents. If there is neither a surviving spouse nor any surviving direct descendant of the intestate, the estate will be distributed to the intestate's parents or, if the parents are not surviving, to the intestate's siblings by representation. If there are no surviving persons in any of these categories, the estate will go to surviving grandparents and their direct descendants. In this way, the family tree is constantly expanded in search of surviving relatives.

If none of the persons specified in the law of intestate succession survive the testator, the intestate's property ultimately goes to the state. This is known as *escheat*.

The laws of intestate succession make no provision for friends, in-laws, or stepchildren. Children adopted by the testator are treated the same as natural children for all purposes.

Spouse's Elective Share

State law will often provide a testator's surviving spouse with certain benefits from the estate even if the spouse is left out of the testator's will. Historically, these benefits were known as dower, in the case of a surviving wife, or curtesy, in the case of a surviving husband. In place of the old dower and curtesy, modern statutes give the surviving spouse the right to elect against the will and, thereby, receive a share equal to at least one-fourth of the estate. Here again, state laws vary. In some states, the surviving spouse's elective share is one-third. The historical concepts of dower and courtesy are in large part a result of the law's traditional recognition of an absolute duty on the part of the husband to provide for the wife. Modern laws are perhaps better justified by the notion that most property in a marriage should be shared because the financial success of either partner is due to the efforts of both.

Advantages to Having a Will

A will affords the opportunity to direct distribution of one's property and to set out limitations by making gifts conditional. For example, if an individual wishes to donate certain property to a specific charity, but only if certain conditions are adhered to, a will can make such conditions a prerequisite to the donation.

A will permits the testator to nominate an executor, called a personal representative in some states, to watch over and administer the estate in accordance with the testator's wishes and the law of the state where the will is being handled. If no executor is named in the will, the court will appoint one. A will permits the testator to give property to minors and to regulate the timing and uses of the property given (i.e., funds to be used exclusively for education).

If the testator has unusual types of property, such as antiques, artwork, publishable manuscripts, or intangibles, such as copyrights, trademarks, patents, and the like, it is a good idea to appoint joint executors, one with financial expertise and the other with expertise in valuation in the genre in question. If joint executors are used, some provision should be made in the will for resolving any deadlock between the two. For example, a neutral third party might be appointed as an arbitrator who is directed to resolve any impasses after hearing both sides.

It is also advisable to define the scope of the executor's power by detailed instructions. A lawyer's help will be necessary to set forth all of these important considerations in legally enforceable, unambiguous terms. It is essential in a will to avoid careless language that might be subject to attack by survivors unhappy with the will's provisions. A lawyer's assistance is also crucial to avoid making bequests that are not legally enforceable because they are contrary to public policy (i.e., if an individual gets married, the bequest will fail).

ESTATE TAXES

In addition to giving the testator significant posthumous control over division of property, a carefully drafted will can greatly reduce the overall amount of estate tax paid at death. The following information on taxing structures relates to federal estate taxation. State estate taxes often contain similar provisions, but state law must always be consulted for specifics.

Gross Estate

The first step in evaluating an estate for tax purposes is to determine the so-called *gross estate*. The gross estate will include all property over which the deceased had significant control at the time of death. In addition to certain bank accounts, examples would include properly held residences, investments that have been structured to avoid probate, certain life insurance proceeds and annuities, jointly held interests, and revocable transfers.

Under current tax laws, the executor of an estate may elect to value the property in the estate either as of the date of death or as of a date six months after death. The estate property must be valued in its entirety at the time chosen. However, if the executor elects to value the estate six months after death and certain pieces of property are distributed or sold before then, that property will be valued as of the date of distribution or sale.

Valuation

Fair market value is defined as the price at which property would change hands between a willing buyer and a willing seller when both buyer and seller have reasonable knowledge of all relevant facts. Such a determination is often very difficult to make, especially when items such as a nonpublicly traded business, artwork, antiques, other collectibles, and intangibles, such as intellectual property, are involved. Although the initial determination of fair market value is generally made by the executor when the estate tax return is filed, the Internal Revenue Service may disagree with the executor's valuation and assign assets a much higher fair market value.

When an executor and the Internal Revenue Service disagree with regard to valuation, the court will decide the matter. In most cases, the burden will be on the taxpayer to prove the value of the asset. Thus, expert testimony and evidence of the sale of the same or similar properties will be helpful. In general, courts are reluctant to determine valuation by formula.

The Taxable Estate

Figuring the taxable estate is the second major step in evaluating an estate for tax purposes, after determining the gross estate. The law allows a number of deductions from the gross estate in determining the amount of the taxable estate. The taxable estate is the basis upon which the tax owing is computed. Some of the key deductions used to arrive at the amount of the taxable estate are discussed below.

Typical deductions from the gross estate include funeral expenses, certain estate administration expenses, debts and enforceable claims against the estate, mortgages and liens, and, perhaps most significant, the marital deduction and the charitable deduction.

Marital Deduction

The marital deduction allows the total value of any interest in property that passes from the decedent to the surviving spouse to be subtracted from the value of the gross estate. The government will eventually get its tax on this property when the spouse dies but only to the extent such interest is included in the spouse's gross estate. The spouse, of course, may limit or eliminate the estate tax on his or her estate by implementing certain estate-planning procedures. This deduction may occur even in the absence of a will making a gift to the surviving spouse, since state law generally provides that the spouse is entitled to at least one-fourth of the overall estate regardless of the provisions of the will.

Charitable Deduction

The charitable deduction refers to the tax deduction allowed upon the transfer of property from an estate to a recognized charity. Since the definition of a charity for tax purposes is quite technical, it is advisable to insert a clause in the will providing that, if the institution specified to receive the donation does not qualify for the charitable deduction, the bequest shall go to a substitute qualified institution at the choice of the executor.

Calculating the Tax

Once deductions are figured, the taxable estate is taxed at the rate specified by the *Unified Estate and Gift Tax Schedule*. The unified tax imposes the same rate of tax on gifts made by will as on gifts made during life. It is a progressive tax, meaning the percent paid in taxes increases with the amount of property involved.

The rates rise significantly for larger estates. For example, the rate increases from 18%, where the cumulative total of taxable estate and taxable gifts is under $10,000, to 49%, where the cumulative total is over $2 million. Federal estate tax is also reduced by state death tax credit or actual state death tax, whichever is less.

Tax credits result in an exemption that is available to every estate. For tax years 2006, 2007, and 2008, the exclusion amount is $2 million. In tax year 2009, the exclusion amount is $3.5 million.

Paying the Tax

There is also an additional exemption for families with qualifying businesses or farms. These exemptions, combined with the unlimited marital deduction, allow most estates to escape estate taxes altogether. For those estates with estate taxes due, generally, estate taxes must be paid when the estate tax return is filed (within nine months of the date of death). Arrangements may be made to spread payments out over a number of years, if necessary.

IN PLAIN ENGLISH

It is not uncommon for executors to be forced to sell properties for less than full value in order to pay taxes. This can be avoided by obtaining insurance policies, the proceeds of which can be set up in a trust. (See the "trust" section of this chapter for more information.)

DISTRIBUTING PROPERTY OUTSIDE THE WILL

Property can be distributed outside the will by making inter vivos gifts (given during the giver's lifetime), either outright or by placing the property in an irrevocable trust prior to death.

Advantages

A potential advantage to distributing property outside the will is that the property escapes the delays and expense of probate, the court procedure by which a will is validated and administered. It used to be that there were also significant tax advantages to making inter vivos gifts rather than making gifts by will, but, since the estate and gift tax rates are now unified, there are few remaining tax advantages. One remaining advantage to making an inter vivos gift is that if the gift appreciates in value between the time the gift is made and death, the appreciated value will not be subject to estate tax. If the gift were made by will, the added value would be taxable, since the gift would be valued on the estate tax return as of date of death (or six months after).

IN PLAIN ENGLISH

This difference in value can represent significant tax savings for the heirs of someone whose business suddenly becomes successful and rapidly increases in value.

Annual Exclusion

The other advantage to making an inter vivos gift involves the yearly exclusion. A yearly exclusion of $12,000 per recipient is available on inter vivos gifts. For example, if $15,000 worth of gifts were given to an individual in one year, only $3,000 of its value will actually be taxable to the donor, who is responsible for the gift tax. A married couple can combine their gifts and claim a yearly exclusion of $24,000 per recipient, though each can gift only $12,000 tax free. Note that the $12,000 gift tax exemption is subject to change, and while it is in effect in 2005, Congress has indicated that it is likely to increase. You should, therefore, check with your accountant to determine what the actual amount of the exemption is on the date the gift is made.

Three-Year Rule

Gifts made within three years of death used to be included in the gross estate on the theory that they were made in contemplation of death. Amendments to the tax laws, however, have done away with the three-year rule for most purposes. The three-year rule is still applicable to gifts of life insurance and to certain transfers involving stock redemption or tax liens. The rule also applies to certain valuation schemes, the details of which are too complex to discuss here.

Gift Tax Returns

The donor must file gift tax returns for any year in which gifts made exceeded $11,000 to any one donee. It is not necessary to file returns when a gift to any one donee amounts to less than $11,000. However, where it is possible that valuation of the gift will become an issue with the IRS, it may be a good idea to file a return anyway.

Filing the return starts the three-year statute of limitations running. Once the statute of limitations period has expired, the IRS will be barred from filing suit for unpaid taxes or for tax deficiencies due to higher government valuations of the gifts. If a taxpayer omits includable gifts amounting to more than 25% of the total amount of gifts stated in the return, the statute of limitations is extended to six years. There is no statute of limitations for fraudulent returns filed with the intent to evade tax.

In order to qualify as an inter vivos gift for tax purposes, a gift must be complete and final. Control is an important issue. If a giver retains the right to revoke a gift, the gift may be found to be testamentary in nature, even if the right to revoke was never exercised (unless the gift was made in trust). The gift must also be delivered. An actual, physical delivery is best, but a symbolic delivery may suffice if there is strong evidence of intent to make an irrevocable gift. An example of symbolic delivery is when the donor puts something in a safe and gives the intended recipient the only key.

Trusts

Another common way to transfer property outside the will is to place the property in a trust that is created prior to death. A trust is simply a legal arrangement by which one person holds certain property for the benefit of another. The person holding the property is the trustee. The trustee can be an individual or an institution, and in some situations, it may be beneficial to have more than one trustee. Those for whose benefit the trust is held are the beneficiaries. To create a valid trust, the giver must identify the trust property, make a declaration of intent to create the trust, transfer property to the trust, and name identifiable beneficiaries. If no trustee is named, a court will appoint one. The settlor (creator of the trust) may also be designated as trustee, in which case segregation of the trust property satisfies the delivery requirement. Trusts can be created by a will, in which case they are termed testamentary.

Inter Vivos Trusts

Generally, in order to qualify as an inter vivos trust, a valid interest in property must be transferred before the death of the creator of the trust. If the settlor fails to name a beneficiary for the trust or to make delivery of the property to the trustee before death, the trust will likely be termed testamentary. Such a trust will be deemed invalid unless the formalities required for creating a will were complied with.

A trust will not be termed testamentary simply because the settlor retained significant control over the trust, such as the power to revoke or modify the trust. For example, when a person makes a deposit in a savings account in his or her own name as trustee for another and reserves the power to withdraw the money or to revoke the trust, the trust will be enforceable by the beneficiary upon the death of the depositor, providing the depositor has not, in fact, revoked the trust.

IN PLAIN ENGLISH

Many states allow joint bank accounts with rights of survivorship to serve as valid will substitutes.

As Part of the Gross Estate

Property transferred and passed outside the will need not go through probate. However, even though such an arrangement escapes probate, the trust property will probably be counted as part of the gross estate for tax purposes because the settlor retained significant control. In addition, if the deceased settlor created a revocable trust for the purpose of decreasing the share of a surviving spouse, in some states the trust will be declared illusory—in effect, invalid. The surviving spouse is then granted the legal share from the probated estate and from the revocable trust.

Life Insurance Trusts

Life insurance trusts can be used for paying estate taxes. The proceeds will not be taxed if the life insurance trust is irrevocable and the beneficiary is someone other than the estate, such as a friend or relative in an individual capacity or a business. This is especially important for businesspeople, since, without a life insurance trust, their survivors might be forced to sell estate assets for less than their real value in order to pay estate taxes.

PROBATE

Briefly described, probate is the legal process by which a decedent's estate is administered in a systematic and orderly manner and with finality. The laws that govern the probate process vary among the states. One of the principal functions of probate administration is to provide a means to transfer ownership of a decedent's probate property. Accordingly, probate administration occurs without regard to whether the decedent died testate or intestate.

In the course of probate administration, the following occurs:
- a decedent's will is admitted to probate as the decedent's last will;
- someone (referred to as the personal representative, executor, or administrator) is appointed by the court to take charge of the decedent's property and financial affairs;
- interested persons are notified of the commencement of probate administration;
- information concerning the decedent's estate is gathered;
- probate property is assembled and preserved;
- debts and taxes are determined, paid, and/or challenged;
- claims against the decedent's estate are paid and/or challenged;
- conflicting claims of entitlement to the decedent's property are disposed of; and,
- at the conclusion of the process, remaining estate property is distributed to the appropriate persons or entities.

While probate administration is pending, distributions of the decedent's property are suspended to allow creditors, claimants, devisees, and heirs the opportunity to protect their respective rights.

Probate property consists of the decedent's solely owned property as of the date of death. Property jointly held by the decedent and another person with the right of survivorship (i.e., a residence or stock certificates owned jointly with right of survivorship) passes to the survivor and is not a part of the decedent's probate estate. Likewise, the proceeds of life insurance on the decedent's life are not part of the probate estate (unless the estate is the designated beneficiary). It is, therefore, possible for a wealthy individual to die leaving little or no probate property.

Glossary

401(k). A type of plan provided by an employer for its employees that requires periodic payments during employment so that the employee can obtain post-retirement income benefits. Its name is derived from the initial section of the Internal Revenue Code, which created it.

A

acceptance. A term used in contract law to describe an element of a contract, which occurs after an offer has been made.

accountant. A trained professional who provides accounting services such as setting up and maintaining a company's books and tax preparation. *See certified public accountant.*

accounts payable. An accounting term used to define monetary obligations owed by one to another.

accounts receivable. An accounting term used to define monetary obligations that one is entitled to from another.

action. Sometimes referred to as cause of action, this is the legal claim or right that one has against another. It is frequently written in the form of a legal document known as a complaint, which is filed in court and used to begin a lawsuit.

addendum. A document attached at the end of another document that is customarily intended to supplement the terms of the document to which it is attached.

adjusted basis. The basis of an item is its cost or fair market value that is adjusted for tax purposes by deducting depreciation and other offsets allowable under the Internal Revenue Code. This concept is frequently used when valuing property for tax or related purposes.

affidavit. A statement sworn to or affirmed by the party making the statement, who is known as an affiant. Affidavits are written and the signature is notarized. Because of this, affidavits carry a great deal of weight and may be used in legal proceedings or other official purposes, such as in real estate transactions or in legal proceedings when a sworn oath is required.

agency. The relationship between one person, known as the principal, and another, known as the agent. Customarily, the agent works for or on behalf of the principal and is subject to the principal's control or right of control. Typically, the agent owes a duty to the principal.

agent. *See agency, principal.*

agreement. An arrangement, written or oral, whereby two or more parties reach an understanding. When conforming to the requirements of contract law, it is known as a contract. If one or more of the requirements for a legal contract are missing, the agreement may be subject to certain legal defenses and, thus, not enforceable.

amendment. A term used when an agreement is modified, as when a contract is changed.

Americans With Disabilities Act of 1990 (ADA). A federal statute enacted by Congress for the purpose of providing individuals with defined disabilities the opportunity to obtain fair treatment in employment, housing, transportation, and the like. The courts have been wrestling with the definition of disability for purposes of interpreting the statute and with the amount of reasonable accommodation required to be provided under the Act.

antidilution. A term used in trademark law to describe one of the forms of protection available to trademark owners under the law. It prohibits another from weakening, tarnishing, disparaging, or otherwise undermining the strength and credibility of the protected trademark.

antitrust laws. The laws used to prevent monopolies and unlawful arrangements which are intended to manipulate or control a particular market and unlawfully affect pricing, as well as other key market factors. The antitrust laws are enforced by both government regulation (federal and state) and by litigation.

apparent authority. A legal term used to define the authority an agent appears to have when dealing with third persons. This is intended to protect the third person's reasonable expectations when dealing with the agent, and is available for third-person protection even when contrary to the express instructions of the principal.

appreciate and appreciation. Financial and accounting terms used to define the increase in value of property, whether tangible or intangible, which occurs over time. Thus, a house frequently appreciates in value as real estate prices increase. Similarly, a copyright, which is intangible, may increase in value when the protected work has received positive critical acclaim or popularity.

articles of incorporation. Legal document filed with the state in which a company desires to do business as a corporation, and is the charter or creating instrument for the corporation. It defines the authority granted by the state for the company to be conducted in the corporate form, and is analogous to a constitution. All business corporations are created under the law of the state in which they are incorporated, and may do business in other states by filing the appropriate document(s) in those states as a foreign (corporation chartered in another state) corporation doing business in that state.

articles of organization. A legal document filed with the state in which a business desires to do business as a limited liability company (LLC), and is the charter or creating instrument for the LLC. It defines the authority granted by the state for the company to be conducted as an LLC, and is analogous to a constitution. All LLCs are created under the law of the state in which they are created, and may do business in other states by filing the appropriate document(s) in those states as a foreign (LLC chartered in another state) LLC doing business in that state.

asset. Financial or accounting term used to describe cash or property. The property can be tangible, such as real estate and office equipment, or intangible, such as intellectual property and goodwill.

assignment for the benefit of creditors. A legal term used in bankruptcy and collections law to define an arrangement whereby assets of a debtor are assigned to another, either the creditor, trustee, or receiver, for the benefit of one or more creditors. This can take the form of a formal court-administered plan or an informal arrangement worked out between the parties.

attorney. A professional who has been licensed to practice law in the state or other jurisdiction by which the license has been issued and whose conduct is regulated by state bar associations and the highest court of the state or jurisdiction. Attorneys must be licensed to practice in every court in which they appear. Customarily, attorneys are graduates of post-graduate law schools and have passed one or more bar examinations.

attorney-client privilege. A legal doctrine established for the purpose of enabling a client to communicate freely with his or her attorney. All communications between the client and attorney (or attorney's staff) which are not in the presence of any other person are privileged and may not be disclosed by the attorney without the client's permission.

attorney-in-fact. A person who is not actually a lawyer but, rather, is a person authorized to perform a specific act or combination of acts described in a document known as a power of attorney on behalf of the person granting the power. The person granting the power must sign this document and that person's signature must be notarized. The power may be general or specific, as defined in the document. In some jurisdictions and for some purposes, a power of attorney may be recorded; that is, filed with the appropriate governmental agency.

audit. An accounting term used to describe a review, typically of financial statements or tax returns. The audit is intended to verify the accuracy of the document and is conducted by an auditor, who is typically a skilled professional.

B

bankruptcy. The legal term defining the consequences of insolvency. In other words, when liabilities are greater than assets or when bills cannot be paid in the ordinary course of one's business, one is technically insolvent or bankrupt. Laws have been enacted which provide relief for those who are insolvent, as well as for their creditors.

blue sky law. A common term used to define state securities laws enacted for protection of those who invest in businesses. The term comes from a statement in Congress during the aftermath of the 1929 depression which referred to the victims of the depression who bought securities whose values were artificially inflated as people who obtained nothing more than chunks of "blue sky."

board of directors. The governing board of a business entity charged by statute with responsibility for administering the business and affairs of that entity. It is frequently used in the context of corporate boards of directors, though it can refer to the administrative board of other types of entities, such as nonprofit corporations, limited liability companies, or the like.

branding. The term used to describe the identification and reputation of a product or service. This modern accordion concept has been used by businesses to describe the process of identifying the qualities, unique characteristics, reputation, market awareness, and the like of specific products or services. One of the most famous brands in the world today is Coca-Cola.

business plan. A document used to describe the process of developing a new or existing business.

buy-sell agreement. A document customarily used by business organizations for the purpose of establishing a formal arrangement whereby the ownership interest in the business may be sold or transferred only in accordance with the terms of the agreement. These agreements typically impose restrictions on sale or transfer to outsiders and establish methods for valuing the interest when the owner desires to transfer the interest, dies, or becomes incapacitated. These agreements are frequently used in closely held businesses, as distinguished from those that are publicly traded.

bylaws. Formal documents adopted by corporations for administering the internal affairs of the company. They typically cover the rules and regulations for calling meetings, defining key positions, and the like. Bylaws may not be broader in scope than the company's articles of incorporation. Articles of incorporation are analogous to a constitution, and define the boundaries of a company's power and authority. The bylaws are analogous to laws and statutes, and are the rules and regulations for implementing the powers and authority. Bylaws are not filed with any governmental agency, but are kept in the corporation's minute book.

C

cash discount. A reduction granted a customer for paying cash on delivery, rather than obtaining credit and delaying payment.

cashier's check. Purchased from a bank and is issued by the bank.

certificate of incorporation. The document issued by many states evidencing the formation of a corporation in that state. It is used to establish that a corporation is in good standing in that state. It may be required when a corporation desires to do business in another state.

certified check. A check that has been certified by the issuing bank, which means that the bank segregates adequate funds from the depositor's account to pay the check, and the certification means that the bank is guaranteeing payment of the check.

Certified Public Accountant (CPA). A professional who has passed the examinations required by the appropriate state agency to provide kinds of accounting services. These services include, for example, setting up and maintaining a company's books and tax preparation. One of the services unique to CPAs is providing audited financial statements.

Chapter 7. A type of federal bankruptcy for individuals and businesses whereby all nonexempt assets are made available to creditors, who are paid in a prescribed order according to an approved schedule, and the debtor is discharged from all further outstanding obligations to the listed creditors.

Chapter 11. A type of federal bankruptcy for businesses, which permits the debtor to propose a plan to pay creditors according to a specific schedule and discharge all outstanding debts.

Chapter 13. A type of federal bankruptcy for individuals, which permits the debtor to propose a plan to pay creditors according to a specific schedule and discharge all outstanding debts.

check. A financial instrument whereby the payor (person writing the check) instructs the bank to pay the defined amount to the order of the designated payee (person or entity to whom the check is written).

civil law. The body of law adopted in some jurisdictions, including Louisiana and California, based on the Napoleonic Code and following prescribed rules or statutes, rather than adhering to past practices or precedent, as in the *common law.*

civil liability. The legal process for recovery of money or property or compelling the doing of things for the benefit of individuals and businesses, rather than imposing penalties or extracting obligations to the governmental jurisdiction. It is administered by private attorneys and individuals, rather than through a district or prosecuting attorney on behalf of the government.

closely held business. A business owned by a small number of people or another business, rather than one that is publicly held or traded on the stock markets. It is frequently a business arrangement between one or more family groups or groups of friends, though the term could describe a larger group of owners, so long as the group is small enough to avoid the necessity of complying with the technical requirements set forth in the state and federal securities laws for publicly held businesses.

collateral. The term used to define assets of a borrower which may be available to a lender as a means of repaying a loan. For example, when a bank is asked to lend money, it will usually require the prospective borrower to provide a list of the borrower's available assets in order to determine whether the borrower has sufficient assets, if liquidated, to repay the loan. The bank may or may not require the assets to be *secured* or *encumbered* for the purpose of guaranteeing repayment.

collective works. Works defined by the federal copyright statute as including periodicals, anthologies or encyclopedias in which contributions consisting of separate and independent works themselves are assembled into a collective whole.

collusion. A legal term defining an unsavory arrangement between two or more entities for an improper purpose.

commingling. Combining assets from two or more sources. The commingling could be legitimate where, for example, a husband and wife have a joint checking account. It could also be improper, as in situations where a mom and pop corporation pays the personal obligations of the owners from corporate funds and/or corporate obligations from the owners' individual funds.

common law. The legal system based on English Common Law that follows past practice or legal precedent, known as *stare decisis*. In this process, rules established in court cases become binding and are followed until modified, extended, or reversed. This should be distinguished from civil law, which is based upon the Napoleonic Code and is limited to statutory pronouncements.

common stock. The form of stock issued by a corporation that has unrestricted voting rights, dividend rights, and ownership in the corporation. It is the kind of stock every corporation must have, and is distinguished from preferred stock, which must, by definition, have some form of preference in either dividends or distribution on dissolution, or both.

complaint. The legal document filed in a court that begins a lawsuit. This document, along with the summons, must be properly served on behalf of the complainant (plaintiff) on the other party (defendant) in order to continue the lawsuit.

confirming memorandum. A written document sent by one party to another for the purpose of confirming the terms of an oral arrangement.

conflict of interest. An ethical concept whereby a party has divided loyalties. For example, when a partner in a partnership is given a cash payment of $10 for a service rendered and belatedly realizes that, instead of one crisp $10 bill, there were two stuck together, the partner is forced to decide whether he should disclose to his partner the fact that the client overpaid. A lawyer who represents two parties who have opposing interests is in a conflict of interest and may, under the rules of many bar associations, be required to suspend representation of both parties. Alternatively, if the conflict is merely theoretical, then most bar associations permit the lawyer to continue representing both parties, provided the facts are disclosed to both parties in writing and there is an appropriate written waiver of the theoretical conflict by all.

consideration. A contract element, which requires the giving or receiving of something of value by one party in exchange for something of comparable value from the other party. Consideration can be in the form of money, property, services, or an agreement to refrain some action. Historically, consideration did not have to be comparable, as when token consideration was used for transactions, such as the classic use of *a* single peppercorn. Today, the law tends to require the parties to give or receive things of comparable potential value in order for the consideration to be deemed valid.

consignment. A legal arrangement whereby the property of one party is entrusted to another for purposes of sale. The person who entrusts the property, who must be the owner or lawful possessor, is known as the consignor and the person receiving the property is known as the consignee. The consignment agreement may be oral or written and, if in writing, it may be recorded with the appropriate government office. Many states have enacted special legislation dealing with unique forms of consignment, such as fine art, crafts, and collectibles.

Consumer Price Index (CPI). A financial tool used to define the increase or decrease in a defined list of consumer products and services in a particular geographic area during a specified period of time.

contract. A legal concept whereby one offers consideration to another in exchange for the others providing comparable consideration. To be legally valid, all contracts require an offer, acceptance, and consideration. They may oral or written. The are other legal requirements for certain types of contract; for example, contracts for the sale of real property (land) and contracts for personal property worth $500 or more must be in writing. *See acceptance, consideration, offer.*

cooling-off period. Concept whereby a consumer is given a specified period of time to reflect on an otherwise valid contract and, if desired, rescind it before it is performed by either party. For example, many states permit a three-day period within which a consumer may cancel contracts obtained by door-to-door salespeople.

copyright. The right whereby any original work of authorship that is put in a tangible form is protected by law. In the United States, the copyright laws have been enacted pursuant to the enabling provision set forth in Article I of the United States Constitution. The most copyright statute was enacted in 1976 and became effective January 1, 1978. This law continues to evolve and has been amended a number of times. It is known as the Copyright Revision Act of 1976, as amended. There are numerous treaties throughout the world dealing with copyright on a multinational level.

corporate shield and corporate veil. The terms used to define the limited liability available for those who conduct business through corporate or other business entities. It is said that shareholders in corporations and owners of limited liability companies are shielded by the limitation of liability available to them when they properly conduct business through these entitles. Creditors cannot pierce the corporate veil or penetrate the corporate shield without establishing a valid legal reason to do so, and the reasons available are very limited.

corporation. A business entity created by one or more persons pursuant to the corporate code of the state in which the business is to be formed.

counteroffer. An offer presented by an offeree, or recipient of an offer, from another, which rejects the original offer and provides a new offer. It converts the original offeror into an offeree. Once the give and take is completed and an agreement is reached, there is a contract.

creditor. One who is owed an obligation by another, known as a debtor. In business, the term is more commonly used to define one who is owed money.

D

damages. The compensation sought or awarded for legal injury sustained.

debentures and bonds. Legal debt instruments frequently used by corporations to evidence debt. When the debt is secured by one or more identified assets, such as a mile of railroad track, the instruments are bonds. When the debt is secured by all of the debtor's assets, the instruments are known as debentures. Bonds are also issued by governmental entities for specific designated purposes, such as building libraries, schools and the like, or funding a particular project.

debt. An obligation owed by one (debtor) to another (creditor).

debtor. One who is owes an obligation to another, known as a creditor. In business, the term is more commonly used to define one who owes money.

defined benefit plan. A retirement plan that pays a specific amount after the employee retires. This payment stream is used to determine the method and amount necessary to fund the plan.

defined contribution plan. A retirement plan that establishes the amount to be paid into the plan, and the benefits then flow from the preretirement contribution.

depreciate and depreciation. Financial and accounting terms whereby the useful life of an item is guesstimated and the value of the item is reduced on a yearly basis according to a prescribed schedule. For tax purposes, the Internal Revenue Service has established prescribed periods of depreciation for various items.

derivative work. A copyright concept whereby a work is taken from, or based on, a prior work.

design defect. A defect in the design of a product that results in the product being defective and may result in liability for the designer of the product. This should be distinguished from a manufacturing defect, where liability would fall to the manufacturer of the product.

discharge. The legal concept whereby a debtor in bankruptcy is permitted to extinguish all prebankruptcy debts when the legal requirements of the bankruptcy law are followed.

disclaimer. A legal device whereby a party may avoid responsibility for warranties that have either been expressly given or are implied by law. In order for a disclaimer to be valid, it must comply with the legal requirements set forth in the statute governing warranties and disclaimers.

dissolution. An entity, such as a corporation, limited liability company, limited partnership, or the like, may end its existence by a formal process known as dissolution. This can either be mandatory, by court order, or voluntary. It can also be involuntary, as when the annual report required by state law, and the accompanying annual fees are not tendered.

dividend preference. A payment defined by a preferred stock instrument setting forth the amount (in either dollars or percentage) which must be paid to the holders of the preferred stock before any dividends are paid to the holders of common stock.

E

e-commerce. Shorthand for electronic commerce, which is the practice of engaging in commercial activities using the computer network known as the Internet and/or World Wide Web.

electronic signature. The electronic communication adopted by a party for purposes of taking advantage of the E-SIGN statute and consummating contracts through e-commerce.

Electronic Signature in Global and National Commerce Act (E-Sign). A federal statute which prescribes a method whereby an electronic signature may be used for purposes of validating contracts in cyberspace, which contracts are binding in the same manner as they would be if entered into through traditional means.

employee stock option plan (ESOP). A plan established by a business entity using the company's stock for purposes of funding an employee retirement plan.

express warranty. A statement of fact or representation by a seller with the respect to quality or other attributes of particular goods to be sold. See also implied warranty.

F

fair use. A copyright concept developed by case law and codified in the Copyright Revision Act of 1976, as amended, to provide a defense for one who copies the protected work of another when the copying satisfies the guidelines set forth in the statute.

Federal Trade Commission (FTC). The federal agency charged by Congress with responsibility for policing interstate commerce and trade within the United States and at its borders. It has also assumed responsibility for policing activities on the World Wide Web when those activities affect commerce in the United States.

fiduciary. The term used to define one who owes a duty to another. The scope of that duty varies from relationship to relationship, and has been more carefully defined in the myriad of cases dealing with individuals who owe or are owed the duty. Classic examples of fiduciary relationships are the agency relationship (where both parties owe a fiduciary duty to each other) and the trust relationship (where the trustee is held to owe a fiduciary duty to beneficiaries).

first sale doctrine. A copyright concept whereby the copyright owner may control the first sale of a copyrighted work. Resales of that work, absent an agreement to the contrary, may be made without involving the copyright owner. For example, a book publisher may, by virtue of the copyright in the book, control the first sale of that book but, absent some agreement to the contrary, a purchaser may resell the book without involving the publisher in the resale.

foreign corporation. *See corporation.*

franchising. A process whereby a successful business pattern is licensed by the originator (franchisor) so that a licensee (franchisee) can create comparable businesses. In order for a franchising arrangement to be legal, the franchisor must comply with federal and state requirements and provide potential franchisees with the disclosures, known as a franchising disclosure document, required by those laws.

full disclosure. The concept of providing all relevant and pertinent information when securities are offered for sale or sold. It was first discussed by the U.S. Congress, later by state legislatures, and the securities laws require full and fair disclosure of all material facts relevant to the transactions involved.

G

general partner. The person or entity who has full personal liability in a partnership. A general partner can be one of the parties involved in a general partnership, which is defined as two or more persons who are co-owners engaged in a business for profit, or the person or entity who runs a limited partnership and has full personal liability for the acts, contracts, or omissions of that business entity.

goodwill. An intangible, which has been defined in cases as the propensity of customers to return to a business. It has also been defined as including the business' reputation, marketability, and success.

gray market. The market that develops when a legally licensed product is introduced into a market other than the one in which it is licensed. For example, a trademark owner in the United States may license the use of its mark in Canada, since the owner has captured the U.S. market. If the Canadian licensee begins selling the Canadian-licensed products in the United States, those sales of otherwise legally licensed merchandise in the restricted market of the United States would be gray market sales.

H

holographic will. Typically, it is handwritten, signed by the person writing it, and properly witnessed.

I

implied contract. A contract created by the law for the purpose of preventing injustice. It is a contract that the parties may or may not have expressly agreed to. For example, when a merchant sells a product without an appropriate disclaimer, the law implies a contract whereby the purchaser may expect the product to be "merchantable," even though merchantability was never specifically bargained for.

implied warranty. A warranty implied by law that exists whether or not the parties have negotiated for it. Classic implied warranties are the implied warranty of merchantability, the implied warranty of fitness for a particular purpose, the implied warranty of title, and the implied warranty that the item is not infringing the intellectual property rights of another. Implied warranties may, if the party against whom it is enforceable complies with the statute, be disclaimed.

independent contractor. A person who engages in his or her own independent business and provides goods or services to another. An independent contract must be distinguished from an employee, who is employed by another for purpose of providing goods or services. The legal distinction between these two categories is that an employer has the right of control over the conduct of an employee's activities, whereas the employer does not have a right of control over the conduct of an independent contractor's activities; rather, the employer contracts for the results.

Individual Retirement Account (IRA). This is a form of pension account created by Congress by individuals.

inherently dangerous goods. Items which, by virtue of their design or manufacturing defects, may expose the seller to liability in the event an injury is sustained from the defect. An example of an inherently dangerous item is a vehicle tire with a design defect such that it blows out when the vehicle on which it is mounted exceeds 40 mph.

intellectual property. The body of law that deals with products of the mind. It includes patent law, copyright law, trademark law, trade secret law, and other forms of protection for creative works.

Internet Service Provider (ISP). A business that provides access to the Internet/World Wide Web, usually for a fee. Examples of ISPs include MSN, America Online, and Netscape.

inter vivos trust. A trust created by one during his or her lifetime.

intestate. The legal term defining a person who dies without a will.

J

joint and several. The term used to define the liability of two or more individuals who are each liable for the entire amount of any damages awarded, or a pro rata share of those damages, depending on the wishes of the person in whose favor the damages are awarded.

joint venture. An arrangement between two or more persons to accomplish a specific task. It is distinguishable from a partnership, in that a partnership is established for the purpose of conducting an ongoing business, whereas a joint venture is created for the purpose of achieving a specific goal. Thus, if two or more persons get together for the purpose of building an apartment complex, it would be a joint venture; if the agreement goes on to say that they will continue to manage it on an ongoing basis, it would be a partnership. A joint venture can be expressed, when the parties work out their terms, or implied, when the parties merely perform the identified task.

joint work. The term defined by Section 101 of the Copyright Revision Act of 1976, as amended, as a work created by two or more persons contributing their creative elements and intending that those elements be combined into a unitary whole. Cases have established that the contributions of each must be independently copyrightable. A classic example of a joint work is an illustrated text, where one creates the illustrations and the other prepares the text.

judgment creditor. A person or entity in whose favor a court has rendered a money judgment.

judgment debtor. A person or entity against whom a court has awarded a money judgment.

jurisdiction. The word used to define a place where a lawsuit may be properly filed, a corporation may be created, a building may erected, or the like. It is a geographic area that has been defined by statute or case law for specific purposes. In the context of litigation, jurisdiction refers to the court system within which a case may be filed; for example, the United States District Court will accept jurisdiction of only those cases that deal with federal questions or involve citizens of different states or foreign countries, and amounts in excess of $75,000; state and local courts, on the other hand, have different jurisdictional requirements.

K

key-person insurance. A type of insurance procured on the life of a person key to a business. It is typically obtained by the business entity to compensate it for the loss it will sustain when the key person dies.

L

lawyer. *See attorney, attorney-in-fact.*

license. A permitted use. In business, licensing is typically used to permit one to use the intellectual property of another. For example, a copyright owner may license the use of a copyrighted use. Licensing may also refer to other permitted uses, for example, states issue driver's licenses and municipalities issue business licenses.

life insurance trust. A form of trust created for the purpose of owning a life insurance policy and distributing the proceeds of that policy when the insured party dies.

limited liability company (LLC). A business form that allows those who conduct business through it to enjoy the benefits of limited personal liability while electing the method by which the entity is to be treated for tax purposes. It was created to overcome the restrictions imposed on small business that could qualify for so-called S-corporation status.

limited liability partnership (LLP). Similar to a limited liability company except that it was created for the purpose of allowing partners in partnerships to have a personal liability shield similar to those who conduct business through corporations.

limited partner. A person or entity who owns an interest in a limited partnership but who is a passive investor and who enjoys limited liability.

limited partnership. A partnership having one or more general partners with full personal liability and one or more limited partners who may enjoy limited liability but may not play an active role in conducting the business of the limited partnership. It is created by statute and the partnership must comply with the limited partnership statute of the jurisdiction in which it is created.

liquidation. The process of converting assets to cash and distributing the cash. It should be distinguished from dissolution, which refers merely to the legal relationship between those who are conducting the business. For example, when a general partner in a general partnership dies, there is a dissolution by virtue of the death of a partner. The remaining partners may, if their agreement permits, continue the partnership or, if the agreement does not or they do not wish to, they may then liquidate the partnership by converting its assets to cash and properly distributing the cash.

litigation. The term used to describe filing and prosecuting a lawsuit.

M

Magnuson-Moss Warranty Act. A federal statute that imposes requirements for warranties when products are sold in interstate commerce.

merger and acquisition. The terms used to define corporate and other business entity arrangements whereby two or more entities are formally combined, or one entity is acquired by another. A merger is a situation where two or more business entities are combined together and the combined entity emerges as a single entity. Acquisitions are when one business entity acquires another business entity or only the assets of another entity. Both mergers and acquisitions are regulated by statute. That is, the business organization statutes regulate the process and the federal, as well as state, securities laws also impose requirements on entities covered by them.

minutes. State statutes governing corporations, LLCs and other business entities typically require those entities to have annual meetings and permit those entities to have periodic meetings. Written records of these meetings are known as *minutes* and are customarily kept in the organization's *minute book*.

money order. A financial instrument purchased from an authorized seller, which includes banks, post offices, and many retailers. *See also cashier's check, certified check.*

multilevel marketing (MLM). A form of doing business whereby a product or service is distributed through a multitiered structure. The structure is referred to as a down line and, customarily, each person in the line receives some compensation for down line sales. It is referred to as multilevel marketing, since each person is able to both sell product or service and enlist down line distributors, who can establish their own sales and distribution networks as well. The consumer who pays for the product or service is actually providing a revenue stream that flows up through all distribution levels. Classic examples of successful multilevel marketing are Amway and Mary Kay Cosmetics.

O

offer. An element of contract whereby one party, known as the *offeror*, presents an opportunity, known as the *offer*, to another party, known as the *offeree*. If the offer is accepted, a contract is made.

operating agreement. The document that defines the internal workings of a limited liability company. By statute, the agreement can be extremely flexible, and the law provides the parties creating the agreement the ability to determine whether the organization will be run by its owners, a panel of owners, or a single manager; whether the organization will be taxed as an *entity* or not. In fact, the law makes it clear that the drafters have extraordinary flexibility in creating the organizational arrangement they desire, so long as the limited legal requirements of the law are adhered to. This document is not filed with any governmental agency, but is kept in the organization's minute book.

P

partner. *See general partner, limited partnership, limited liability partnership.*

partnership. *See general partnership, limited partnership, or limited liability partnership.*

partnership agreement. The agreement between two or more persons who desire to conduct business in a partnership form. A partnership agreement can be expressed, when the parties work out the arrangements between themselves;

implied, when they merely conduct their business as a partnership; oral; or written. When the parties do not work out the details of a formal partnership agreement, the law imposes certain terms on the relationship.

patent or letters patent. Legal document issued by the government to those who comply with the strict and technical requirements of the patent law. It is a form of intellectual property.

pension plan. A plan adopted for the purpose of providing a pension for individuals who retire so they can augment the Social Security payments obtained from the government.

preferred stock. A form of stock that contains some form of preference. The preference can either be in the payment of a dividend; that is, the holders of this type of stock must receive a dividend payment before any dividends may be paid to holders of common stock. The preference may also be in the form of a liquidation payment; that is, when the entity is dissolved and liquidated, holders of preferred stock with liquidation preferences must be paid the preference before holders of common stock will receive any payment on account of their interest in the liquidated company. Preferred stock can have either or both of these forms of preference.

principal. The term used to define the person on whose behalf an agent acts and who controls or has the right to control the conduct of the agent. This term also refers, in a financial context, to the amount upon which interest is calculated.

product liability. The legal doctrine that applies to situations where a defective product results in injury to person or property. The defect can be a design defect or a manufacturing defect.

profit-sharing plans. Plans whereby business owners agree to share business profits with participants in the plan. These plans are very technical and require specialists to assist in their formation and administration.

Q

qualified plan. Refers to a pension or other plan that qualifies for special tax treatment under the Internal Revenue Code and state taxing statutes.

R

receiver. A person who is appointed on an interim basis to administer a business for the benefit of creditors or others. A receiver is typically appointed by court order and reports to the court.

reorganization. The process whereby a business may be restructured for the purpose of satisfying its creditors when it is unable to pay them in the regular course of business. Reorganizations can involve use of the business entity's stock or ownership interest as vehicles for payment. Non-insolvency reorganizations can occur when businesses are restructured for the purpose of accomplishing other goals; for example, a business may reorganize in order to change its business form, add or delete new product lines, or the like.

royalties. Periodic distributions paid pursuant to a licensing agreement.

S

S corporations. Corporations that comply with the requirements set forth in the Internal Revenue Code and elect to be treated, for tax purposes, as if they were still run as sole proprietorships or partnerships.

Securities and Exchange Commission (SEC). A federal agency, charged by Congress with responsibility for policing the securities market.

securities exemption. The term used to define specific and technical requirements necessary to avoid having to register securities with either the federal Securities and Exchange Commission or the state securities agency (in every state in which the security is to be sold). The two most common federal exemptions are the so-called intrastate offering exception, for securities that are offered for sale and sold only within the boundaries of one state, and the exemption available for those potential purchasers of the security who are deemed sophisticated or wealthy enough not to need the protection of the securities laws.

security interest. The interest created by statute in favor of a party, known as the secured party, in the assets of another for the purpose of protecting an obligation owed the secured party by the other party. A security interest may be perfected by having the proper document filed with the appropriate governmental agency.

service mark. A trademark used to identify a particular service with its provider. Service marks may be registered with the federal Trademark Office and appropriate state offices, as well. Classic examples of service marks for airlines providing travel services are Western Airlines' slogan "The only way to fly" and Braniff's "We move our tail for you."

shareholder. The person or entity owning stock in a corporation.

shareholder or annual meeting. The meeting required by the state corporation code for every corporation. It must be held at least once a year for the purpose, among other things, of electing the corporation's board of directors.

shareholders' agreement. The agreement between a corporation's shareholders and the corporation governing certain rights and restrictions of the owners with respect to their stock.

shareholder's derivative action. A cause of action provided the owner of stock in a corporation to vindicate a right or redress a wrong to the corporation. A shareholder's derivative action may be brought by the holder of even one share of stock in a corporation, though certain procedural restrictions are imposed when the ownership interest is small.

Simplified Employee Pension Plan (SEPP). A type of pension plan permitted by statute for employees.

sole proprietorship. The term used to define a business owned by a single individual.

Statute of Frauds. A law that was first enacted in England for the purpose of preventing fraud and perjury. It recognized the fact that certain transactions are so touched with the public interest that they should not be permitted enforcement over the objection of a party unless they were evidenced by a writing signed by that party, though parties could voluntarily perform the transactions if they wished. Since the English feudal system was a governmental process based on land ownership, one of the first transactions covered by the law was real estate transfers. The law was later extended to cover transactions in goods in excess of a certain value. The law also prohibited oral wills, since it would be too easy for unscrupulous individuals to misstate the wishes of a dead person. These laws have been refined and adopted in the United States.

stock. Refers to the ownership interest in a corporation and, traditionally, was evidenced by a stock or share certificate. The stock can be common or preferred. In addition, both common and preferred stock may be issued in different *classes*, typically identified by alphabetical designations.

stock or share certificate. The document used to evidence stock ownership in a corporation. Historically, it was a steel-engraved form, though some companies created unique and distinctive versions of their certificates. Today, many stock transactions are electronic, and no physical certificates are issued.

stockholder or shareholder. The individual or entity owning stock in a corporation.

stock option. A method by which an individual or business may acquire the right to obtain corporate stock at a defined price for a limited period. Options themselves are tradable and, in fact, there is an option exchange. Those who deal in options are said to trade on equity, since their exchanges are for the appreciation in the value of the underlying stock, rather than trading in the stock itself.

T

tax. The term used to define a government's right to extract payment from its citizens. In the United States, the federal income tax was initially declared unconstitutional, as confiscatory, and voided. Unfortunately for the taxpayer, the Constitution was amended to permit an income tax.

trade dress. A form of intellectual property law that was initially developed through cases for the purpose of protecting the unique and nonfunctional characteristics of product packaging. It was later extended, by case law, to cover everything from product design to the look and feel of businesses. It has even been used to protect the distinctive characteristics or look and feel of an artist's distinctive style.

trademark. Any words, phrases, name, symbol, logo, or combination of them, when used to identify a product or service. When used in connection with services, they are referred to as service marks.

trust. A legal arrangement whereby a person, referred to as the settlor, trustor or creator, conveys property to another, referred to as the trustee, for the benefit of one or more persons or entities, known as beneficiaries. The trustee is a fiduciary, owing a duty to the beneficiaries.

trustee. *See trust.*

Truth-in-Lending Act. A federal statute requiring certain lenders (usually institutional lenders) to comply with its requirements when loans are made.

U

Uniform Commercial Code (UCC). A body of commercial law, adopted in every state of the United States, though its periodic modifications may not have been universally accepted.

Uniform Offering Circular. The document required by statute to be used when franchises are offered for sale.

unincorporated association. An association of two or more persons who have not adopted a legal business form. Since the individuals are conducting business without having the benefit of a liability shield, such as through corporations, LLCs, or the like, they are legally partners and, thus, have full personal liability for the debts and other obligations of the business.

V

venture capital. Funding obtained from business speculators who provide money in exchange for ownership interest, control, and other defined benefits of the business. Since venture capitalists frequently provide large sums of money in a single block, they are customarily in a position to extract more rewards than individuals or businesses that invest modest amounts. Many venture capitalists were burned by the so-called technology meltdown and, thus, the availability of venture capital today is limited.

venue. The legal requirement imposed in litigation defining the specific court where a case must be filed and tried.

vesting. The process whereby an individual's interest in a retirement or pension plan is secured. For example, many pension plans provide that plan participants are vested 20% per year for five years; thus, an employee who leaves the company after three years will be 60% vested and entitled to receive only 60% of the amount that would otherwise have been available to a fully vested participant.

voting trust. An arrangement whereby shareholders or owners of interests in other business entities pool those interests and agree to have them voted in a particular way. These are typically formal arrangements embodied in technical documents that comply with the business code of the state in which the entity is created.

W

warranty. A form of guarantee that is either expressed or implied by law and provides protection to the purchaser when the characteristics warranted are not present.

winding up. The process whereby a business completes its activities and prepares to end its operations. This can be a technical dissolution and liquidation.

works made for hire. The copyright term used to define works created by employees within the scope of their employment, or by independent contractors whose work is specially ordered or commissioned and the arrangement is embodied through a written contract, which arrangement falls into one or more of the categories enumerated in the statute.

World Intellectual Property Organization (WIPO). A multinational organization created for the purpose of administering the interface of copyright laws between its member nations.

Z

zoning. The government's designation of limitations on the use of land and structures. Classic examples of zoning laws are those that prohibit commercial activities in residential areas and those that prohibit individuals from living in commercial structures.

Index

B

C

About the Author

Leonard D. DuBoff is an internationally recognized expert who has lectured on legal issues throughout the world. He began his legal career in New York, and then relocated to Palo Alto, California, where he started teaching at the Stanford Law School. Subsequently, he moved to Portland, Oregon, where he taught law at Lewis & Clark Law School. DuBoff spent almost a quarter of a century teaching business and intellectual property law.

While a full-time law professor, DuBoff was also Of Counsel to law firms and maintained that relationship until 1994 when he left full-time teaching to found his own law firm that specializes in business and intellectual property law. DuBoff has received academic awards from President Lyndon Johnson, New York Governor Nelson Rockefeller, and in 1990, he received the Governor's Arts Award from Oregon Governor Neil Goldschmidt.

In addition to practicing law, DuBoff has also been involved in its creation. In the late 1980s, he testified in support of the *Visual Artist's Rights Act of 1990* at the request of Senator Edward Kennedy of Massachusetts. He has also provided Congress with testimony related to several cultural and intellectual property treaties and has worked with state legislatures on their legislation as well.

A prolific author, DuBoff has written numerous articles for scholarly journals, practical articles for lawyers' bar publications, and articles for nonlawyers as well. He has regular columns in several publications. He is coauthor of the law school text *Cases and Materials on Art Law*.

He has also written a host of other books including:
Art Law: Domestic and International
The two volume *Deskbook of Art Law*
The Book Publishers Legal Guide
The Antique and Art Collector's Legal Guide
Art Law in a Nutshell

His business encyclopedia series includes:
The Crafts Business Encyclopedia
The Art Business Encyclopedia
The Entertainment Business Encyclopedia
His (In Plain English)® series includes:
The Law (In Plain English)® for Small Business
The Law (In Plain English)® for Crafts
Business and Legal Forms (In Plain English)® for Craftspeople
The Law (In Plain English)® for Craft Galleries
The Law (In Plain English)® for Writers
The Law (In Plain English)® for Photographers
Hi Tech Law (In Plain English)®
The Law (In Plain English)® for Health Care Professionals
The Law (In Plain English)® for Restaurants and Others in the Food Industry

DuBoff continues to serve as an educator by presenting continuing legal education programs for attorneys and seminars for nonlawyers.